The Book of the
EDWARDIAN & INTERWAR HOUSE

ABOVE: *recreation of an Edwardian interior (Geffrye museum)*

ABOVE: *a parlour (c.1904)*

ABOVE: *Interwar interior by Vanessa Bell (1934)*

ABOVE: *Interwar interior by Ellen Nicholson (1925)*

The Book of the
EDWARDIAN & INTERWAR HOUSE

Richard Russell Lawrence

First published in 2009 by Aurum Press Limited, 7 Greenland Street, London NW1 0ND

Copyright © 2009 Richard Russell Lawrence

A catalogue record of this book is available from the British Library.

ISBN 978 1 84513 340 5

1 3 5 7 9 10 8 6 4 2

2010 2012 2013 2011 2009

Designed by Richard Russell Lawrence

Printed in China

FRONT COVER: *montage of Edwardian & Interwar exteriors*

HALF-TITLE PAGE: *pair of semi-detached houses in a London suburb (1913)*

TITLE PAGE: *speculatively built semi-detached suburban houses (1914–15)*

THIS PAGE: *semi-detached suburban houses (1921)*

BACK COVER: *montage of Edwardian & Interwar interiors*

TABLE OF CONTENTS

ABOVE: *a suburban detached house (c.1911) 'cottage style'*

ABOVE: *terraced house (1923)*

ABOVE: *Edwardian neo-Georgian semi-detached house (c.1910)*

INTRODUCTION

The Book of the Edwardian and Interwar House describes the architecture, plans and interiors of typical houses of the Edwardian and Interwar periods (1901–39). It also includes some exceptional houses of those eras. Although the reign of King Edward VII began in 1901 and only lasted until 1910, as far as domestic architecture is concerned the Edwardian period extends until the end of the First World War. Because of the war, there was a virtually no house building between 1915 and 1918. However during the Interwar period, 1919–39, 4 million homes were built.

This book distinguishes between exceptional houses such as country houses and typical urban houses which are, in turn, identified as large, medium and small. The phenomenal aspect of both periods was the remarkable achievement of building millions of medium-sized and small houses, mostly in the expanding suburbs. The houses are presented as front, plan and back. The front shows the development of their domestic architecture. Plan shows the development of their interiors. Back shows their services and their gardens.

Part One describes the background and origins of the houses: the stylistic influences upon their exteriors and interiors, the way that building was organised up to 1900 and significant developments such as the Garden City movement and the first 'council-houses'. Part Two describes Edwardian town houses. Part Three describes several Edwardian country houses and some Edwardian and Interwar country house gardens. Part Four presents Interwar town houses. In Part Five, the functional and decorative details of houses of both periods, such as roofs and bathrooms, are presented.

A comprehensive glossary of terms and concise biographies of influential designers and thinkers is included, as well as some suggestions for places to visit and sources of further information.

I would like to thank all those who have assisted me in preparing this book – Piers, Nithya and Lynn at Aurum Press; Roz Wallinger of the Manor House, Upton Grey; Robin and Charlotte Morrison; Nigel and Dinah Kendal; the staff of various museums, local studies libraries and National Trust properties; my family: my wife, Caroline, my sisters, Liz and Sami, my brothers-in-law, Stephen and Jeremy; and my good friend Charles.

Richard Russell Lawrence
Summer 2008

ABOVE: *the Manor House, Upton Grey (1907)*

ABOVE: *the staircase at Homewood, designed by Lutyens (1901)*

ABOVE: *a wallpaper designed by Voysey, the most prolific designer of the Edwardian & Interwar eras (1926)*

OPPOSITE: *speculatively built suburban terraced house (1911–12)*

I

Social & Economic Background to the Edwardian & Interwar Eras

ABOVE: *an Empire at its peak: Admiralty Arch (1911)*

ABOVE: *because of the Empire, Colman's really could claim to distribute their products 'all over the world'*

The Edwardian period was a time of radical transformation. Between 1901 and 1914, social and economic patterns emerged which would become standard during the twentieth century. At the same time the increasing availability of electricity, the arrival of the internal combustion engine and the introduction of other innovations such as the vacuum cleaner (patented 1901) began to transform the lives of the upper and middle classes – changes which would eventually reach the working classes in the interwar years.

Internationally, Great Britain was at the peak of its powers. One in four people in the world lived in the British Empire and in 1913 British shipbuilders built 60 per cent of the world's new tonnage. But the country's relative economic decline was beginning. Its industrial rivals, Germany and the USA, were growing faster. Between 1893 and 1913 Britain's exports of manufactured goods more than doubled, but Germany's trebled and the USA achieved a fivefold increase. By 1908 Germany was producing twice as much steel as Britain.

ABOVE: *RMS Olympic (1910), built when Great Britain dominated the world's shipbuilding*

However, this relative decline was not widely recognised because Britain still enjoyed considerable invisible earnings from its worldwide empire which kept the country's balance of trade looking healthy. Between 1901 and 1905, average annual net imports were £471.5 million while exports were £269.9 million. The deficit was easily offset by income from 'invisibles': £116.6 million from services and £112.9 million from interest and dividends. The same pattern applied between 1911 and 1913.

Wartime inflation caused the pound to be overvalued, which led to trade deficits and substantial gold outflows after 1925. International competition affected British industry – for example, the textile industry, which had been dominant before the war, faced serious rivalry from France and Austria. Consequently, Great Britain struggled with low growth and recession during most of the second half of the 1920s. But the country did not slip into severe depression until early 1930, and its peak-to-trough decline in industrial production was roughly one-third that of the United States: 16.2 per cent compared with 46.8 per cent in the USA. The economy stopped declining soon after Great Britain abandoned the gold standard in September 1931, although genuine recovery did not begin until the end of 1932.

ABOVE: *new industries developed in and around London – part of the Hoover building (1931–35)*

OPPOSITE: *speculatively built suburban terraced house (1908–10)*

The Depression chiefly affected the older industries such as shipbuilding, coal and cotton in the North. On a national scale this was partly counter-balanced by the development of new industries in and around London. This created a need for more housing. The working classes were obliged to buy homes because there was a lack of rented accommodation in those areas where the new industries were situated. The speculative builders met this demand on an unprecedented scale so the working class was able to continue to follow the middle class out to the suburbs.

ABOVE: *front cover of a 1928 edition of* Home Chat *(first published in 1895)*

The Edwardian period saw important developments in welfare. National Insurance began in 1911, giving the British working classes the first contributory system of insurance against illness and unemployment; benefits were paid at the new labour exchanges. At the same time labour was moving towards organisation on a national scale via the amalgamated trade unions and the system of labour exchanges. In 1910 Churchill, advocating the new labour exchanges, stated 'Modern Industry has become national.'

In politics, the Labour Party was emerging as a significant force. By 1914 it had 179 constituency parties and was supported by a network of related organisations such as the Fabian Society. The housing conditions of the working classes had become an important social and political issue.

Compulsory education had begun in 1870. It created new markets which were catered for by publishers including Alfred Harmsworth's Amalgamated Press, which published the *Daily Mail* from 1896. Women's magazines aimed at the increasingly literate mass market that had appeared since the 1870s. Amalgamated Press published *Home Chat* which reached a circulation of 186,000 by 1895.

The country's population grew from 41.5 million in 1901 to 45.2 million in 1911. The birth rate was declining but infant mortality was decreasing faster. Life expectancy was rising due to better medicine, housing and hygiene. After 1900 the urban population, which by then made up 77 percent of the total, continued to become increasingly suburban, a trend which had begun in the mid-Victorian period.

It was the spread of the suburbs that largely accounted for a surge in building during the final years of the nineteenth century. An annual average of 150,000 houses was built between 1898 and 1903. But by 1905 the building trade was becoming depressed. By 1909 there was serious unemployment in the industry, which meant that employers could pick the best available employees with a consequent effect on the standard of Edwardian building.

At first, the outbreak of the First World War made little difference. In the closing months of 1914 building continued as if the war would indeed be over 'by Christmas' but during 1915 it ceased as resources were diverted to the war effort. When building resumed after the war, service flats would take the place of speculatively built large town houses, medium-sized houses would be built for sale rather than rent and small houses for the working classes would be either publicly funded or speculatively built for sale. Many of the occupants of the new suburbs would become 'owner-occupiers'.

THE GROWTH OF THE MIDDLE CLASSES

Much more apparent to most people than Britain's relative economic decline were the major social and demographic changes that were underway. The Edwardian period saw a vast expansion in the number of 'white collar' jobs offering good pay and regular hours, and the people who filled these jobs increasingly demanded better housing and a more salubrious environment than that provided by the centres of the great Victorian cities.

From 1891 to 1911 the accumulation of social legislation and the enlargement of the armed

RIGHT: *population growth 1801–1931*

FAR RIGHT: *proportion of population living in towns 1901, 1911 and 1931*

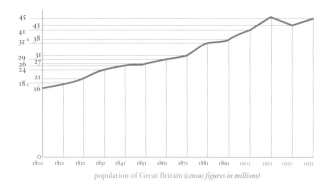

population of Great Britain *(census figures in millions)*

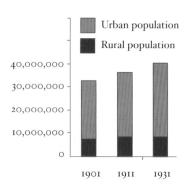

LEFT: *suburban terraced houses (1911–12)*

ABOVE: *new retail outlets, Oxford Street (1909)*

forces led to a doubling in the number of 'white collar' jobs in both central and local government. The civil service cost £22.5 million in 1895, but £61.5 million in 1914. At the same time there was a corresponding growth of similar jobs in commerce. This was due to the proliferation of joint stock, limited liability companies and to the absorption of family businesses by larger corporate entities. Amalgamations and federations were taking place in iron and steel, brewing, cement, salt, wallpaper, tobacco, railways, shipping, oil, banking, chemicals, glass, textiles and mining. The Fine Cotton Spinners' and Doublers' Association Ltd was formed from thirty-one firms in 1898; it had incorporated another sixteen by 1905. In addition, the new retail outlets which were spreading across the country also required salaried staff. In 1911, income from salaries was 10.5 per cent of total national income. This had grown to 20.5 per cent by 1924, and 24 per cent by 1938. The resulting growth in the number of middle-income earners created a vast market for suburban houses of all types.

ABOVE: *Arding & Hobbs, a suburban department store, rebuilt in 1910 after a fire in 1909*

CHANGES IN THE SUBURBS

The term 'suburbia' had come into use during the 1890s. In *The Suburbans* (1905), T.W.H. Crossley wrote of:

> penny buses, gramophones, bamboo furniture, pleasant Sunday afternoons, Glory Songs, modern language, teas, golf, tennis, high school education, dubious fiction, shilling's worth of comic writing, picture postcards, miraculous hair restorers.

Walter Besant wrote in 1909: 'The suburbs have developed a social life of their own; they have dances, dinners, subscriptions.' There were new forms of leisure activities such as archery, badminton, golf, hockey, ping-pong and skating as well as football and cricket, cheaper and better music halls, the picture palace, the cheap periodical and books. The *Daily Mirror* and *Daily Express* were both launched on to the market in the early twentieth century. Daily newspaper readership

ABOVE: *Boots, 'the largest retail Chemists in the World', Windsor (1904)*

ABOVE: *during the Edwardian period, the new retail outlets were equipped with cash registers.*

ABOVE: *Barton & Walton, a Birmingham suburban station (from an Edwardian photograph)*

ABOVE: *Southall, west London, in 1909*

RIGHT: *terraced houses in Victoria Park, Manchester*

doubled from 1896 to 1906 and again by 1914. Retail centres opened as stall-holders and itinerant traders were displaced. Specialist shops had begun to appear during the 1880s. These included multiples like Lipton's, Maypole, Home & Colonial, Dunn's, Freeman, Hardy & Willis, Lyons restaurants and Boots chemists. During the Edwardian period they would be equipped with the new cash registers.

By 1914 department stores, multiple shops and co-ops accounted for 16–20 per cent of all retail sales. By the time of its founder's death, the high-class grocers, Williams of Manchester, had opened thirty branches in the middle-class suburbs. The faster growing chains relied on limited stocks and higher turnover. 'High-class provisioners' such as Williams stocked 2,000 items.

But during the Edwardian period something new began to happen: the working class began to follow the middle class out to the suburbs, which now differentiated themselves into distinct inner and outer 'belts'. Better-paid manual workers were able to travel to work on trams and buses which were less socially exclusive than the railways. A return fare cost 2d. In London, Metropolitan Electric Tramways Ltd opened an electric tramway from Finsbury Park to Wood Green and Tottenham in 1904. Tram services also 'fed' railway stations such as Bruce Grove on the GER. In the south-west of the capital, 'tramway suburbia' stretched as far as Hounslow. Such services allowed an inner ring of working-class suburbs or 'artisan belts' like Tottenham and Enfield to develop. Birmingham, Leeds, Liverpool and Manchester also developed tramway systems, as did even comparatively small towns like Wrexham. As early as 1903 the *Birmingham Daily Mail* regretted that the suburbs of Olton, Solihull, Knowle and Ackock's Green had been abandoned to 'the smaller house – the house adapted to the means of a man of limited income who likes to live just outside the artisan belt encircling the city'.

Higher income earners lived further out where they were served by trains. Liverpool had Everton, Prince's Park, Sefton Grove and Fulwood Park; Birmingham, Edgbaston; Leeds, Headingley Hill; Newcastle, Gosforth and Jesmond; Brighton, Kemp Town and Hove; Bristol, Clifton, Cotham and Redland; Nottingham, Wollaton and Mapperley Park; Manchester had Victoria Park, Preston Park, Didsbury, Alderley Edge, Hale and Bowden. This trend was largely a product of the second

FAR LEFT: *Bruce Grove,
north London, a working-class
suburb, in 1913*

LEFT: *a tram in Rayne's Park,
south London (1907)*

generation of railway development which had focused on suburban lines. The process had begun in London and the South East but the rest of the country soon built its own suburbs. By 1904 Leeds had over forty suburban railway stations. As soon as a station opened in an area close to a town with a commercial or administrative centre the speculative builders would move in.

A second new development had begun. In 1914, 90 per cent of the urban population rented their homes but the Edwardian period would be the last in which large, medium and small town houses were built for rent. Already in the new suburbs houses were beginning to be speculatively built for sale; by 1909 an advertisement for houses in Wembley was describing the time as one 'when people are buying their houses in preference to renting them'. It was in response to such preferences that, in 1904, the Halifax Building Society raised the level of mortgages it was prepared to offer from 75 to 90 per cent of valuation on freehold properties valued at up to £300. It was in houses built for sale that new designs were most apparent. In the interwar years permanent building societies turned to the financing of house building for sale and their investors' funds were used to fund owner occupation.

Between 1919 and 1939 an average of 17,500 houses were completed each month. A total of four million homes were built in twenty-one years. But in the aftermath of the First World War

LEFT: *a suburban terrace
built in 1914*

private house building for rent was no longer viable. Building costs had risen so much that the rent required for a landlord to recover his costs was prohibitive. By the end of the war the cost of building a small house was four times what it had been in 1914. Rents had been kept down by law since 1915. Newly built houses were not subject to fixed rents but they were too expensive for their intended occupants. This was a deterrent to small-scale investors even after the abolition of rent controls in 1923.

As well as those with middle-sized incomes, the incomes of those on lower wages had risen enough to make them prospective home-owners. The government helped by granting tax relief on mortgage interest payments. Builders agreed to smaller deposits than previously. Deposits fell to below 20–25 per cent of the purchase price.

Building societies' total lending rose from £66 million in 1914 to £700 million in 1938. They advanced £32 million to mortgagees in 1923 and more than £103 million in 1933. Borrowing peaked in 1936 when £140.3 million was lent. The number of borrowers in 1928 was just over half a million. This had grown to 1.3 million by 1936.

Mortgage interest rates kept going down. By the early 1930s building costs were at their lowest since 1914. Houses were being sold for £350 to £550, which was affordable for those earning £3.50 to £4.50 per week. The better-paid manual worker could afford to become an owner-occupier.

By the mid-1930s builders began to anticipate demand being met. They thought they would have to try to appeal to others, apart from mature married men in secure jobs, such as the elderly and the newly married. This required different types of housing such as bungalows which were represented as 'labour-saving' and therefore suitable for the elderly. Bungalows could be built on cheaper, marginal sites which could not support the weight of a two-storey house. Another alternative was flats which were aimed at single people, businessmen or professionals whose families lived out of town.

ABOVE: *terraced houses with cast-iron balconies in Ilford (c.1907), an area of exceptional growth*

AREAS OF EXCEPTIONAL GROWTH

In the conurbations of the North East, around Tyneside and Wearside, the population grew from 200,000 to two million between 1855 and 1895, producing coal, iron and steel, ships and armaments. The term 'conurbation' was invented during the Edwardian period by Patrick Geddes. In *Cities in Evolution* (1915) he defined a conurbation as 'a cluster of contiguous urban administrative districts'.

The 1901 census showed that Blackpool, Edmonton, Gillingham (Kent), Ilford, Smethwick, Southampton and Wallasey had been areas of exceptional growth during the preceding decade. From 1901 to 1911 the fastest growing locations were Coventry, Hendon and Southend-on-Sea. Some of the fastest growing locations were new iron and steel producing centres such as Barrow, Middlesbrough and Scunthorpe; new railway workshop centres like Ashford, Crewe, Darlington, Derby and Swindon; new shipbuilding centres such as Birkenhead; new glass and chemical towns such as St Helens and Widnes; new coal entrepots like Cardiff; or new light engineering towns such as Coventry (bicycles and motor cars). Others were established centres where former cottage-scale industries had expanded to factory-scale production, such as Swindon, with its Great Western Railway works and station, 'noisy, new, cheap and Liberal, full of every accent'; Ransomes of Ipswich had grown to 2,500 employees by 1911, Marshall's of Gainsborough had 5,000 in 1913; in Lincoln, Clayton & Shuttleworth had 2,300 in 1907 and Ruston's 5,500 in 1912.

ABOVE: *a 1904 tram from Lowestoft, Suffolk*

Leeds could claim the fastest growth (115 per cent) from 1861 to 1911. This was due to the expanding manufacture of engineering, cloth and leather goods.

Nottingham's population grew from 75,000 in 1861 to 260,000 by 1911, with the workers producing lace, leather goods and hosiery as well as Raleigh's bicycles, Player's tobacco and Boot's drugs. Some towns attracted business because they were already centres of trade and transport; for example, Reading, which became 'biscuitopolis' – Huntley & Palmers bakery employed 5,000 by 1914.

Seaside and leisure resorts were some of the fastest growing towns. The population of Southend grew from 3,000 in 1861 to 63,000 in 1911; Blackpool from 4,000 in 1861 to 58,000 in 1911; Bournemouth from 1,940 in 1861 to 79,000 by 1911. Folkestone was successfully developed for the visits of fashionable and intellectual society. King Edward VII himself was a regular visitor.

All this was a cause of concern in the upper echelons of the intelligentsia, which were rife with anti-urbanism. In *Modern Manufacture and Design* (1859) Ruskin had contrasted medieval Pisa and contemporary Rochdale as 'brightness and blight'. William Morris contemplated a 'cockneyised countryside' with 'no rest, no beauty, no leisure anywhere: all England become like the heart of Lancashire is now'.

ABOVE: *the Great Wheel at Blackpool in 1906*

CHANGES IN TRANSPORT

In 1900 road transport was entirely horse-drawn. In 1901 the newspaper editor, R.D. Blumenfeld wrote in his diary that a hansom cab driver had told him:

> Them automobiles are all right as playthings, but you can't depend on 'em. Besides they are dangerous and you can't guarantee getting your fare to the place he wants to reach. You'll never beat my old horse.[1]

Blumenfeld predicted: 'We are on the eve of great electrification movements. The automobile has come to stay, and there are even some people who predict that in another generation our traffic will be horseless...'

Blumenfeld was right – the decade 1900–10 was to be the age of the 'disappearing horse'; by 1910 the motor bus had taken over. This affected the farmland surrounding the cities where fodder had been grown for horses. The demand for its staple product gone, the land became available for building.

Railway passengers were predominantly middle-class, while trams were used by the working class. A 1905 report by the Royal Commission on London traffic stated that 500 million passengers

ABOVE: *a horse bus in 1899*

LEFT: *the Grand, Folkestone, a fashionable leisure resort. King Edward VII regularly stayed at the Grand. Spectators waited outside to catch a glimpse of him in the glazed conservatory, which was known as 'the monkey-house'*

RIGHT: *commuters at a
suburban station in 1908*

ABOVE: *a type 'B' motor bus*

ABOVE: *a 1912 LCC tram*

ABOVE: *a Wolverhampton
trolleybus (Black Country
Living Museum)*

were carried annually by 4,000 horse-drawn omnibuses but only 165 million by LCC tramways.
London's tramways compared unfavourably with those of Liverpool and Manchester. Only 30 of
London's 107 miles of tramway had been electrified and the electrified sections were fragmented.
Until 1906 there was a ban on trams on Thames bridges and the embankment.

The efficient and reliable type 'B' motor bus was introduced in October 1910. It was a 30hp
vehicle that not only saw off the horse buses but also virtually ended new tramway construction.

Liverpool introduced motor buses in 1911, Birmingham in 1913. By 1914, eighteen local
authorities ran bus services. Tramways survived throughout the interwar years because the bigger
railway companies such as the Great Eastern employed them to feed their rural stations.

In 1911 Leeds and Bradford introduced a new form of transport, the trolleybus: this was an
electrically powered bus which ran on pneumatic tyres rather than rails. It gained its power from
a trolley which ran on overhead cables using a pair of trolley poles pressed against the overhead
cables to keep the wheels of the trolley in position. They were cheaper than trams because they
did not require tracks. Their design was improved during the interwar years. They continued to
operate in London until 1962 and in Bradford until 1972.

The expansion in the ownership of private vehicles was another factor. The 1861 Locomotives
on Public Highways Act had been repealed in 1896. This was the Act which imposed a speed limit
of four miles per hour and required that a man carrying a red flag had to walk in front of any self-
propelled vehicle on a public road. The possibilities of the motor car were under consideration.

At first motoring was regarded as a sport. Chauffeurs joined the households of the rich as
very expensive higher servants. In 1904 there were 8,645 private cars, 4,000 goods vans and 5,345
public transport vehicles. By 1914 the numbers had increased to 132,015 cars, 82,010 lorries and
52,167 public transport vehicles.

The most popular car was the Model T Ford, which had made its world debut at the 1908
Olympia Motor Exhibition. This boosted sales of Ford vehicles in Britain so that a London
dealership was set up and 400 cars were sold within the year. Production of Model T Fords began
in Britain in 1913 at a disused tram works at Trafford Park just south of Manchester. The decision
to make them only in black was taken in 1914. In 1919, 40 per cent of the cars on the road in
Great Britain were Model Ts. During the 1920s the Ford management looked for somewhere to

ABOVE: *a Model T Ford (1908); in 1919 they made up 40% of the cars on British roads*

operate on a vast scale. They chose a 500-acre site on the banks of the Thames near the small village of Dagenham in Essex.

The motor car brought country houses within easy reach of London society for weekend house parties. Mrs C.S. Peel, a well-known social commentator and, from 1914, editor of the women's page of the *Daily Mail*, described:

> As the motor car came into more general use, the week-end habit grew, and well-to-do folk ceased to use the Park and went further afield for their Saturday to Monday pleasuring. Even people of no account like ourselves were affected. We went to quantities of all kinds of parties and when we could get away took a holiday abroad or rented a house in the country, sufficiently near London for Charles to travel up and down to his office and for me to keep in touch with my newspapers.[2]

The big development in trains which began during the Edwardian period was electrification. Cheaper to run than steam trains, electric trains allowed better services with an increase in traffic. Suburban electric trains encouraged the expansion of the outer suburbs where managers and professionals could afford to live. Outlying towns, such as Bromley, Chislehurst and Croydon became satellites connected to suburban stations by bus services. In *Town Planning* (1940) Thomas Sharp stated that the remedy for over-centralisation was 'not decentralisation but sub-centralisation round a lessened centre maintained for other purposes'.

ABOVE: *an electric suburban train at Aldershot*

As motor traffic increased in the 1920s, the disadvantages of trams became apparent; in particular the fact that they obstructed the free circulation of traffic. As a result the motor bus became the most common form of public transport. By 1923 buses were beginning to carry more passengers than trains. But London was the exception. Although there were 3,522 motor buses in the capital with services extending as far as Windsor, Barnet and Epping, London had another popular form of transport: the Underground Railway. It had begun as the Subterranean Railway during the 1860s. The 'Twopenny Tube' was electrified during the Edwardian period and changed its name to the cleaner sounding 'Underground'. Its first escalators were built in 1911.

In 1921 Edgware was a village in Middlesex; by the 1930s the Northern Line had been extended from its original terminus at Golders Green. It had become the busiest line in London. In 1921

ABOVE: *1924 edition of*
Metro-land

ABOVE: *a laundry press;*
laundry was an integral and
intensive part of domestic
labour

ABOVE: *advertisement for the*
first Daily Mail Ideal Home
Exhibition *(1908)*

Hendon's population was 58,000; by 1939 it had grown to 146,000. The Cockfosters extension of the Piccadilly line from Finsbury Park had a similar effect.

The Metropolitan Railway (Met) was a transport service provider which also became a property developer. Before the war it had gained the power to use land which it had acquired adjacent to its lines for housing development. The Met transformed the area to the north west of London, in Middlesex, Hertfordshire and Buckinghamshire, into the commuter land that became known as Metroland. It was named after a publication, *Metro-land*, which appeared annually from 1919 to 1932. *Metro-land* promoted the Met's new residential estates following the route of its line out through Neasden, Wembley Park, Northwick Park, Eastcote, Rayners Lane, Ruislip, Hillingdon, Pinner, Rickmansworth and Amersham. The electrification of the suburban rail network south of the Thames had a similar effect, resulting in the large-scale residential development of south-east and south-west London. Car ownership meant that builders had to think about accommodating the family car. By the early 1930s builders were willing to construct a brick-built 'motor house' for an additional £30–£60.

'THE SERVANTLESS HOME'

Traditionally the population of London had grown through immigration and the majority of London immigrants were women aged 15–30, drawn by the prospects of domestic service and the possibility of marriage. Country-wide, the 1891 census had shown that 2.33 million men and women were employed in domestic service (16.1 per cent of the entire population but 11.1 per cent of the adult female population). Wealthy establishments might have a cook and two maids, perhaps also a children's nurse and a gardener or groom, though not all would live in. The minimum was a 'cook general' who would receive £20–£26 per annum plus board. In 1913 as many as one-third of all girls leaving Middlesex elementary schools went into domestic service.

Even before the First World War, although the rich could afford servants, many middle and working-class homes could not afford much help and an increasing number who aspired to middle-class status could afford little or none. A British Commercial Gas Association advertisement of 1918 predicted:

> After the war domestic labour will probably be both scarce and dear, and the servantless home will, through force of circumstances, tend to become the rule rather than the exception ... convenience, cleanliness, economy, efficiency, and comfort, without unnecessary labour, are signs of progress which no woman can afford to disregard.

This continued a trend that was already underway before the outbreak of war. As early as 1903 a new magazine, *Women's World*, was aimed at homes without servants, as were books such as A.E.L.'s *How She Managed without a Servant* (c.1901) and Mrs D.C. Peel's *How to Keep House* (1902).

IDEAL HOMES

The growing number of suburban houses in which families lived with little or no domestic help led to increased interest in their design, especially as it affected the ease and convenience of day-to-day life. Shops and department stores offered advice on interior design. Gamage's in High Holborn offered goods in their catalogue which were available by mail order and hire purchase. This was aimed at both the middle and artisan classes.

This new market was the one for which the *Daily Mail* Ideal Home Exhibitions were intended. The first was held in 1908: at each exhibition, full-sized show houses were built on site. The show houses were some of the most popular exhibits. Different styles were featured, such as the 'Tudor Village' of 1910. The *Daily Mail* described: 'Streets of a town lined with hundreds of bright little buildings of varying shape and design – red roofed cottages, brown bungalows, and gaily coloured pavilions – and moving between them endless lines of interested visitors.' The exhibitions also drew attention to the latest equipment, such as electrical appliances.

Exhibitions were showcases for contemporary concerns such as health and convenience. This concern with health was a reaction to the dirt and disease of the inner city. Indeed, health had been a major public preoccupation since 1871 when the future King Edward VII had nearly died of typhus attributed to 'bad plumbing'. Since then public awareness of hygiene had become acute. An International Health Exhibition was held in 1884. 'Sanitary' became the new watchword.

By 1900 improvements in hygiene resulted in a surplus of births over deaths. The movement outwards to the suburbs made a considerable difference to health. There was a national trend towards smaller families. Women's health benefited from reductions in family size and birth rate. By 1900 women formed the majority of the national population. In 1901 there were 17,752,000 males and 18,934,000 females.[3]

ABOVE: *1908 Underground poster*

The new suburbs were represented as healthy or, as in a 1908 Underground poster, a 'place of delightful prospects'. House advertisements emphasised features such as height above sea-level: in 1909, Telford Park, Streatham Hill was advertised as '180 feet above sea-level'. Hilly ground, like Preston Park, Brighton, was regarded as desirable because of the health-giving fresh air and the views it offered. Built-in furniture or 'fitments' as they were known at the time were intended to reduce areas where dust and dirt could collect in the house. They were introduced to the public at the 1884 International Health Exhibition. By 1900 fitted cupboards and dressers were standard in kitchens and living-rooms. They were listed as part of the fixtures and fittings when a house changed hands.

ARCHITECTS VS BUILDERS

During the Edwardian period, architects' attitudes towards builders changed. There were two types of builders: building contractors and speculative builders. Builders who undertook both kinds of work called themselves 'Builders & Contractors'. Architects used building contractors to execute their designs. Previously, architects had mainly worked for a rich, upper-class clientele and left the market for medium-sized and small houses to the speculative builders who would copy the architects' latest designs if they thought they would appeal to their market and could be produced cheaply.

ABOVE: *a cartoon depicting the results of 'jerry building'*

The vast majority of urban housing since the seventeenth century had been speculatively built. The suburban growth of the second half of the nineteenth century was undertaken by speculative builders. But it was in the suburbs that architects and speculative builders became rivals. Architects were becoming aware that there might be opportunities for them in the growing market for suburban houses. In 1910 the architect Sir Lawrence Weaver declared: 'The time has come when the educated should shake off the shackles of the speculative builder and turn their backs on the desirable villa residence.'[4]

Architects and designers began to pour scorn on speculative builders. Walter Crane judged that 'the mass of modern London consists of the erections of the speculative builder – miles of absolutely uninteresting house fronts, chiefly composed of the repetition of one pattern, and that of the meanest and most uninventive kind crowded together.'[5]

ABOVE: *a builder's yard in 1909*

In 1911 the architect Ernest Newton declared: 'The speculative builder gaily devastates whole districts, his only ideal being the greatest apparent accommodation for the least actual cost'. Newton had noticed 'the virtually new class who had made their fortunes from commerce. Their first step towards fulfilling their ambitions was to buy land and build a house'.[6] He concluded that it was the time of the 'smallish house' which, due to its scale, needed an intimate touch which the speculative builder failed to achieve.[7]

Speculative building, as opposed to building contracting, was building in advance of demand. Since the mid-nineteenth century it had been relatively easy to anticipate demand. As soon as

Right: *a detached house in
Gerrards Cross, built soon
after the station opened
(c.1907)*

Y. J. LOVELL & SON.
GERRARD'S CROSS (AND BEACONSFIELD).

Above: *a 1910 advertisement
for a firm of builders based
in Gerrards Cross, which was
developed after the railway
arrived in 1906*

transportation became available to an area near to a town or city the builders would move in – for example, Gerrards Cross in 1906. Landowners would then grant building leases to builders who were given a limited period of time to build on the land. During this period the plots were let at a low ground rent on the understanding that the lessee built, at his own expense, a house or number of houses of an agreed character. If the builder failed to 'cover in' by the end of the period of low rent, he lost everything he had put into the plot and it became the property of the landlord who would get another builder to finish the job. 'Covering in' meant completing the shell of the house up to the roof ridge. The successful builder could continue to be the lessee or sell the lease on to a landlord who would rent the houses out. At the end of the lease, the house or houses on the plot became the property of the ground landlord.

Until the Edwardian period, virtually all speculative building was houses which would be rented. Because speculative builders worked at their own expense they were inclined to make savings wherever they could. This could result in some very poor quality building, especially when it came to small houses. This kind of bad practice became known as 'jerry building' during the early Victorian period (1837–50). Critics sometimes lumped speculative builders and 'jerry' builders together.

Robert Tressall described, from personal experience, how competition for work led to cost-cutting practices: 'The successful tenderer has to cut the price so fine that to make it pay he must scamp the work, pay low wages, and drive and sweat the men whom he employs'.[8]

Builders did not need architects because they could find designs in pattern books and publications such as the *Illustrated Carpenter and Builder*. Since the eighteenth century, they had been able to create both exteriors and interiors. Pattern books such as Batty Langley's *The Builder's Jewel* (1767) and Nicholson's *Builder's & Workman's Director* (1825) provided them with instructions and working drawings. By the late eighteenth century they could also follow the formula for large houses without an architect. This formulaic approach provoked William Morris's description of late Georgian houses as 'brown brick boxes'.

LEFT: *speculatively built terraced houses in Hanwell, a west London suburb (c.1904)*

ABOVE: *Church Farm, Hendon, one of the farms which produced fodder for horses but lost its livelihood after the introduction of the internal combustion engine. The farmland was sold for building*

After 1900 the speculative builders were paying attention to designs by Voysey, Lutyens and others. Speculative builders were becoming organised on an increasing scale. The first change had been in the supply of materials as they became mass produced and available, on credit, through builders' merchants such as Young & Marten. Then the builders began to become developers who worked closely with estate agents. Estate agents had formerly been rent collectors with some responsibility for the management and maintenance of properties. But as new land became available for building, landlords were able to sell the land itself. This had been impossible on land which was held by traditional, aristocratic landlords such as the Dukes of Bedford or Westminster because, under the terms on which they inherited, their estates could not be sold. But farmers who had lost their livelihood to the internal combustion engine faced no such obstacle. Some builders worked for estate companies which had been formed by landowners and entrepreneurs. The estate companies acted as principals providing capital and organisation.

Some speculative builders formed their own companies to buy the land. This reduced the risks they faced and allowed them to work on an altogether larger scale. Ilford was on the Great Eastern Railway's main line to Ipswich. It had become an urban district in 1894. It also became the location of a new type of building enterprise: speculative building for sale rather than rent. After W.P. Griggs bought the Cranbrook Park estate, he built houses on it which were offered for sale. By 1904 he had built 2,000 houses. Another speculative builder, A.C. Corbett, built over the Clements House, Grange House, Downshall and Goodmayes estates; by 1903 he had sold over 3,000 houses in the Ilford area.

Architects developed new concepts such as lower density housing and different forms of grouping. But during the interwar period even the most idealistic designers, like Raymond Unwin, failed to match the awareness of the speculative builders when it came to what the market wanted. The 1934 National Housing Committee recommended a type of house of not less than 760 square feet, to be let at under 10s per week, inclusive of rates. But it should not have a parlour since it is 'not so necessary for healthy and decent family life as the other rooms ... and

ABOVE: *the new suburbs were healthier; Ilford (c.1900)*

PART ONE:
BACKGROUND
& ORIGINS

RIGHT: *terraced houses in
Ilford (c.1901)*

the bathroom will be placed on the ground floor ... but may serve more readily as a wash-house if placed adjacent to the scullery'. The speculative builders were well aware of what people wanted. They were successfully selling three-bedroom houses with parlours and upstairs bathrooms. In 1944, *The Dudley Report* found:

> There is a considerable difference of opinion in this matter between those producing agencies which have an interest in the collective architectural effect of the houses they build and the consumers generally, who are principally concerned with the convenience of the individual house. This is not just necessarily a financial choice, it is a reflection of taste.[9]

ABOVE: *Coleherne Court, west London (1903–04)*

In 1934, even the *Journal of the Royal Institution of British Architects* admitted: 'articles in the architectural press about the need to "educate the spec builder" were missing the point; the builder built what the public wanted'.

Immediately after the First World War, architects continued to design in a similar manner to before the war. Speculative builders were faced with very different circumstances because building for rent was no longer viable. The Permanent Building Societies had to find an alternative use for their small scale investors' funds. The solution to the problem was the financing of owner occupation. Ironically, this was similar to the original purpose of the terminating building societies which ceased to exist once their members were all housed.

Wage earners' incomes had risen enough to make them prospective home owners. As the proportion of national income from salaries grew, the government helped by granting tax relief on mortgage interest payments. Speculatively built medium and small houses met the interwar need for housing. The biggest speculative builders began to go public during the 1930s: Wimpey in 1934; Taylor Woodrow, Costain and New Ideal Homesteads were floated in 1935.

Unlike the builders of publicly funded houses, the speculative builders were able to respond to changes which personnel on the spot might suggest or customers demand. During construction of the Canons Park estate, John Laing himself realised that some of the houses would be sunless; he had the whole layout redesigned in a week. Such speed was not only necessary to catch the market, it kept down costs.

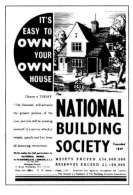

ABOVE: *interwar building society advertisement*

The speculative builders saved money by employing non-union labour and using prefabricated components. The houses they built had the characteristics of the pre-First World War semi, but with improvements resulting from the modernisation of the building supply industry and the availability of electricity and of kitchen and bathroom equipment.

They also economised on design. In January 1935 a leader in the *Illustrated Carpenter and Builder* said, 'At present the great majority of builders work to plans produced in their own offices ... it is undeniable that a sound well-planned house can be erected almost equally well from a series of sketches on the back of an old envelope as from a neatly executed and carefully coloured working drawing'.

During the Edwardian period, architects had also found new opportunities designing blocks of flats. It was the first time, in Britain, that flats became a real alternative to houses. Wealthy town dwellers might occupy a service flat and escape to their rural cottage at the weekend. In 1910 E.M. Forster described the growing number of blocks of flats as 'bricks and mortar rising and falling with the restlessness of the water in a fountain, as the city receives more and more men upon her soil'.[10]

2

Introduction to Edwardian Domestic Architecture

OPPOSITE: *a timber-framed
house in Hampstead Garden
suburb, designed by M.H.
Baillie-Scott, 1908–09.*

dwardian architects acknowledged that they were the heirs of a tradition of domestic architecture. In fact they were unashamed of 'borrowing from the past' features such as timber framing. But they also wished to distinguish themselves from their immediate predecessors, the Victorians, whom they criticised because they had been merely 'revivalist'. By 'revivalist' they meant copying earlier styles wholesale. In 1901, Charles Holme, the editor of *The Studio*, wrote:

> One of the features which characterise the opening year of the twentieth century is the renewal of
> general interest in architecture and decoration, more especially in their relation to the construction
> and ornamentation of the home. The last century was chiefly remarkable for the numerous attempts
> to revive styles belonging to the past, most of which have failed in a greater or less degree owing
> to the fact that they have misrepresented modern conditions and modern requirements. That the
> new century should generate a style characteristically its own, borrowing from the past only those
> features that are strictly in accordance with present-day needs, is the desire of all who have given
> close attention to the principles that govern truly artistic work. Some progress in the right direction
> has been made in the course of recent years, and it is not only interesting now to observe the
> present-day phases of architecture and decoration, but it will be of value in time to come to look
> back upon what are probably but the initial stages of a large and important movement.[1]

The origins of English domestic architecture lay in the rural cottage. Other plans developed from that. Cottages could be detached or built as a row or terrace. The rooms of a cottage were placed side by side. The cottage plan had to be adapted in towns where space was limited so the rooms were placed one behind the other. The structure was usually timber-framed with a brick-built fireplace. The frame was filled in with local materials. Additional accommodation was provided by adding more storeys. The jetty form of construction gave additional floor space to the upper storeys. It also threw off rainwater and made the structure stronger.

Timber-framed buildings easily caught fire and could quickly become unhygienic. Brick, which had been brought to Britain by the Romans, was less hazardous but more expensive. Brick buildings began to appear during the fifteenth century. The front range of the medieval manor

ABOVE: *a timber-framed
house in East Grinstead,
Sussex (1599)*

ABOVE: *rural plan, house
next door shown in grey*

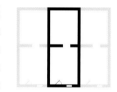

ABOVE: *urban plan; houses
on either side shown in grey*

BELOW LEFT: *a seventeenth-
century detached rural cottage
(Weald & Downland
Museum)*

ABOVE: *Sissinghurst manor
(c. 1490) one of the first brick
buildings without a timber
frame*

RIGHT: *a row of timber-framed houses of jetty construction in Staplehurst, Kent*

ABOVE: *the Banqueting House, Whitehall, one of the first classically styled buildings in Britain (1622)*

ABOVE: *early classically styled houses (c.1641), which have been attributed to Inigo Jones. They form part of the original development of Lincoln's Inn Fields*

of Sissinghurst (c.1490) was one of the earliest brick buildings without a timber frame. Brick buildings were fashionable throughout the sixteenth century.

During the first half of the seventeenth century, a fashion for classical design was introduced by Inigo Jones. In 1616 Jones was commissioned to design the Queen's House, Greenwich for King James I's wife, Anne of Denmark. (It was finally completed for King Charles I's Queen, Henrietta-Maria, in 1635.) Other commissions followed including the Banqueting House, Whitehall (1622) and the first flat-fronted brick-built terraced houses, for the Duke of Bedford, in the north-west corner of the piazza in Covent Garden.

The wealthy and influential could choose either classical proportion and harmony or the native brick-built tradition. The Great Plague (1665) and the Great Fire of London (1666) finally led to the introduction of building regulations which prohibited the construction of timber-framed buildings in the capital. Northampton, Marlborough and Bury St Edmunds had been damaged by large fires before the Great Fire of London; consequently the London Building Acts became a pattern for other local authorities to follow – for example, Warwick, which was destroyed by fire in 1694. It was rebuilt under an Act of Parliament modelled on the 1667 London Act.

Building in brick became standard in towns. The late seventeenth and early eighteenth centuries saw a fusion of classical proportions and the native brick-built tradition in what the Edwardians regarded as the English Renaissance. This included the Queen Anne (1702–14) and early Georgian (1714–50) periods.

But just as the brick-built terrace achieved its greatest success, it began to lose its appeal for Edwardian designers. By the mid-eighteenth century, terraced houses as developed in Bath by John Wood, father and son, had become desirable dwellings for those with landed income when they wished to stay in town for business or pleasure. Builders elsewhere copied their buildings but eventually the classically proportioned terraced house was reduced to a 'drab uniformity', according to John Ruskin. This was the result of successive health and safety regulations and the efforts of speculative builders to meet demand. Though William Morris had dismissed the classically proportioned terraced house as a 'brown brick box' in 1893, he did admit that the late Georgian form of the terraced house had 'some style about it and even some merit of design, if only negative'.[2] By this he meant that it was formulaic. The 'golden rectangle' could be applied

LEFT: *the oldest surviving brick-built terraced houses in London, on Newington Green (1658)*

to the façade of a large terraced house. But the strict proportions that did this were easily copied. The Edwardians acknowledged that they used the term 'Georgian' only loosely, but in their version of 'neo-Georgian' style they emulated the features of the Queen Anne and early Georgian periods. The Edwardian architect W.H. Bidlake expressed his approval; although he viewed classical architecture as 'a new and alien fashion' compared with 'the irregular and picturesque grouping of gables'. By the eighteenth century, it had become part of the English tradition:

ABOVE: *Queen's Square, Bath (1729–39), developed by John Wood, the elder, as desirable dwellings for the wealthy*

> Classic forms had now become quite acclimatised and English Renaissance architecture, in the hands of the architects of the eighteenth century, became as distinctive and as thoroughly national as English Gothic architecture had been in an earlier age ... the architectural forms of the day, although in the main classic, were yet capable of adaptation and change: they had not become stereotyped: they were still living. It was not until the latter days of the eighteenth century that the literal copyism of ancient classic forms sapped the life from the English Renaissance.[3]

Despite its critics the terraced house continued to develop in response to the demand for new housing. The Edwardians found the domestic architecture of the first half of the nineteenth century disappointing. Something new was needed. Bidlake:

> ... in this hour of direst need Mr. Norman Shaw began to address himself to the problems of house building ... Mr Shaw was not slow to perceive that the brick Renaissance houses of the eighteenth century – houses in the 'Queen Anne style' so called – more nearly answered the requirements of the present day; and it is by the revival, or more correctly the adaptation and development of this style, and its application to the town house and the small country house, as well as to the country mansion, that Mr Shaw has rendered such inestimable service to the advance of domestic architecture. Mr Philip Webb, Mr Eden Nesfield, Mr Ernest George and Mr John Belcher, not to speak of many others of lesser note, have each assisted nobly in the good work.[4]

ABOVE: *an early example of the domestic revival, cottages in Penshurst, Kent, restored by George Devey c.1850*

The Edwardians were so pleased with the development of their native traditions that they rejected any other forms; even those of Charles Rennie Mackintosh and the Glasgow School. Bidlake justified the Edwardian architects' use of tradition 'only as a base to work on'. He insisted: 'We do not want a new style.'[5] But the forms of the past might be adopted to meet current needs – for example, the use of the hall as a living room.

OPPOSITE TOP: *an original
Queen Anne house of 1705
in East Grinstead*

LEFT: *Edwardian neo-
Georgian detached house in
Hampstead Garden Suburb
(1909–11)*

The German observer, Hermann Muthesius, agreed about the beginning of the domestic revival: 'A movement opposing the imitation of styles and seeking closer ties with simple rural buildings began over forty years ago.'[6]

He gave the credit for the change in English domestic architecture to 'three architects who took the bold step of abandoning mere pastiche in architecture. They looked to simple country buildings in particular houses in villages and small towns.' 'The three men were Philip Webb, Eden Nesfield and Norman Shaw.'[7]

The one who had the greatest influence was Shaw. Muthesius explained that he 'invariably uses traditional forms, though he is not bound by them; he takes liberties with them and uses them only as an instrument for his own ideas', continuing: 'To this extent he was the first of the modern architects'.[8] Like Webb and Nesfield, Shaw mainly designed houses for the wealthy such as Leyswood, Sussex (1866) which was built in the local Wealden style. But it was Shaw's designs for medium-sized houses for the middle classes which had the greatest impact; in particular, his designs for the new suburb of Bedford Park in West London came as 'a complete revelation to the contemporary world'.[9]

OPPOSITE BELOW: *Queen
Anne Revival in Bedford Park
(1875)*

BEDFORD PARK

Bedford Park was an attempt to build an estate of small houses on artistic principles. It was a success in that the fashionable people the estate was intended to attract moved in. The family of the poet W.B. Yeats were among the early residents. Bedford Park became a sight 'which no American passing through London could miss seeing'.[10]

But it had a far wider impact. Drawings of the estate were published in the *Illustrated Sporting & Dramatic News*, *Building News* and the *British Architect*. Bedford Park soon became the subject of cartoons and satirical drawings in *Punch*. Easily available drawings and widespread approval were invitations to the speculative builders. Bedford Park was the classic example of truly significant design because speculative builders could copy it.

Speculative builders were always conscious of fashion because they built houses which were for rent; in the Edwardian period 90 per cent of the population lived in rented accommodation. Many of their tenants moved every few years. Many of Shaw's details, such as red brick and white

ABOVE: *Edwardian neo-
Georgian detached house in
Hampstead Garden Suburb
(c.1910)*

RIGHT: *the illustration of Bedford Park which appeared in* Building News

ABOVE: *a speculatively built terraced house (1886–67) with Queen Anne Revival features*

ABOVE: *the Edwardian speculative builder's version of half-timbering in Victoria Park, Manchester*

banding, were easily copied. The speculative builders' goal was to meet the demands of the public who happily moved into the new 'Queen Anne' style houses which featured tiles, tall chimneys, steep roofs with dormers, gables, bay windows, balconies and stained glass.

The 'Queen Anne' style, or Queen Anne Revival, developed into two formulas which the speculative builders could use: red brick and half-timbering. Architects like Shaw had intended red brick to be the urban form and the half-timbering its rural equivalent. By the Edwardian period speculative builders were introducing more half-timbered features into urban houses. The speculative builder's version of half-timbered was purely cosmetic – wooden strips nailed to brickwork. There was an excuse for such subterfuge. By-laws regulating building stipulated that external timbers, for example on a gable, could only be used if there was solid brickwork behind them.

LARGE, MEDIUM & SMALL

Since the late eighteenth century, typical English urban houses had fallen into three categories: large, medium and small. The London Building Act of 1774 was the culmination of various building regulations which had been passed since the Great Fire of 1666. It categorised buildings into seven rates.

Only the first four rates dealt with 'dwelling houses'. The first rate was for great or exceptional houses of over 900 square feet in size. The Building Act described them as being 'for the nobility'. The second rate was for houses of 500–900 square feet. It described them as being for 'merchants'. Typical large town houses were of the second rate. They were rented by the rich. The third rate (medium) was for 'clerks'. These houses were 350–500 square feet. The fourth rate (small), for 'mechanics' or artisans, was up to 350 square feet.

The London Building Act of 1774 resulted in entire streets of identically sized houses being built because it specified the minimum street width in relation to the height of the houses. It also provided formulae which builders could follow without incurring the additional expense of an architect. Large, medium and small houses could be built in the same style.

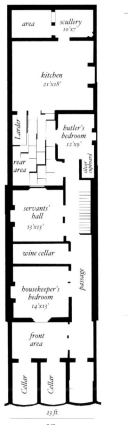

FAR LEFT: *plans of a typical large Georgian house*

LEFT: *plans of the basement (left) and ground floor (right) of a typical large Regency house. The main reception room was still on the first floor*

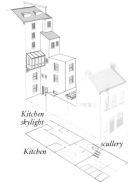

ABOVE: *changes to the plan – the kitchen and scullery were moved to the back of large houses between 1811 and 1850*

ABOVE: *paired front doors (1891–92)*

DEVELOPMENT OF THE PLAN

The ground plan of late Georgian houses was two rooms to each floor with the kitchen and the services in the basement. The chief developments in the plan during the early nineteenth century were the introduction of the dining room and the removal of the kitchen towards the back. In large houses, the kitchen was removed out of the main body of the house during the Regency and early Victorian periods (1811–50). At the same time, a new service room, the scullery, was introduced for washing-up.

During the eighteenth century, tables and chairs were arranged against the walls of reception rooms when not in use. When the occupants wished to dine, tables and chairs were moved temporarily to the middle of the room. But between 1811 and 1850, in large houses, one of the reception rooms began to be allocated as a permanent dining room. This change was not applied to medium-sized houses until the mid-Victorian period (1851–75).

The most important reception room in large houses had been on the first floor, but by the late nineteenth century, the drawing room remained on the 'piano nobile' only in large houses in the inner city. Further out, in the suburbs, it was on the ground floor so it could connect with the garden.

The most important distinction within the house was the separation of 'family' and 'service' areas. In *The Diary of a Nobody* (1894) the aspiring clerk, Mr Pooter, insists that tradesmen use the side, or service, entrance of his medium-sized, end-of-terrace house in a London suburb. By 1900 the distinction was still apparent, even in medium-sized houses where there was a step down to the kitchen in the rear extension.

By the mid-Victorian period, basements had gained an unhealthy reputation. During the late Victorian period (1876–1900) the kitchen and the services were moved to the back where they were accommodated in a rear extension or 'service wing'. Up-to-date medium houses no longer had a basement although cellars remained part of the house. In terraces, the rear extension was coupled with that of the house next door. The front doors were aligned with the rear extensions, so they, too, became paired.

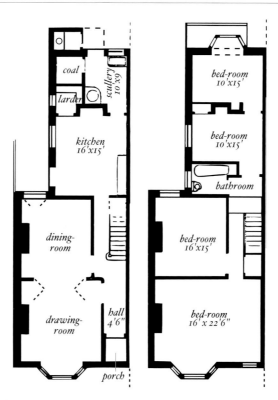

OPPOSITE: *terraced house with bay window but without basement (1886)*

FAR LEFT: *recreation of a late Victorian interior with a bay window (Geffrye Museum)*

LEFT: *ground and first floor plans of late Victorian medium terraced house showing the kitchen in the rear extension*

coal

larder

scullery 10'x9'

kitchen 16'x15'

dining-room

drawing-room

hall 4'6"

porch

bed-room 10'x15'

bed-room 10'x15'

bathroom

bed-room 16'x15'

bed-room 16' x 22'6"

By the late Victorian period, medium-sized houses were being built with bathrooms, while in older properties, bedrooms were converted into bathrooms.

In the suburbs there was less need for more storeys. A medium-sized house with a split-level rear extension could accommodate two reception rooms, four bedrooms, kitchen, scullery, bathroom and WC on two floors.

By 1900 a new plan was appearing in the suburbs. The broader plots allowed more rooms in the main body of the house. These included the kitchen and scullery. One of the reception rooms gained direct access to the garden via a conservatory or French doors.

BAY WINDOWS

The abolition of glass and window taxes in 1851 allowed builders to add bay windows to the front of both large and medium-sized houses. This helped the alignment of the doors and windows of medium-sized houses. Plate glass had arrived in 1832. For the next fifty years, the lights of sash windows were subdivided into, at most, four panes with thinner glazing bars. The bay window would remain a popular feature throughout the Edwardian and interwar periods. It took several forms: cant or straight sided, square and segmental.

DEVELOPMENT OF THE BACK

Originally, the backs of town houses were simply sites for the temporary storage of sewage, ash and refuse. After the 1875 Public Health Act the backs of houses became much more pleasant because every newly built house had to have adequate provision for the disposal of sewage and the storage and removal of ash from the coal fires. In the suburbs, where more space was available, one of the attractions was a back garden. But even when the drains were connected to the main sewers, enjoyment of the garden could be spoilt by leaks and smells. The introduction of the disconnecting trap prevented the smell from the sewer venting back into the house and garden when the WC was flushed.

ABOVE: *cut-away view of the connection to the main sewer showing improvements to drainage and sanitation*

ABOVE: *the vital improvement to the back – the disconnecting trap*

OPPOSITE: *a Victorian semi-detached villa (c.1870)*

LEFT: *the by-laws created unrelieved rows of working-class houses – Barrow Hill, Derbyshire (c.1902)*

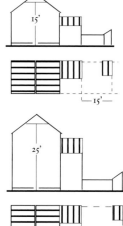

ABOVE: *the Model By-laws specified minimum space allocated to service areas at the back, according to the height of the building*

BY-LAW HOUSING

The 1875 Public Health Act was more effective than any preceding legislation in dealing with WCs, water supplies and sewers. It was followed by the 1877 Model By-Laws. These obliged local authorities to issue their own by-laws regulating street width in relation to the height of the buildings. The by-laws also dictated the minimum space which could be allocated to the service areas at the back, relative to the height of the building. This resulted in streets being laid out in rigid grids. These new streets were an improvement on earlier small houses which had become health hazards. Some towns developed into miles of parallel streets of identical by-law houses. In south Middlesbrough a single type of house with the same type of back lane was built further and further out until the early 1900s.

By 1901, many influential figures had noticed the uniformity of these working-class suburbs. In 1907, the Archbishop of Canterbury complained, in a House of Lords debate, that 'nothing could be more deplorable either aesthetically or from the point of view of health than the miserable monotonous rows of long, ugly, mean streets which are growing up around London...'

THE SEMI-DETACHED VILLA

The first villa suburb was St John's Wood in London, which was built during the Regency and Early Victorian periods (1811–37; 1837–50). The idea was to build gracious detached houses in their own grounds on the outskirts of town. As a speculation, St John's Wood was not a success, but as a prototype it was widely emulated elsewhere. In cities like Birmingham and Manchester, the rich preferred to move out to the healthier outskirts because the centres were becoming overcrowded and unhealthy.

Villas could be built in pairs as two separate dwellings which could each enjoy a greater sense of privacy than a terraced house. These semi-detached villas were the prototypes of the homes that became characteristic of the interwar years. But during the nineteenth century the description 'villa' was frequently applied to speculatively built suburban houses whether they were detached, semi-detached or even terraced – indeed, some terraced houses bore plaques with names such as 'Hanover Villa'.

By the Edwardian period some of the earlier suburban villas were being demolished to allow the land to be developed as new suburban streets of medium-sized or small houses. Terraced houses were still the most numerous type of dwelling built during the Edwardian period. But half the total number of houses built during the interwar years would be semi-detached.

ABOVE: *an end of terrace house (c.1870) with its original name plaque: 'Hanover Villa'*

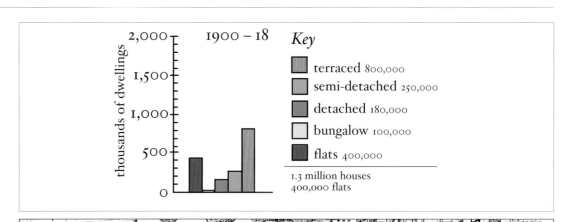

2,000 ― 1900 – 18

1,500 ―

1,000 ―

500 ―

0 ―

thousands of dwellings

Key

■ terraced 800,000
■ semi-detached 250,000
■ detached 180,000
□ bungalow 100,000
■ flats 400,000

1.3 million houses
400,000 flats

RIGHT: *chart showing numbers (in thousands) of each type of house built 1900–18*

RIGHT: *a middle-class family depicted in the garden of their recently built suburban house (c.1875). Note the builders' ladders at the backs of the, as yet unfinished, neighbouring houses*

ABOVE: *re-creation of a Georgian garden with gravel walks and flower beds edged with box hedges (Geffrye Museum)*

RIGHT: *a mid-Victorian garden with lawn, flower beds and gravel paths*

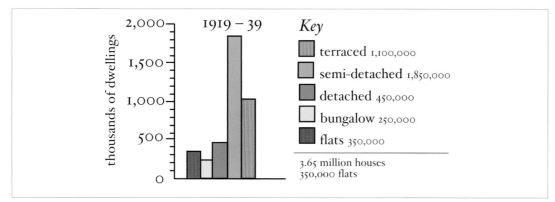

thousands of dwellings	1919 – 39	Key
2,000		terraced 1,100,000
1,500		semi-detached 1,850,000
1,000		detached 450,000
500		bungalow 250,000
0		flats 350,000

3.65 million houses
350,000 flats

LEFT: *chart showing numbers (in thousands) of each type of house built 1919–39*

GARDENS

One of the attractions of the suburbs was that a family could enjoy their own 'bit of garden'. In *Sketches by Boz*, Charles Dickens had observed that if 'the regular City man, who leaves Lloyds at five o'clock, and drives home to Hackney, Clapton, Stamford-hill, or elsewhere, can be said to have any daily recreation beyond his dinner, it is his garden.' Dickens continued: 'There is another and a very different class of men, whose recreation is their garden. An individual of this class, resides some short distance from town – say in the Hampstead-road, or the Kilburn-road, or any other road where the houses are small and neat, and have little slips of back garden.'

The gardens of Georgian town houses were formal, with gravel walks. The flower beds, edged with box hedges, held potted plants, herbs, flowers and bulbs. But this changed after the lawn mower was invented during the 1830s. It was advertised with a smartly dressed 'gentleman' in control to convey the idea that gardening was socially acceptable for the middle classes. The Victorian middle classes preferred not to grow vegetables because that was something the working classes might do: lawns and flowers were the proper objects of their attention.

The Victorian garden featured carpet bedding in shaped flower beds with topiary, hedges and geometric designs. Carpet bedding had developed during the 1860s. The surface of a bed was planted with a close cover of foliage that would provide a backdrop for flowering plants. This broke up the visual monotony of the earlier massed bedding techniques. The plants were kept clipped to a regular height and often planted in elaborate patterns or even sculptured forms. Another advantage was that the plants lasted longer than the flowers of a massed bedding system. Popular annuals were Dahlia 'White Aster', hyacinth 'L'Innocence'; nasturtium; pelargonium 'Mrs Pollock'; sweetpea 'Painted Lady'; Tulipa 'Peach Blossom'; and the rose 'General Jaquemine'.

ABOVE: *detail of a Victorian garden with topiary and box hedges*

ABOVE: *gardening was presented as socially acceptable*

LEFT: *Victorian shaped flower beds*

ABOVE: *carpet bedding*

A NEW CENTURY

Even before the death of Queen Victoria, a new generation was beginning to assert itself. By 1901 this generation not only belonged to a new century, it had a new monarch. Edwardian architects claimed what they were doing was 'modern' and wished to distance their work from that of the Victorians whom they condemned as revivalists. Edward S. Prior, writing in 1901, stated:

> If we want English homes, we want them also to be of the twentieth century: not to be Classic, nor Mediaeval, nor Tudor, nor Georgian; still less to be of the unwise Victorian habit of the nineteenth century, which masqueraded so determinately in the fancy housing of every century but its own.[11]

OPPOSITE: a suburban end of terrace house with a deep gable; it was built by W.H. George, a speculative builder, for himself (1914)

Early twentieth-century commentators distinguished between domestic architecture (exteriors) and the applied arts (interiors), which they described as 'the construction and ornamentation of the home'.[12]

The predominant Edwardian style of domestic architecture was 'cottage style'. This was a development from the domestic revival which had been led by Norman Shaw and followed by the speculative builders. A new generation of architects like C.F.A. Voysey and Edwin Lutyens designed houses which were lower and wider. They designed vernacular features in ways which were consistent with Arts & Crafts principles, such as using local materials and blending designs into their surroundings. Like Philip Webb before them, both Voysey and Lutyens designed as many of the interior details as their budgets allowed. Voysey's work began to appear in *The British Architect* from 1893. Like the earlier work of Norman Shaw, Voysey's and Lutyens's designs had a wide impact because the speculative builders could copy the features they favoured, such as rough-cast finishes and deep gables.

ABOVE: The Orchards, Chorleywood, designed by Voysey with deep gables and rough-cast finish (1899)

The designs of Voysey and Lutyens were more rural than Shaw's. They were wide, like the traditional cottage plan, and horizontal in emphasis. This was achieved by designing deep roofs and gables which came down to first-floor level. Because the available plots were wider, the speculative builders could emulate these features in the suburbs. Rough-cast finishes allowed builders to economise on the brickwork behind them.

'Cottage style' became the norm throughout the Edwardian and interwar periods. From 1910 onwards, neo-Georgian emerged as an alternative. Speculative builders quickly followed the architects' example by adding neo-Georgian features such as red brick and round-headed door arches to their repertoire.

But the Edwardian and interwar styles were mostly formed by the millions of homes built by speculative builders. They could emulate either 'cottage style' or neo-Georgian but they reacted to their market rather than the opinions of the architects. The new council houses had a very definite effect on style. Although the first estate of council houses was designed by the LCC's in-house architect W.E. Riley as a 'cottage estate' with rough cast and deep gables, it soon became apparent that the compact forms of neo-Georgian were better suited to the needs of publicly subsidised housing. The first post-war Garden City at Welwyn in Hertfordshire showed how well neo-Georgian met the need. During the 1920s neo-Georgian terraces would become standard for local authority housing. Once people began to own their own homes, they wished them to be clearly distinct from those rented from the local authority. Because of this, speculative builders preferred to avoid neo-Georgian as the new owner-occupiers wanted their homes to be clearly different from council houses. The feature they included in their designs to further distinguish them from council houses was the bay window.

ABOVE: neo-Georgian detached house (1914)

Manchester's equivalent to a garden suburb, Wythenshawe, was built during the 1930s. It was a mixture of local authority housing and private development. But it was an exception to the interwar norm because the local authority housing was built in a vernacular style and the speculatively built houses were neo-Georgian. The council houses were short vernacular style terraces. The majority of the houses built for sale were semi-detached neo-Georgian with lightly-built bay windows.

RIGHT: *the garden front at Standen, designed by Philip Webb (1892–94)*

BELOW: *a house near Winchfield, Hampshire, designed by Ernest Newton (c.1901)*

TOWN & COUNTRY

Despite the evidently urban nature of the English population, there was a particular relationship between town and country which affected house design. Muthesius observed that:

> In England one does not 'live' in the city, one merely stays there. England differs from all the other countries in the world in that even the royal residence is not in the capital, but far away in the country and the town palace is now used only for overnight stays. All the aristocracy and every well-to-do commoner lives in the country in his well-appointed country-seat, some of them of royal dimensions and most in splendid, though remote and isolated, natural surroundings. These men possess smaller town houses where they stay on visits to the capital and for a brief period during the so-called season, that is, during the spring months. Those whose daily work takes them to the city seek their place of residence as far out as possible in a suburb that has retained its rural appearance and they do not begrudge the sacrifices that this entails. Others who are obliged to live in the city at least rent a country-house in some pleasantly situated village, either for the summer months or for the whole year, where they regularly spend the time between Saturday and Monday and where they leave their family throughout the warm season. All this indicates a flight from the metropolis and an instinctive urge on the part of each individual to preserve his direct link with nature and to seek his life's contentment nowhere but in his own house.[13]

ABOVE: *the conservatory and terrace of Standen*

Standen, near East Grinstead, Sussex, was built in 1892–94 as a state-of-the-art country house and a showpiece for the Arts & Crafts movement. It was a house in the country rather than a country house because its owner did not derive his income from its surrounding land. Standen was built for a London solicitor and businessman, James Beale, who had accumulated a fortune through his various companies in Birmingham and London. The architect, Philip Webb, incorporated a farmhouse and other existing old buildings into the layout. He also designed the interiors himself, including every single fireplace and many of the artefacts, such as the metal fireguard in the dining room.

ABOVE: *the fireplace in the dining room at Standen, with metal fireguard designed by Webb. ©NTPL/Michael Caldwell*

Webb paid equal attention to the needs of the family and their staff but he followed the normal practice of keeping family and servants' quarters separate. The family rooms are light with plain panelling in harmony with the colour and pattern of the wallpapers, fabrics, tapestries and furniture. These were provided by Morris and Co. The house was fitted with its own generator for electric light. W.A.S. Benson designed the pendant electric light fittings, the table lamps and the lights over the billiard table. Webb himself designed the copper wall-hung light fittings in the drawing room.

By the Edwardian period many other architects were designing country houses for a similarly middle-class clientele, for example Ernest Newton's design for a house near Winchfield, Hampshire. Walter Shaw Sparrow explained that the architects' country house designs ranged 'from simple cottages to houses that would suit the professional man and the man of business, either as homes or places of retirement in which to pass the final years of their life, or else as places of rest for the week-ends or from the street noises of houses in town.'[14]

ABOVE: *Standen;– the lights over the billiard table were designed by W.A.S. Benson ©NTPL/Michael Caldwell*

The speculative builders picked up ideas from the design of country houses to add to town houses. For example, improvements such as electric light first appeared at Cragside, which was fitted with its own hydro-electric plant circa 1868.

To live in a country house was not only an achievement, it was an aspiration. Country house living represented peace, tradition and tranquillity as well as beauty. In both fact and fiction Edwardians dreamt of putting down roots in the English countryside.

Edward Hudson was the owner of a printing works who started the magazine *Country Life* in the late 1890s. The principal features of *Country Life* were articles on country houses. In addition,

RIGHT: *a small house near Royston, Hertfordshire, designed by John Belcher (c.1901)*

ABOVE: *Mr C.D. Harrod's premises 1901*

ABOVE: *the drawing room at Standen; furnishings by Morris & Co. ©NTPL/ Michael Caldwell*

the magazine tried to cover every aspect of rural life because it made two assumptions: that life in the country was better than life in the town and that the life of an English country gentleman was the best life of all. The urban middle classes were inclined to believe it. They were doing their best to escape to the country, if only at the weekends.

Until the last quarter of the nineteenth century, owning land was the basis of power and wealth. Those who owned land built houses on it. A country house was the physical representation of individual status. Land had always been a safe investment for the traditional English upper classes. If they did not farm themselves, landowners derived their income from the rents paid by tenant farmers. Land couldn't burn down or be lost at sea. But by 1894 the price of wheat had fallen from its 1875 price of £8.80 per tonne to £3.80. British farmers suffered a depression as a result. Families who had relied on income from their land suffered too. The landowning classes were forced to be more open to business. Those in business were eager to enjoy country living too.

By 1900 the landowning class had relaxed their objections to business or 'trade'. They had been forced to find new sources of income themselves or to marry their sons to the daughters of rich bankers, industrialists or brewers. Country house hospitality helped social mobility. 'A Foreign Resident' on *Society in the New Reign* (1904):

> The interval separating the social life of retail traders from that of the professional classes has been largely bridged over by the rural hospitalities of others who, during business hours, stand behind their Bond Street counters. The strawberry feasts, at which the head of a hair-cutting dynasty entertains his customers, almost next-door to the Rothschilds at Gunnersbury, are still smartly patronised... Latter-day Liberalism has found a notable supporter in Mr J. Barker, head of a mammoth drapery firm in Kensington. After long and lavish expenditure on party objects, he is now in Parliament, and, if with good reason expectant of a baronetcy, is not likely to let a title shame him out of his trade. Mr C.D. Harrod is visited by academics and parliamentarians at his hunting-box in the Exmoor region. Mr. Whiteley, of Westbourne Grove, from among his young ladies, provides wives for Indian staff-officers.

Aspiring owners of country houses were more likely to build than existing owners. The new owners' taste in country houses was progressive. They employed architects like Voysey and Baillie-

Scott. They received plans featuring grey-green Delabole slates, white-washed, rendered or oak-framed exteriors and uncomfortably original furniture within. The result was a house in the country rather than a country house. A fictional example of this appeared in *Howards End* by E.M. Forster (1910). When Henry Wilcox and Meg Schlegel become engaged, they 'look out for something in the spring'. They decide to 'go down to Sussex and build' near Midhurst. When Meg looks at the plans, she remarks: 'We are to have a good many gables and a picturesque skyline.'

Country Life featured newly built country houses but preferred more traditional properties. Vita Sackville-West extolled the merits of houses which were 'essentially part of the country, not only in the country but part of it – "a natural growth".'[15]

The eponymous country house, *Howards End,* was an example of this. In a letter to her sister, Meg, Helen Schlegel wrote:

> It is old and little, and altogether delightful – red brick... From the hall you go right or left into dining-room or drawing-room. Hall itself is practically a room. You open another door in it, and there are stairs going up in a sort of tunnel to the first floor. Three bedrooms in a row there, and three attics in a row above. That isn't the house really but it's all that one notices – nine windows as you look up from the front garden. Then there's a big wych-elm – to the left as you look up – leaning out a little over the house and standing on the boundary between the garden and meadow. I quite love that tree already. Also ordinary elms, oaks – no nastier than ordinary oaks – pear trees, apple trees and a vine. No silver birches though... Oh the beautiful vine leaves! The house is covered with a vine... 'The dog roses are too sweet. There is a great hedge of them over the lawn – magnificently tall, so that they fall down in garlands, and nice and thin at the bottom, so that you can see ducks through it and a cow. These belong to the farm which is the only house near us.[16]

Henry Wilcox disagreed with Vita Sackville-West's criteria:

> Well. Howards End is one of those converted farms. They don't really do, spend what you will on them. We messed away with a garage all among the wych-elm roots, and last year we enclosed a bit of the meadow and attempted a rockery. Evie got rather keen on Alpine plants. But it didn't do – no, it didn't do. You remember, or your sister will remember, the farm with those abominable guinea-fowls, and the hedge that the old woman never would cut properly, so that it all went thin at the bottom. And, inside the house, the beams – and the staircase through a door – picturesque enough, but not a place to live in.[17]

LEFT: the morning room at Standen. The pendant lights were designed by Benson, the wall-hung lights by Webb.
©NTPL/Michael Caldwell

MODEL DEVELOPMENTS

Bedford Park was just one of a series of model developments that introduced innovations in design and layout which had significant influence on Edwardian and interwar houses. They were designed by architects and copied by speculative builders. The common element to all these schemes was space and light. This was achieved in ways which contrasted with the monotony of the uniform streets which followed the 1877 by-laws, a monotony evoked by J.B. Priestley describing surviving by-law streets in Swindon in 1934:

> Here there were no gardens and the houses were built in immense unbroken rows. It was a town laid out for Victorian artisans, who no doubt considered themselves lucky to be there. I seemed to walk miles between these brick facades, for ever the same height. Each street seemed exactly like the last. Nowhere did I see one house bigger or older or newer or in any way better or worse than the others. Everywhere, the same squat rows. It was like wandering through a town for dingy dolls. There was nothing to break the monotony. If a number of bees and ants, cynically working in bricks and mortar, had been commissioned to build a human dormitory, they could not have worked with a more desolating uniformity.[18]

As early as the 1870s, Lord Shaftesbury, George Cadbury, Joseph Rowntree and Ebenezer Howard came to the conclusion that 'the root of most social evils lay in the bad housing conditions in which all too many had to live.'[19]

ABOVE: *a by-law street in Salford*

The Shaftesbury Park Estate, in Battersea, was a small scheme developed by the Artisans', Labourers' & General Dwellings Company, a co-operative movement of small builders and workmen. The Company's aim was to provide healthy housing for working people. Lord Shaftesbury showed his support by laying the foundation stone in 1872 and allowing the estate to be named after him. He also advised George Peabody to make housing for the poor the beneficiary of his goodwill. The result was the Peabody Trust which was responsible for building one of the first blocks of flats for workers, or 'tenements', Farringdon Road Buildings (1874). Municipal tenements like these were not regarded as desirable by contemporaries. The novelist George Gissing described them as 'terrible barracks'.[20]

The Shaftesbury Park Estate contained twelve hundred houses which accommodated eight thousand people in low-rise houses with gardens. The new residents were mainly better-off workers and clerks. The Artisans', Labourers' & General Dwellings Co built a second estate in Kilburn, north-west London, in 1877.

ABOVE: *Shaftesbury Estate, low rise houses with gardens (1872–73)*

As we have seen, Bedford Park was one of the most significant developments. Built from 1875 onwards, its street layout avoided the grid by winding round existing trees and planting others. The streets were laid out to resemble a village. The gardens had wooden fences.

The development consisted of the full range of medium-sized house types: terraced, detached and semi-detached but the interior layouts were similar. The general interior layout was a drawing room at the front, dining room at the back with kitchen on the ground floor. Above were three bedrooms, bath and WC with additional bedrooms on the attic floor. There were no basements. Sculleries and stores were placed in single storey rear extensions.

Bedford Park's suburban location and proximity to public transport were also the shape of things to come. Its style was more red brick than rural but elements of rural style such as hanging tiles were there for all to see.

William Hesketh Lever founded Port Sunlight in 1888 to house the workers at his soap factory. It was intended to be a garden village. The maintenance and upkeep of the village was subsidised with a portion of the profits from his company. It featured a variety of vernacular styles including the local Cheshire style. Lever employed nearly thirty different architects to design the blocks of cottages, including Edwin Lutyens and Ernest Newton. The houses were laid out in smaller blocks of between three and ten, with standardised interiors. A high quality of building materials was coupled with careful detailing.

ABOVE: *Port Sunlight; cottages designed in the local Cheshire style (1902)*

RIGHT: *Letchworth, a theory that was realised as short terraces with gables (1903–07)*

ABOVE: *Bournville, 'a small contribution to the solution of a great problem'*

ABOVE: *New Earswick, a 'garden' village*

In 1895 George and Richard Cadbury moved their works from the centre of Birmingham to Bournville, which was then a rural area, four miles out of the city. Cadbury 'was himself fond of country life, and knew its material and spiritual advantages over life in crowded industrial areas, and when the factory was thoroughly established in its new environment he began to seek ways and means of giving more and more people the opportunity to enjoy it. He did not, however, contemplate a scheme only for the benefit of his own workpeople; rather, his idea was to make what he called "a small contribution to the solution of a great problem" – the problem of housing as affecting large industrial towns.'[21]

The Cadburys were Quakers, as were the Rowntrees. In 1901 Joseph Rowntree commissioned two provincial architects, Barry Parker and Raymond Unwin, to design a new 'garden village' for the employees of his cocoa and confectionery business just outside York. New Earswick was to be a balanced village community. Rents were to be kept low but they were supposed to generate a modest return on the capital invested. Houses in New Earswick were to be open to any working people, not just Rowntree employees. The houses were to be 'artistic in appearance, sanitary, well built and yet within means of men earning about 25s (£1.25) per week.' Rowntree hoped that New Earswick would become a model for other developments elsewhere.

Rowntree insisted that the houses had gardens with fruit trees and enough ground to grow vegetables. The Joseph Rowntree Village Trust, which was set up in 1904 to build and manage New Earswick, safeguarded the open green spaces. All the grass verges were planted with trees. Parker and Unwin were forced to cut costs by standardising components and by using rectangular shapes. They took their experience with them on to their next project.

Perhaps the most radical of all these model developments was the Garden City at Letchworth, which was not only intended to be a mixed community but to include residential and industrial areas. It was to be the first step in a radical programme of social reform and renewal, a solution to the 'great problem'. The idea of a 'garden city' was the conception of Ebenezer Howard, whose vision gathered a considerable amount of support, including that of the Cadburys and the Rowntrees. Howard explained:

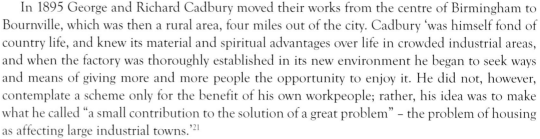

My proposal is that there should be an earnest attempt made to organise a migratory movement of population from our overcrowded centres to sparsely-settled rural districts; that the mind of the public should not be confused, or the efforts of organisers wasted in a premature attempt to accomplish this work on a national scale, but that great thought and attention shall be first concentrated on a single movement yet one sufficiently large to be at once attractive and resourceful.[22]

Howard and his supporters held conferences at which their ideas and plans were discussed. They formed a Garden City Association. The aim of the Garden City movement was to regenerate the entire country by relocating industry in rural areas to avoid conurbations. Garden cities would be established across the country. Ultimately, authority would be decentralised. In May 1900 the Association decided to form a limited company with share capital of £50,000 for a new town. The company bought some land near the village of Letchworth in Hertfordshire.

Ebenezer Howard's original idea had been entirely theoretical. As he later admitted, 'it was purely an idea – a theory which had not stood the test – the severest test always of an endeavour to realise it, and in my book I said very little about the steps which must be taken if the idea of a garden city was to be realised.'[23]

It fell to Parker and Unwin to realise 'the idea of a garden city'. Unwin had given a paper to the Garden City Conference in 1902, in which he stated that natural features should be incorporated into new developments. In April 1904 the Rowntrees sponsored a competition to design the first Garden City at Letchworth. Three architectural partnerships submitted plans. Those offered by Parker and Unwin were the only plans which were not symmetrical with formal centres. By the time they received the commission they had already moved to the site.

ABOVE & BELOW LEFT:
Letchworth; use of paths and grouping around greens

Their design placed a central square on the highest point of the site. The axes and termini culminated in views and prospects. Both peripheral and central roads were intended to funnel traffic away from the residential areas, showing the planners' awareness that motor traffic would probably become a major factor.

Their layouts achieved low density housing by grouping the houses in short terraces and placing groups of houses around village greens. They introduced the cul de sac to provide access to building plots. The cul de sacs were extended to enclose ornamental greens which further separated the housing from roads. Footpaths gave access to gardens. They used single gables to unify main elevations and angled houses across corners. Unwin planned in a comprehensive way, from interiors up to town and regional plans, but had a continual struggle to ensure adequate

RIGHT: *houses set back around a communal green in Hampstead Garden Suburb, designed by Geoffry Lucas*

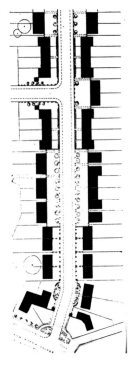

ABOVE: *block plan of Rotherwick Road, showing how Unwin's grouping worked: houses are grouped in blocks with the same building line*

ABOVE: *a view of the Heath along a street radiating from the central square of Hampstead Garden Suburb*

quality control while keeping costs to a level at which the houses would remain cheap enough for workers to rent.

The Cheap Cottages Exhibition (1905), held at Letchworth, gave the impression that cottages were for 'week-enders' as well as agricultural labourers or artisans. The factory area filled up more quickly than expected: Greshams, an engineering firm, Idris, a mineral water producer, and the Garden City Press moved in. The biggest problem was lack of finance: the development was under-funded, which resulted in plots being sold off, and as a result, the estate became a patchwork of small sites.

BEAUTY IN THE SUBURBS

The next project undertaken by Parker and Unwin was Hampstead Garden Suburb, another attempt to create a mixed community, for which they were appointed architects in March 1906.

The scheme arose out of one woman's wish to save part of Hampstead Heath, on what were then the outskirts of London, from being built over. In 1902 Henrietta Barnett's peaceful retirement in Hampstead was threatened when permission was granted to build an extension of the newly electrified Underground Railway to a new terminus at Golders Green. She at once set about rallying support for a scheme to save the threatened part of the Heath. She formed a syndicate with the Earl of Crewe, Earl Grey, the Bishop of London and others. They gained the Heath 'extension of eighty acres and surrounding land' on which to develop 'a garden suburb for all classes'. The Hampstead Garden Suburb Trust wanted to meet the housing problem by putting within reach of working people the opportunity of taking a cottage 'within a 2d fare of Central London and at a modest rent'.[24]

A local Act of Parliament was necessary to exempt Hampstead Garden Suburb from the 1877 by-laws covering road construction. Henrietta Barnett's notes on Unwin's original plan had designated seventy acres of houses for the 'industrial classes at ten per acre'. But the Act was passed only in return for an agreement that the site density would be eight houses per acre. Unfortunately this limited the ability of the scheme to provide a complete range of housing 'for all classes', an ambition with which Unwin was very much in sympathy. He disapproved of building large areas of housing of exactly the same size and type. He thought it was 'bad, socially, economically and aesthetically. It is due to the wholesale and thoughtless character of town development'.[25]

The Suburb Trust acquired land from the church commissioners to build Rotherwick Road to connect the Suburb with the station. The buildings at the junction of Rotherwick Road and the Finchley Road became one of the gateways into the Suburb.

Hampstead Garden Suburb took beauty in the suburbs to a whole new level. Almost immediately features and techniques used there began to be copied in neighbouring streets. Golders Green station was opened by David Lloyd George on 22 June 1907. Prospective purchasers and tourists came to marvel. Within ten days of the station's opening, Virginia Woolf was one of the first to come to view the completed development. She recorded in her diary:

> The Twopenny Tube has now burrowed as far as Golders Green; so that sinking into earth laid with pavement and houses at one end, you rise to soft green fields at the other ... Well, we all of us got out at Golders Green; which term I take to apply to a dusky triangle between cross roads ... occupied by a cluster of idle people sucking like bees at some gaudy and profuse flower. Their little island was a refuge from motor cars which shot constantly past ... no real country road ... is raked so persistently by huge barrelled motor cars; nor do strings and knots and couples of brightly dressed people fill all the way, so that you must steer to get past them.

During the interwar years the Suburb expanded from its original landholding as far as East Finchley station. Unwin left to dedicate himself to planning in 1914, but he continued to live in the Suburb. Barry Parker became the architect of Wythenshawe, Manchester's municipal satellite. He began to plan the development during the 1920s, but building was delayed until the 1930s.

ABOVE: *a building angled across a corner of Rotherwick Road, one of the original entrances to Hampstead Garden Suburb, designed by Charles Wade Paget in Unwin's Hampstead office (1909)*

LEFT: *houses around a green, in Hampstead Garden Suburb, designed by Edwin and James Palser (1908–10)*

WELWYN GARDEN CITY

After the First World War, the Garden City movement made a second attempt at Welwyn. In 1919 Howard put down a deposit for part of Lord Desborough's Panshanger estate near Welwyn. This consisted of 1,458 acres, acquired at a cost of £51,000. Second Garden City Ltd was formed in 1920, with capital of £250,000.

Louis de Soissons FRIA was appointed to plan the town. His proposals were similar to Unwin's planning style as detailed in *Town Planning in Practice*. He chose a local version of red brick neo-Georgian rather than rough-cast vernacular and included features like Mansard roofs and the occasional bay window to enliven a terrace.

The new development was one of the first to benefit from the 1919 Housing Act. In 1921 the local authority included houses for rent in its own plans, which were to be built under the overall direction of de Soissons. To reduce the costs of the services, roads followed the contours of the land wherever possible and the use of cul de sacs reduced the service expenditure. A frequent layout was the close of about twelve houses. The original grass verges were not suitable for cars and by 1927 it was already clear that the courts and cul de sacs were also too narrow to accommodate them.

The cottages and terraced houses at Welwyn were similar to those at Letchworth. They consisted of three bedrooms with fireplaces in two of them, a bath in the scullery and a covered way to the external WC. There were no fitted cupboards, but a fuel store and larder were provided. Every Garden City cottage or terrace had gardens, at both front and rear. Even the smallest had intimate fireplace alcoves in the living room, wooden ceiling beams, window seats and French windows opening out onto terraces in the garden.

Like Letchworth and Hampstead Garden Suburb, plots had to be sold off to finance the development. These plots became medium or large houses so, once again, it was the better off who ended up living in the improved environment.

OPPOSITE ABOVE: *Welwyn Garden City; a terrace enlivened with occasional bays*

OPPOSITE BELOW: *Welwyn Garden City; a short terrace with hipped rooves*

ABOVE: *Welwyn Garden City; a medium sized house*

LEFT: *Welwyn Garden City; a terrace showing the passage which gave access to the back*

THE FIRST COUNCIL HOUSES

Council houses – small houses built by local authorities for rent by the working classes – began to appear in significant numbers during the Edwardian period. They would become a substantial proportion of the national housing stock during the interwar years. There was an increasing concern about the housing problem for several reasons. There was, obviously, a housing shortage. A survey of the health of workers recruited during the Boer War (1899–1902) had made the poor quality of housing a political issue. High building costs caused housing shortages, which allowed landlords to charge higher rents. In 1876 the *Derby Mercury* had reported that rents of six shillings per week were being charged for two rooms in an article entitled 'Overcrowding and Unhealthy Habitations'.

The 1890 Housing of the Working Classes Act encouraged local authorities to improve the housing in their areas. The Act gave them permission to build housing for rent but they were not obliged to do so. However, they were given powers to compel the sale of land for this purpose. Local Authorities in Liverpool, Manchester, Sheffield and London became the pioneers. Other cities, such as Birmingham, set up committees to examine the housing problem. One of the difficulties was the high cost of land in areas where it was needed, such as Battersea. A second Housing of the Working Classes Act, in 1900, gave local authorities powers to purchase land outside their boundaries. This enabled the London County Council (LCC) to obtain suitable land at much less cost. At first, they took care to site their new estates where there was cheap travel: two pence for a workman's daily return fare.

The LCC's first estate of council houses was at Totterdown Fields, just off the Upper Tooting Road. This was served by the Council's first electric tramway. Between 1903 and 1911 roads were laid out and 1,299 houses were built on what was referred to as a 'cottage estate'. The houses were built in terraces of twenty, set back five to fifteen feet from the road. There were a variety of exterior designs but all the houses had paired front doors, set at an angle to each other. The fronts were finished in rough cast or hanging tiles, with deep gables. They were designed by the LCC's in-house architect, W.E. Riley.

Each house had a small garden. The cheaper houses had a living room, two bedrooms and a scullery. The larger ones had a living room, parlour, three bedrooms and a scullery with bath. The rent for a three-bedroom cottage was 7s (35p) a week. The average tenant earned about 32s (£1.60) per week. Only those in regular employment were able to afford the new houses.

The LCC built an estate outside its area of jurisdiction, at Norbury, between 1906 and 1910. This was poorly served by electric tramways, unlike the White Hart Lane Estate, built between 1904 and 1915, which was half a mile from Bruce Grove station, GER. A tram service was soon provided to cover the distance to the station where a twopence daily workman's return fare was available. W.E. Riley again designed the houses, this time in a variety of styles including vernacular and neo-Georgian. He also varied the building lines and grouping. Almost all the houses had a bath. Rents for two to five rooms varied from 6s to 13s per week. The LCC only built one more cottage estate before the outbreak of the First World War. Its final pre-war estate was built at Old Oak in Hammersmith and was almost a mile from any public transport.

Manchester, Liverpool and several London authorities completed blocks of flats which were known as municipal tenements or dwellings.[26] In 1903 Manchester purchased Heaton Park, for the use of the people of Manchester, and set about the building of a Corporation housing estate at Blackley. Bristol City Council made its first attempt to provide homes for rent in 1905 with a common lodging house in Wade Street, St Judes. But contemporary opinion preferred houses to blocks of flats. Sheffield built municipal housing in straight terraces (1903–05) on the Flower Estate, Wincobank. This estate was a mixed development, part of which was a garden suburb. The earlier council houses proved so expensive that the later ones were built without bathrooms. In 1907, Wincobank became the site of the North Midland Cottage Exhibition. The council subsequently bought the exhibition houses.

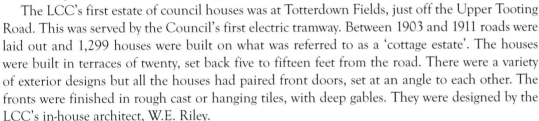

OPPOSITE: *council houses on the LCC's first 'cottage estate' at Totterdown fields (1903–11)*

ABOVE: *tile hung gable on the LCC's estate at White Hart Lane (1904–15)*

ABOVE: *paired front doors on the LCC's estate at White Hart Lane (1904–15)*

ABOVE: *council cottages at Totterdown Fields*

ABOVE: *council cottages at White Hart Lane*

'HOMES FIT FOR HEROES'

During the First World War very few new homes were built. As a result rents soon rose until there was a threat of civil disorder. In 1915 the government fixed both the rents of smaller houses and mortgage interest at pre-war levels. By the end of the war the cost of building a small house was four times that of 1914. Wholesale materials and labour were both in short supply. By 1920 the cost of materials was still three times that of 1913.

The housing shortage was such that an estimated 600,000 to 850,000 dwellings were required in England and Wales. Rents were still kept down by law. Newly built dwellings were not subject to fixed rents but they were too expensive for those for whom they were intended. Private enterprise was unable to meet the demand for housing. The government had to act before the returning servicemen became revolutionary.

In November 1918 the Prime Minister, David Lloyd George, proclaimed in a speech in Wolverhampton: 'What is our task? To make Britain a country fit for heroes to live in.' Housing was clearly an urgent political issue. 'Homes fit for heroes' became an election slogan. In 1919 King George V said publicly: 'If unrest is to be converted into contentment the provision of good housing may prove one of the most potent agents in that conversion.'[27]

In July 1917 the government had set up a committee to consider plans for postwar housing, led by Sir Tudor Walters MP. The committee's report came out in 1919. It was mostly the work of Raymond Unwin, the pioneer town planner. It stressed the importance of open layout with no more than twelve houses per acre, a minimum of seventy feet between rows of facing houses and still greater width on roads carrying through-traffic. It stipulated that the houses themselves should be at least 760 square feet, with three bedrooms, a living room, sunny aspect, a small parlour, a reasonably sized scullery and a bathroom and WC accessible under cover.

In response to the Tudor Walters report, Dr Christopher Addison, the Minister for Health, introduced the Addison Act which made local authorities responsible for providing low-rent housing. The Act guaranteed that losses would be made good by the national government. It was

LEFT & BELOW: *council houses built at Knebworth, Hertfordshire (c.1924). Red-brick neo-Georgian was the predominant local style*

estimated that 500,000 houses should be built. But only 214,000 had been built by the time the threat of civil disorder had receded and funds began to run out. By 1923 most local authorities had stopped building.

The new council houses were subject to the standards specified in the Tudor Walters report. To achieve this, local authorities had to build on cheap land at locations on the fringes of the cities, such as Finchley or Enfield on London's northern borders. They also needed to build in areas served by public transport. The new small houses quickly began to appear around suburban railway stations like Earlsfield in South London. Manchester City Council's Old Moat Estate (1927) was served by trams. Birmingham, Leeds and Liverpool also extended their networks of electric trams.

Towns like Derby reacted by planning two types of houses. One type had a parlour, living room, scullery, three bedrooms and bathroom for a rent of 12 shillings (£0.60) per week. The other only had a living room, scullery, three bedrooms and bathroom for a rent of 10 shillings (£0.50) per week. Actual building began about 1922. The delay was due to a debate about the design of small houses which would continue throughout the interwar period. Influential planners such as Unwin considered that a parlour was unnecessary and baths could be taken in the scullery. Derby Corporation built 7,050 houses during the interwar years.

The largest council housing estate was at Becontree, where over 25,000 houses were built between 1921 and 1932. One hundred thousand people moved into the estate, which lay within the parishes of Dagenham, Barking and Ilford, in Essex.

Welwyn in Hertfordshire was one of the first places to begin building. It had just become an Urban District Council and coordinated its efforts with the Garden City development which was being built there at the same time. This adopted the red brick neo-Georgian style which was the predominant local form of architecture. Other local authorities followed their example. Neo-Georgian terraces and semi-detached forms became the interwar standard for council-houses until efforts at slum clearance and reducing overcrowding made it necessary to build flats.

Introduction to Edwardian Interiors

he most obvious influence upon Edwardian interior design was the Arts & Crafts movement. But William Morris and the other designers generally grouped together under the Arts & Crafts heading were only one of a number of groups which came together in the latter half of the nineteenth century in reaction to the first generation of factory-produced or machine-made products as exhibited at the Great Exhibition of 1851. All shared an abhorrence for what their hero, John Ruskin, had described as 'soulless, repetitive industrialism'[1] and believed that inspiration should be sought from direct observation of what Ruskin called 'the beauty of the natural world'.[2]

One such group was the Design Reform movement which was influential in setting up the National Art Schools, where drawing from nature became a standard practice. The National Art Schools trained several designers who influenced Edwardian style, including Christopher Dresser, Archibald Knox and Gertrude Jekyll. Another was the Aesthetic Movement, a loose grouping of people who valued individuality and beauty. They were particularly interested in the applied arts and gained their title in 1878 when Charles Eastlake suggested the use of lighter, more 'aesthetic' styles with simplicity being the desired effect.[3] Jonathan Carr's development of Bedford Park was considered to be an attempt to develop an estate of Aesthetic houses because it was intended for well-educated, middle-class people of moderate means rather than 'carriage folk'. Carr's original choice for Bedford Park was the exemplary Aesthetic designer, Edward Godwin. The Aesthetic Movement's most distinctive taste was for Japanese fans and blue-and-white china. The magazine which favoured Aesthetics was *The Burlington*, founded in 1881. The most obvious feature of Aesthetic interiors was the over-mantel, on which works of art could be displayed.

OPPOSITE: *an 1890s Aesthetic interior. Note the elaborate overmantel*

ABOVE: *a caricature depicting an Aesthetic couple admiring a teapot.*
Aesthetic Bridegroom: 'It is exquisite, is it not?'
Intense Bride: 'It is indeed! Oh, Algernon, let us live up to it!'

FAR LEFT: *an Aesthetic Gothic room, the Ante-room of The Grove, Harborne, Birmingham, 1877–78, designed by architect J.H. Chamberlain for William Kenrick*

LEFT: *greenery-yallery, a tile in Aesthetic taste and colours*

Right: *Sussex chair by Morris & Co; the model remained in production until the firm's demise in 1940.*

Far Right: *Honeysuckle, a wallpaper designed by William Morris (1876)*

The Arts & Crafts movement itself began through the efforts of a number of individuals to develop alternatives to the 'vast output of poor substitutes for good craftsmanship [which] was poured broadcast over the land'.[4] By 1881 the critic Robert Eddis insisted that consumers should be more critical of the 'products of common industry':

> Ordinary English homes (of twenty years ago) were fitted out either in the dreariest monotony of common places or made gaudy with paper-hangings and floor coverings of vulgar colouring and design. The most formidable obstacle which lies in the way of any attempt to reform the arts of design in this country is, perhaps, the indifference with which people of even reputed taste are accustomed to regard the products of common industry.[5]

Above: *Primrose, a tile designed by William Morris (1862)*

Above: *Fruit, an early Morris wallpaper design (1866)*

The 'products of common industry' were cheap roller-printed wallpapers and textiles woven on Jaquard looms. Morris himself explained that the Arts & Crafts movement had been necessary 'because the applied arts had been "sick unto death"', and that this 'forced us into taking up the dropped line of tradition and once more producing genuine organic art'.[6]

This 'organic' art would be created, it was believed, if the traditionally rigid distinction between Fine and Applied Arts, between designer and craftsman, was abolished. When applied to architecture, for example, this approach would encourage architects to, as far as possible, design the details of their interiors themselves rather than delegating the task.

In 1893 Walter Crane, the president of the Arts & Crafts Exhibition Society, stated that 'life is growing "uglier every day," as Mr Morris puts it'.[7] He also expressed his fear that artists would be seduced by commercial considerations if they catered for the new middle-class market which had opened up through shops because 'if artists cease to be found among the crafts there is great danger that they will vanish from the arts also, become manufacturers and salesmen instead'.[8] This statement reveals another aspect of the Arts & Crafts movement: that it preferred to produce for an exclusive market which could afford hand-made goods. Even Morris admitted that he found himself 'ministering to the swinish luxury of the rich'.[9]

Thus, although the Arts & Crafts movement set up a number of enterprises to produce the hand-crafted designs it advocated, its adherents preferred to ignore the 'people of even reputed taste' to whom Eddis had referred. Crane even disdained the new retail outlets which made the applied arts accessible to this wider market, rejecting larger-scale production of goods for sale through shops as impersonal; it seemed absurd to him that an artist or craftsman should be expected to produce things of beauty for an impersonal and unknown public.

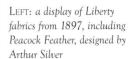

LEFT: *a display of Liberty fabrics from 1897, including Peacock Feather, designed by Arthur Silver*

ABOVE: *silver Cymric tray & coffee service designed for Liberty's (1902–03). The Cymric range successfully competed with the Guild of Handicraft*

ABOVE: *silver jamdish designed by C.R. Ashbee, made by the Guild of Handicraft*

ABOVE: *table lamp standard designed by Roger Fry for Omega workshops (1912–18)*

None of the other Arts & Crafts movement enterprises was as successful as Morris's own company, Morris & Co. This survived through the support provided by Morris's contacts such as G.F. Bodley and Philip Webb, who brought it commissions to provide stained glass and, later, to furnish entire interiors. Various attempts were made to set up workshops to employ craftsmen, such as C.R. Ashbee's Guild of Handicraft. The Arts and Crafts Exhibitions Society was formed to hold exhibitions, in 1888 and 1889, to boost these flagging enterprises. The Guild of Handicraft actually came into direct competition with Liberty's because some of its artefacts were similar to Liberty's Cymric range. Liberty's was an outstandingly successful retail enterprise which catered for the 'people of even reputed taste' of whom Eddis was critical. By 1880 it was importing 'Eastern Art Manufactures' such as Chinese and Japanese bronzes, enamels, jade, ceramics, embroideries and rugs. Its founder, Arthur Lasenby Liberty, went on to commission fabrics, furniture, silver and pewter from designers such as Archibald Knox, Christopher Dresser and Silver Studio. Unlike the Arts & Crafts enterprises, Liberty's is still trading today.

Not even Roger Fry's Omega Workshops lasted more than a few years despite the fact that, like Morris, Fry was well connected. Although the Arts & Crafts movement as a whole disdained shops and the middle-class market, Morris & Co. had a shop on Regent Street and another outlet in Manchester. Morris's wallpapers and a few other products such as their Sussex chair were truly popular. In 1904 Muthesius recorded that Morris's early wallpaper designs, Daisy and Pomegranate, 'are as popular today as they were forty-five years ago when they first appeared.'[10] Morris reverted to the traditional craft-based technique of block printing and developed patterns suited to this. His greatest achievements were in pattern design: wallpapers from 1864, printed textiles from 1873 and carpets from 1875.

Right: *Voysey designs;
desk (1896) and Purple Bird
(1899), a woven silk and
wool double cloth, produced
by Alexander Morton & Co*

Above: *table designed by
Voysey (1903)*

Above: *Clutha glass vase
designed by Dresser (c.1900)*

Above: *Cordofan candlestick
designed by Dresser*

By 1900 the Arts & Crafts aversion to machine production had become a fashionable orthodoxy. But its proponents were being left behind by developments like the first Ideal Home Exhibition, which was held in 1908. The Exhibition was sponsored by the *Daily Mail.* The paper and the Exhibition were designed to attract the middle classes, particularly clerks and women with a certain amount of disposable income. Moreover, innovations such as the telephone and electricity meant that change was inevitable. The introduction of electricity alone made a considerable difference to Edwardian interiors.

The designer, J.D. Sedding (1838-91), who exhibited at the first Arts & Crafts Exhibition Society show, had already conceded that it was unrealistic to imagine that the movement's standards could be universally applied: 'Let us not suppose that machinery will be discontinued. Manufacture cannot be organised on any other basis. We had better make life square with the facts, rather than rebel against the inevitable, in striving for the ideal.'[11]

After 1910 attitudes began to change even more rapidly, as demonstrated by the career of W.A.S. Benson. Benson was Morris's successor as chairman of Morris & Co, yet he also became a founding member of the Design & Industries Association (DIA). The DIA was founded in 1914-15 by designers, businessmen and industrialists. Its slogan 'Nothing Need Be Ugly' reflected a change in the way that products were designed and perceived by the public. Benson's change of allegiance from Arts & Crafts to DIA reflected the gradual acceptance that machine production was an irreversible change that designers should work with rather than against.

It is also important to note that not all designers had been opposed to machinery. Christopher Dresser was an exact contemporary of Morris but he chose to work within the industrial system rather than against it. Dresser, and others such as Owen Jones, led the way towards professionalism in design. Dresser attended the London School of Design where he studied design and botany. The essence of design reform was based on the study of nature rather than copying earlier artworks. Unlike other designers, Dresser never became involved with architecture but worked in a commercial design studio. He produced designs for over fifty companies including the new retail outlets such as Liberty's, for which he designed Clutha glass vases and Cordofan candlesticks. In 1899 he was described by *The Studio* magazine as 'the greatest of commercial designers'. Liberty's did not credit individual designers but they commissioned Archibald Knox and Rex Silver's Silver Studio. Liberty's Art Fabrics earned them the compliment that, in parts of Europe, Art Nouveau was known as 'Stile Liberty'.

New department stores catered for the growing wealthy middle class; Selfridges, Harrods, Debenhams in London; Lewis's and Paulden's in Manchester. The introduction of hire-purchase extended the market further. Specialist shops such as Heal's, Maples, and Waring & Gillow[12] also became patrons of the applied arts. They did so by ordering whole ranges of goods which were designed to be sold through stores rather than in limited numbers as private commissions. Their goods were displayed in showrooms and illustrated in catalogues.

EDWARDIAN PATTERN DESIGN

Edwardian pattern design was based on floral motifs in the tradition established by Morris and his successors. The most prolific Edwardian pattern designer was C.F.A. Voysey. In 1896 *The Studio* stated: 'Now a "Voysey wallpaper" sounds almost as familiar as a "Morris chintz" or a "Liberty silk".' In 1893 Voysey signed a contract to Essex & Co. for whom he created hundreds of designs up until 1930. He tried not to use the 'greenery-yallery' palette of Arts & Crafts interiors, preferring 'crudity, if you will, rather than mud and mourning'.

Until the First World War the British textile industry was predominant. As early as 1897 *The Studio* had reported 'le Stile Anglais' was invading France where 'the majority of designers and manufacturers are content to copy and disfigure English patterns'. Various art movements provided alternatives to the mainstream. During the Edwardian period the alternative was the 'new art', as they called 'Art Nouveau'. Bidlake acknowledged that the 'new art' grew out of the Arts & Crafts movement:

> But excesses of enthusiasm came, wild and foolish excesses that proved to be a reversion to pre-historic barbarity. The 'New Art' craze came into being, and it is still so recent that we can hardly yet realise that it was and is a nightmare and not a permanent reality. Is it not extraordinary, and not a little inconsistent, that those who were advocating the revival of craft traditions should have deprecated the continuance of architectural tradition also, seeking to remove that rudder which, all along the history of the world's architectural development, is seen to be the steadying and steering agent? Thus relieved of guidance and restraint every man did that which was right in his own eyes, until his better sense recoiled at the lawlessness and licence to be witnessed everywhere. To be merely original is easy enough. The New Art having detached itself from the past, sought originality first, an aggressive and self-advertising originality, showing no respect for the virtues of reticence and the sense of fine proportion.[13]

ABOVE FROM TOP: *designs by Christopher Dresser; Kettle (c.1880), cup and saucer (c.1875), curtain fabric (c.1870)*

So Art Nouveau was seen as, at best, eccentric. Bidlake concluded: 'Fortunately, the "New Art craze" has not taken any real hold on British domestic architecture, which has quietly and steadily progressed, unaffected by "New Art" eccentricities.' Despite the opinions of the architects, Art Nouveau found its way into Edwardian houses via fittings like stained glass, fabrics, tiles, fireplace surrounds and ceramics. The builders' responsibility only extended as far as the 'carcase' of the house. This would have included stained glass, tiles and fireplace surrounds, which they might have obtained through a builders' merchant. The landlords were responsible for 'fixtures and fittings' such as dressers, fabrics and wallpapers which could make the property look up to date.

INTERWAR INTERIOR STYLE

In the interwar period Edwardian style continued as the mainstream. The alternatives were Art Deco and Modernism in the form of 'Cubism' and other art movements such as Vorticism. International competition seriously affected the British textile industry. In *Textile Design* (1937) Antony Hunt explained:

ABOVE: *the 'New Art' found its way into homes in the form of tiles and ceramics*

> The anti-Morris, anti-classic post-war style came in as 'Cubism'. It concentrated upon abstract form, and studiously avoided any floral motifs. From France came light, loose cloths mostly of rayon, all spikes, triangles, and crescents, and from Germany heavier, rather simpler designs with squared formations. America with its characteristic enthusiasm for any live new movement quickly plunged into the vortex of Continental Cubism. England sceptically deferred until much later.

The most significant interwar technical development was the invention of screen-printing in the early 1930s. Furnishing fabrics became increasingly important as the modern movement influenced people to choose plain walls instead of patterned wallpapers. England resisted the modern movement until the 1930s, when emigres from Europe such as the Swiss-born designer Marianne Straub brought it with them.

ABOVE: *linen furnishing fabric (1921–26), influenced by Cubism and Vorticism*

4

Large Edwardian Town Houses

By the Edwardian period, the wealthy were either moving out to the suburbs or into 'mansion' or 'service' flats. Consequently most large town houses were being built in the suburbs. In the inner cities, some older large houses were demolished when their leases expired or 'fell in'. Many large town houses were replaced by blocks of flats. In *Howard's End* (1910) the Schlegel sisters lose their family home this way. But despite the fact that fewer large town houses were built in the inner cities, there were some exceptional examples which anticipated developments in the medium-sized houses.

THE DEBENHAM HOUSE

In 1906, Halsey Ricardo designed a spectacular detached house in west London as a family home for Sir Ernest Debenham. Ricardo chose a classical rather than a vernacular style. In this respect he anticipated the trend towards classical architecture which would be copied by the speculative builders. But he executed the commission in a colourful way which could not be copied. When he received the commission in 1905, William de Morgan's ceramic works was closing and Ricardo bought up much of the company's remaining stock of tiles, both plain and decorated, for the interiors. The exterior of the Debenham house is faced with 6,000 glazed bricks: green and blue ones from de Morgan's ceramic works were combined with pale terracotta and coloured glazed bricks from other sources. The green of the lower levels was intended to harmonise with the lawns and the blue of the upper levels and the chimneys with the sky. The roof pantiles are green, to blend with the canopy of the trees.

The facade features classical entablature, eaves, dentils, paterae and pilasters. Facing the street there is only a small back door. The main entrance is at the side. Access from the street was through a covered way which runs parallel with a carriage drive. The covered way is lined with de Morgan's tiles. The windows are framed by semi-circular arches with shutters on either side.

The ground plan of the Debenham house also anticipated what was to come in houses of lesser means by emphasising the hall. The central hall of the Debenham house dominated the

ABOVE: *large suburban semi-detached pair (c.1909)*

ABOVE: *the domed hall of the Debenham house (1906)*

FAR LEFT: *detail of the street façade of the Debenham house showing window arches, paterae, external shutters, pilasters and entablature*

LEFT: *the end opposite the main entrance, showing how the green tiles blend in with the surrounding foliage*

entire plan. A little entrance vestibule is set to the side of the house, with some steps leading from it into the domed central hall. This is lined with mosaics in blues, greens, reds and gold; columns, lintels, balustrades and fireplace are made of a variety of marbles and other veined stones. The dining room is panelled. The small library has mother-of-pearl details on the bookcases. Other leading lights of the Arts & Crafts movement designed some of the details: ornamented ceilings by Ernest Gimson, timber carvings by William Aumonier, enriched glazing for doors and windows by E.S. Prior. Ricardo himself designed the marblework and many of the other details.

OPPOSITE: *7 St James's
Square, re-designed by Lutyens
(1911)*

7 ST JAMES'S SQUARE

After 1910 architects such as Edwin Lutyens were abandoning vernacular for classical style. What Lutyens referred to as 'the High Game of Classicism' took the form of Queen Anne and early Georgian architecture. In 1911 Lutyens redesigned an existing building, 7 St James's Square, as a town residence to be jointly occupied by the Farrer brothers; two solicitors and a merchant banker, who had bought the original building (c.1676) in 1909. Lutyens' exterior featured warm red facing brick, stone string courses and a colonnaded porch over the front door. The sash windows were unrecessed with Portland stone keystones in the window arches. (The Building Acts then current no longer insisted that windows should be fully recessed.) The parapet incorporated stone balustrades. Lutyens added a fourth attic storey lit by dormer windows with stone pediments. His version of neo-classical was one which could be copied.

ABOVE: *Onslow Court
(c.1902)*

Lutyens's designs for the interior of 7 St James's Square were seventeenth century in character. He, too, emphasised the hall by giving the house both a square entrance hall and an inner hall. Several rooms were the full width of the building: the dining room and servery on the ground floor and a library on the first floor. This had a barrel-vaulted ceiling which rose into the second storey. The drawing room and an ante room were also on the first floor. Lutyens' design also set an example by increasing the ratio of bathrooms to bedrooms. There were two bedrooms and a bathroom on each of the second and third storeys. The servants accommodation was in the fourth floor attic storey.

In the inner city, the alternative to a large town house was a flat. In 1910 the architect G.A.T. Middleton, vice-president of RIBA, wrote:

> It is only in comparatively recent times that it has become common in England to provide town dwellings for the middle classes in the form of flats; but now comparatively few separate houses are built, and flat dwelling is customary. The principal reason for this is to be found in the economy of service which is effected, there being fewer servants required for a family living in a flat than for one living in a house, together with the convenience of being able to shut up one's residence and go away at any moment by merely locking the door. Of course, it is rarely possible for a person to own the freehold of a single flat, although this was done in some cases a hundred years ago; but in large towns few persons own their own houses, and the sentimental objection to sharing a house with other people is by no means so strongly felt as it is in the country.[1]

ABOVE: *Coleherne Court
(1903–4)*

Numerous blocks of flats like Drayton Court and Coleherne Court were built in the early years of the twentieth century. Buildings like these contained spacious flats with five bedrooms. Harrods in Knightsbridge (1901) had four floors of 'mansion' flats above the retail premises.

The social commentator Mrs C.S. Peel described how she and her husband rebuilt an older house in Brompton Square:

> Our home was one of the two last lodging houses. We proceeded to modernise it, adding a kitchen, larder, boxroom and storeroom, a large drawing-room, small sitting-room and bathroom, a service lift, electric light and a telephone, not as usual a piece of domestic equipment as it now is.
>
> Neither architect nor builder suggested central heating, a second bathroom, or indeed any labour-saving arrangements.

ABOVE: *Brompton Square*

Right: *Chelsea Park
Gardens, a development
begun in 1914–15*

Above: *suburban houses with
front and back gardens in
Hampstead Garden Suburb
(c.1909)*

This house when rebuilt contained a large basement, three sitting-rooms, what house agents now call a lounge-hall, and seven bedrooms. All the rooms were warmed by coal fires. There were nursery meals to be carried up and down, hot water to be taken to the bedrooms, and we entertained a good deal in a small way. Yet we found little difficulty in running the house with a staff consisting of a Norland nurse, a parlourmaid, a housemaid, and a cook. Later we kept a manservant who had been head footman of three, and asked £70 a year. The cook, and a very fair cook too, earned £28.[2]

By describing it as one of the last of the 'lodging houses', presumably she meant that the house had previously been available for rent.

There was at least one attempt to create a garden suburb environment near the centre of London. Chelsea Park Gardens was begun during the Edwardian period. During 1914–15 the Sloane Stanley estate began to redevelop some earlier housing in Camera Square. The development was interrupted when building ceased during the First World War.

'RUS IN URBES'

Some of the new suburban houses were only town houses by virtue of their suburban rather than rural surroundings. They had gardens or driveways at the front and opened onto gardens at the back. The idea of 'rus in urbes' or a country house in an urban location was close to reality. The larger building plots in the suburbs allowed architects and builders to produce houses which were wider and lower. Consequently, the appearance of these houses had a strong horizontal emphasis. These new suburban houses were as big, if not bigger, than their earlier urban equivalents.

Hampstead Garden Suburb was intended to be a mixed community but the cost of development meant that funds had to be raised by leasing off plots to bring in ground rent. An Act of Parliament had been required to exempt the development from local by-laws. The Act also prohibited more than eight houses per acre: consequently large and medium sized houses predominated. Many of these were designed by architects who introduced numerous innovations. For example, the

Above: *horizontal emphasis
formed by linked arches
and first floor loggias in
Hampstead Garden Suburb,
designed by Parker and Unwin
(1910–11)*

ABOVE & LEFT: *detached
houses with front gardens in
Hampstead Garden Suburb
(1910–12)*

large corner house at Meadway Gate, designed by Edwin & James Palser (1908–10), features an overhanging, hipped roof. This was a feature which would be widely emulated elsewhere and during the interwar period.

Vernacular and neo-Georgian features were often combined in one design. For example, warm red brick with white rough-cast at first-floor level, casement windows with small panes, semi-circular fanlights, projecting hoods, dormer windows, red tiled roofs and tall chimneys could all be included in one design.

ABOVE: *a suburban house
which combined vernacular
and neo-Georgian features
such as red brick on the
ground floor, white rough-cast
on the first; pilasters and arch
over the front door (c.1910)*

LEFT: *large corner house
at Meadway Gate in
Hampstead Garden Suburb,
designed by Edwin and James
Palser (1908–10)*

59

RIGHT: *an inglenook with
a carved oak mantlepiece in
the hall of a house built at
Handsworth Wood (c.1906)*

ABOVE: *the hall and staircase
of a house near Piccadilly
(1901)*

RIGHT: *a design for the side
of a small hall by John Cash
(c.1906)*

ABOVE: *staircases became
a feature in the larger halls
(1906)*

RIGHT: *plans of a detached
house at Hampton in Arden,
Warwickshire (1906)*

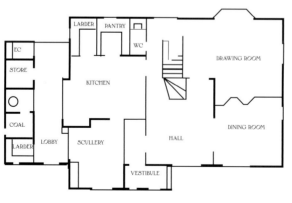

GROUND FLOOR   FIRST FLOOR

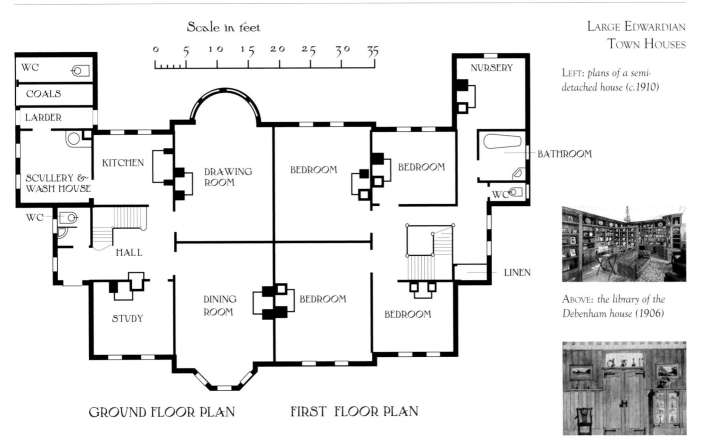

Scale in feet

0 5 10 15 20 25 30 35

WC	
COALS	
LARDER	

KITCHEN

DRAWING ROOM

BEDROOM

BEDROOM

NURSERY

BATHROOM

WC

SCULLERY & WASH HOUSE

WC

HALL

STUDY

DINING ROOM

BEDROOM

BEDROOM

LINEN

GROUND FLOOR PLAN   FIRST FLOOR PLAN

LEFT: *plans of a semi-detached house (c.1910)*

ABOVE: *the library of the Debenham house (1906)*

ABOVE: *a design for the side of a dining-room by John Cash (c.1906)*

ABOVE: *a morning room (1901)*

SUBURBAN PLAN

In the suburbs the wider plots allowed considerable variation in the plan. The hall received greater emphasis and was treated as a reception room and a less formal sitting-room. It now had its own fireplace which might be the grandest in the house with an 'inglenook'. An inglenook was a traditional feature which was originally developed to exclude draughts. The architect W.H. Bidlake professed: 'the fireside ingle has been recognised as one of the most pleasing and luxorious features of modern home planning'.

Sometimes a fireplace with an inglenook was situated on an outside wall: despite the obvious heat loss, appearance was more important than comfort. The larger hall also made it possible to make more of the stairs. Often they began with a couple of broad steps then turned, for effect. Posts and fretwork screens were a further embellishment. The other reception rooms were also on the ground floor. There might also be a morning room, library or study. The drawing room faced the back so it could open onto the garden. The service rooms were often placed to the side where they might be screened off by box hedges. Upstairs numerous rooms were placed around a central landing. To preserve the family's enjoyment of the privacy of the garden, servants' bedrooms were placed so their bedrooms overlooked the side, or even the front, of the house.

Semi-detached houses were similar in plan to detached. The service part of the house was to one side, often set back. The front door opened into an entrance hall or vestibule. There was usually a WC and a lavatory for hand washing. The hall itself was where the service and private parts of the house connected and where the stairs were located. More than a single turn in the stairs could create a stair well. This could make the hall double height. The drawing and dining rooms connected with the hall; the dining room was more likely to be at the front. Upstairs the landing was central with the bedrooms and bathroom opening onto it. It was likely that one of the bedrooms in a large house would be used as a dressing room. The smallest bedroom, or boxroom, would have been the only one without a fireplace.

RIGHT: *plans of a house
in Chelsea Park Gardens
(c.1915); from left – ground,
first and second floors*

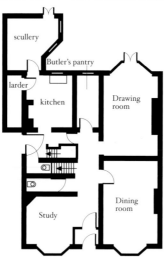

Fitted cupboard

ABOVE: *a Baillie-Scott design
for a dining-room in oak
(1906)*

The houses in Chelsea Park Gardens are double-fronted with rooms on either side of the entrance hall. The dining room was on the ground floor facing the front. In most cases the drawing room was on the ground floor facing the gardens at the back. But several houses in the development retained the drawing room on the first floor. The kitchen and service rooms were within the body of the house but the scullery was in a small rear extension. The stairs were placed centrally rising towards the side of the house. They gave access to a central landing on the upper floors. The master bedroom on the first floor had an en suite bathroom. The larger bedrooms were fitted with built-in wardrobes.

Architects such as Halsey Ricardo or Baillie Scott wished to achieve interiors which were 'airy and spacious'.[3] Their designs often featured oak panelling or furniture. Ricardo regretted: 'most rooms are woefully overcrowded'[4] but the manufacturers of reproduction furniture wanted their customers to furnish their interiors with whole suites in a Sheraton or neo-Georgian style.

RIGHT: *catalogue illustration
of an interior fitted with
reproduction neo-Georgian
furniture*

ABOVE: *an interior design by M.H. Baillie-Scott (c.1901)*

LEFT: *a Sheraton style interior from a contemporary furnishing catalogue*

ABOVE: *oak wardrobe, (c.1910)*

PART TWO:
EDWARDIAN
TOWN HOUSES

RIGHT: *the back of the
Debenham house*

ABOVE: *the front garden of
the Debenham house*

BELOW: *design for proposed
alterations to an existing
house in Nower Hill, Pinner,
showing the entrance and
garden fronts (1901)*

NOWER HILL PINNER
SKETCH FOR ALTERATIONS
CECIL C. BREWER ARCHITECT

LEFT: *the garden front of a house in Stanmore, with terrace and lawn tennis court (1901)*

ABOVE: *the garden front of a suburban villa with a conservatory (c.1899)*

ABOVE: *a design by C.E. Mallows for an outdoor dining room, looking out through a loggia (c.1910)*

LARGE: BACK OR 'GARDEN FRONT'

The Debenham house is surrounded by gardens, with extensive upper and lower gardens at the back. Ricardo designed a classical garden pavilion – which connects to the house through another covered way. The front garden is laid out in a formal Dutch style.

Like country houses, suburban houses in places like Pinner or Stanmore could claim to have 'garden fronts'. This was realised by having bay windows or a terrace overlooking the garden. From the terrace one could, perhaps, step down to a croquet lawn or a lawn-tennis court.

Ideally the garden front faced south to get as much sun as possible. The orientation of interiors towards the garden went as far as attempts to create outdoor rooms 'so that shelters, loggias, arbours and garden-houses take a large place in modern garden design. There is no better moment to enjoy the fresh air and garden outlook than at mealtimes'.[5]

ABOVE: *a suburban back garden with bay window, terrace and lawn (1909)*

LEFT: *a garden front in Hampstead Garden suburb (1909)*

5

Medium Edwardian Town Houses

The majority of medium-sized houses built between 1900 and 1918 were terraced. Out of a total of 1.33 million houses of all kinds, 800,000 were terraced; 250,000 were semi-detached, 180,000 detached and 100,000 were bungalows. In addition 400,000 flats were built. Around 1900 bay windows were being built in a rectangular form with gables decorated with barge boards, finials and ridge tiles. The windows were framed with heavy stone mullions. Terraced houses continued to be built with coupled rear extensions and paired front doors. After 1900 vernacular cottage styles became widespread. Most of these medium sized houses were speculatively built in the new suburbs.

In the Edwardian period, the middle class continued to expand in relation to the rest of the population. The solid middle class consisted of those with incomes of £700–£1,000; the rest of the middle class could only aspire to a four-figure income. Those who were in this 'solid' group were only a small proportion of the middle class. Some were people of independent means but many were in the continually expanding professions – particularly the new professions that went with commerce and industry. Middle management, engineers, accountants and solicitors joined the traditional professions such as the Church, services, law, civil service and teaching. The range of incomes of the middle class was reflected in the variety of sizes of their homes: the medium-sized town houses.

For the average tenant it was necessary for a house to be up-to-date in style with all the latest amenities, yet it was considered better to be safe rather than to be avant garde. A 1905 advertisement in a local journal proclaimed: 'well fitted with hot and cold water, two separate WCs; extra large coal cellar. Tiled halls and forecourts, fitted with gas, speaking tubes, electric bells, and could easily be fitted with electric light, if required. Good gardens all laid out. These houses are well-fitted with every modern improvement.'

Electric light was a strong attraction but, at first, supplies were limited. In Ilford electricity was supplied by the council's own generating station which opened in May 1901. Domestic consumers had to use penny-in-the-slot meters. Over 500 were in use by 1906. By 1912, 4,000 consumers were using the service. A large number of houses in the same locality were lit by gas which was also supplied by the council.

The majority still rented, but that was beginning to change. Large-scale owner occupation began during the Edwardian period. In 1904 the Halifax Building society raised the level of advances from 75 to 90 per cent of valuation on freehold properties valued at up to £300. A four bedroom house in Wood Green, north London, with 20 foot frontage was offered at £250 leasehold in 1904 or £20 deposit followed by £1 19 shillings and sixpence a month. A three bedroom semi-detached house in Golders Gardens cost £425 leasehold. As well as London suburbs like Ilford and Golders Green, owner-occupation began in satellite towns such as Gerrards Cross ,which became ripe for development as soon their railway stations opened. Gerrards Cross station opened in 1906.

In Manchester the middle class moved out to Victoria Park. Even in market towns like Worksop prosperous individuals moved out of the centre to more tranquil locations such as Blyth Grove. Plots in developments like Letchworth and Hampstead Garden Suburb were sold or leased to individuals who commissioned architects and builders to construct their new homes.

OPPOSITE: *medium-sized suburban terraced houses with triangular gables, barge-boards and ridge tiles (1913–14)*

ABOVE: *speculatively built suburban terraced houses in Manchester (c.1904)*

ABOVE: *a medium sized detached house in Gerrards Cross (1906)*

ABOVE: *houses with double gables in Hampstead Garden Suburb, designed by Courtenay Crickmer (1909–10)*

RIGHT: *houses with double gables in Golders Green (c.1911)*

CHANGES IN PRACTICE

The speculative builders were beginning to operate in different ways. Builders like William Moss & Sons of 'Hampstead Way, Hendon' described themselves as 'Builders & Contractors'. 'Builders' meant that they undertook speculative work but building under contract could be as risky as the system of building leases. This was because the builder had to complete at the contract price. Between 1898 and 1903 an annual average of 150,000 houses was built but afterwards the figure declined. Building slowed down but never stopped; consequently there was competition for the jobs that were available. Builders were able to pick and choose the best workmen. This improved the quality of Edwardian workmanship. Charles Booth criticised speculative builders for 'the uniformity of style and a resulting architectural dullness ... rather than inferior workmanship or the use of bad materials'.[1] The problem, as he saw it, was that with mass production every element of a house was being designed and produced on a large scale. Builders obtained their materials from 'regular stock'. The number of builders' merchants, like Young & Marten, grew from 100 in 1870 to 1,300 by 1910. Machinery considerably reduced the cost of work previously done by hand, such as joinery. As standardisation became more widespread, items such as moulded majolica glazed tiles became readily available.

Speculative builders were quick to copy what they thought would appeal to their market. For example, double gables appeared on a house in W.P. Griggs' speculatively built 'garden suburb' on the Valentines Park estate, Ilford, shortly after Courtenay Crickmer designed double gables at a junction within Hampstead Garden Suburb in 1909-10. There were even more significant

ABOVE: *a detached house with double gables on W.P. Griggs' speculatively built 'garden suburb' in Valentines Park, Ilford (c.1911)*

ABOVE: *terraced houses were criticised for their uniformity rather than their quality (c.1910)*

PART TWO:
EDWARDIAN
TOWN HOUSES

RIGHT: *spacious, semi-detached houses in Blyth Grove, Worksop*

ABOVE: *double-fronted terraced house in Ilford (1907)*

RIGHT: *cottage style; a semi-detached pair in Blyth Grove, Worksop*

ABOVE: *medium sized terraced houses in Victoria Park, Manchester*

LEFT: *a new style – semi-detached with red roof tiles, gables, rough cast finish, casement windows and timber framed bays – Golders Gardens (1911)*

ABOVE: *a new style which began to appear in the suburbs– white rough-cast above red brick walls with an oriel window (1905–07)*

changes in practice: builders began to buy rather than lease the land on which they built. W.P. Griggs and Archibald Cameron Corbett purchased a whole series of estates in Ilford. They both became speculative developers who built houses for sale rather than for rent. Builders also began to cooperate with estate agents over sales, for example in Golders Green, 'within sight of Golders Green terminus of the Hampstead tube, half a dozen estate agents' pavilions may be counted dotted among the fields'.[2]

Both terraced and semi-detached houses continued to be built with paired rear extensions and front doors but as the twentieth century progressed new styles and plans were developing.

A NEW STYLE

A new style was appearing in Edwardian suburbs such as Golders Green, as seen in Golders Gardens (1911). The new style was semi-detached with red roof tiles; the elevations of the houses displayed an irregular sequence of window and gable with red-brick walls or cement and rough-cast finish. The white painted windows were casements rather than sashes. The bays were timber-framed on a brick base or tile-hung on a timber frame.

ABOVE: *wooden features such as bargeboards and half-timbering on the gables of the bay and 'cock-loft' dormer windows*

Oriel windows were an alternative to bay windows; their cantilever construction made them cheaper to build. After 1909, in Ilford, A.C. Corbett was building the newer type using more wood externally. Wooden features such as bargeboards, finials and half-timbered effects were re-introduced. The half-timbered 'Old English' look became widespread. This had originally been the rural form of the domestic or 'Queen Anne Revival'. Casement windows further enhanced cottage style. The new casement windows could be side or top hung. They could also be pre-fabricated.

Medium-sized houses varied considerably in size from three to five bedrooms and two to three storeys. Attic storeys were made habitable by the addition of dormer windows. These might be given a pitched-roof and a gable which made them look like a traditional 'cock-loft'.

71

PART TWO: EDWARDIAN TOWN HOUSES

RIGHT: *plans of a double-fronted, suburban terraced house in Cardiff, similar to those in Worksop*

ABOVE: *re-creation of a hall with its own fireplace (Geffrye Museum)*

RIGHT: *plans of the new type of house without a rear extension*

ABOVE: *the hall seen through the entrance to the drawing room (Geffrye Museum)*

RIGHT: *cross-section, ground, first and second floor plans of a split-level, medium-sized, terraced house*

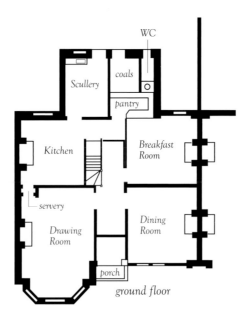

ground floor

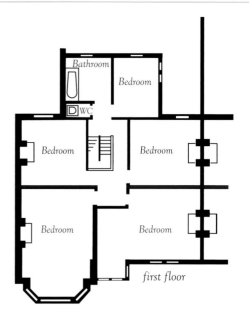

first floor

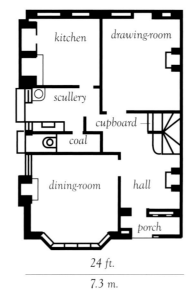

24 ft.

7.3 m.

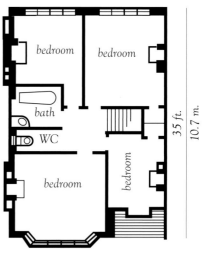

35 ft.

10.7 m.

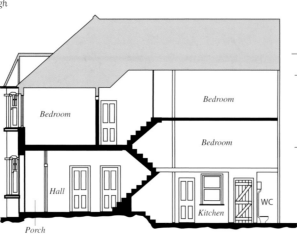

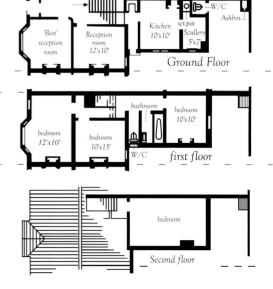

Ground Floor

first floor

Second floor

72

VARIATIONS IN GROUND-PLAN: SUBURBAN SEMI-DETACHED

The wider plots available in the suburbs allowed considerable variation in the ground-plan. The more spacious, semi-detached, medium-sized houses finally broke away from the old plan of one room behind the other with a narrow hall on one side. Medium-sized, double-fronted, terraced houses were also being built in the new suburbs. Each of these types adopted a similar plan to large houses such as those in Chelsea Park Gardens. In medium-sized, semi-detached, suburban houses the hall became a room with its own fireplace.

In the wider suburban plots the reception rooms were placed on either side of a central hall with a third reception room facing the rear. The kitchen and other service rooms came back into the main body of the house to such an extent that there was only a minimal need for any rear additions. The bathroom was upstairs on the first floor. In 1905 the *Hornsey and Finsbury Park Journal* was advertising:

> High class, Substantial, doublefronted and semi-detached villas. Quite up to date. From £550 to £1000. Rentals from £50. Charmingly situated and 350 feet above sea level. 25 minutes to City. Variety of designs, some with full size Billiard Rooms and electric Light.

ABOVE: *re-creation of an Edwardian drawing room* (Geffrye Museum)

MEDIUM-SIZED TERRACED HOUSES

The plan of less-spacious medium-sized terraced houses was a development of the old plan with a slightly wider hall on one side. The combined kitchen and scullery came back into the main part of the house with only a small rear extension. This was for a WC which was entered from the outside. As the twentieth century continued this became the standard type. Until about 1905 terraced houses with rear extensions continued to be built. These included the split level type in which the rear extension contained the kitchen with two floors above. After 1905 the types with full rear extensions, such as the split level type, gradually ceased to be built.

Staircases became more of a feature in the larger halls of medium-sized houses. The hand rail was probably the only piece of hardwood in the entire house. Newel posts might be incorporated into an arch. Fretwork screens separated small areas near the foot of the stairs into cosy nooks. Upstairs, there was a central 'landing' and extra space was available for 'conveniences' such as dressing rooms, linen cupboards and box rooms. Fitments like dressers might be found in the dining room or kitchen.

ABOVE: *staircase of a terraced house. The handrail was hardwood and was left unpainted (1910)*

Furniture was becoming simpler, with an unpolished finish which was consistent with the emphasis on being hygienic, dust-free and easy to clean. Features such as hinges and handles were made of copper, pewter or black-painted ironwork rather than brass. The more affluent occupants of medium-sized houses could afford new furniture of the latest type from Heal & Son or department stores in the suburbs. Companies like Heal & Son used opportunities such as the Cheap Cottages Exhibition of 1905 to promote their craftsman-designed, inexpensive furniture such as a plain oak dresser for £6 15s.

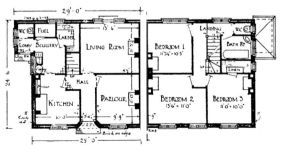

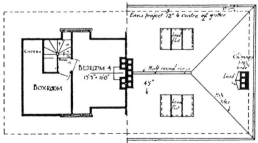

LEFT: *ground, first and second floor plans of a double-fronted, semi-detached house (c.1912)*

PART TWO:
EDWARDIAN
TOWN HOUSES

RIGHT: *hall of a medium
sized terraced house (1910);
the tiled floor, hardwood hand
rail, balusters, newel post and
arch are original*

FAR RIGHT: *re-creation of
a drawing room, showing
a window which would
have overlooked the garden
(Geffrye Museum)*

FAR RIGHT: *re-creation of a
drawing room showing the
double doors from the hall
(Geffrye Museum)*

RIGHT: *a dining room in
Hindhead, Surrey (1906);
a hanging lamp has been
converted into an electric light
fitting*

LEFT: *a drawing room scheme from* Mrs Humphry's Book of the Home *(1909)*

ABOVE: *bedroom scheme from a Waring's catalogue (1910)*

Catalogues for department stores and furniture companies such as Waring and Gillow [3] illustrated interior schemes for middle-class homes. They frequently claimed that their products or schemes were 'Art' or 'Artistic' such as William Wallace & Co's 'Inexpensive Artistic Boudoir Furniture' (1895). By 1908 furniture companies such as Williamson & Cole had dropped their pretensions and were offering 'Luxorious Easy Chairs' from £3 10s. *Mrs Humphry's Book of the Home* (1909) was one of numerous books offering advice on interior design which were specifically aimed at the middle classes. Catalogues and books like these were the equivalent of the illustrations of architect-designed interiors for large houses which were published in magazines like *The Studio*.

ABOVE: *dining room scheme from a Waring's catalogue (1910)*

LEFT: *drawing room scheme from a Waring's catalogue (1910)*

MEDIUM: BACK

Improvements in drains and sewage disposal, especially the intercepting trap, allowed the back of the house to become more pleasant. Other services such as coal bunkers and ash bins could be discreetly located on the paved area to the rear of the house. The older types of terraced houses had accommodated the ash bin and outside WC in a single-storey, lean-to extension; some Edwardian terraced and semi-detached houses still did this. The latest terrace designs, such as those at Letchworth, included arched passageways through the building that gave direct access to the back. Semi-detached houses allowed access to the back through a gate and passage at the open side.

Houses with rear extensions had coupled backs. The rear extension restricted access to the garden. Consequently, in some houses, the dining room was placed in the rear extension and the kitchen was brought back into the main body of the house. In this way the occupants could reach the garden from a reception room.

Those with the newer plan enjoyed more direct access to the garden through French doors which allowed the occupants to enjoy their gardens, even in bad weather. They might also do this from a conservatory if their resources allowed.

Greenhouses and conservatories were becoming increasingly popular. There was a large range of exotic plants with which to stock them: orchids, oleander and freesias could be grown as pot plants. Tender climbers like bougainvillea, abutilon, hoya and plumbago could be planted in large containers or a soil border.

One of the major attractions of the newly built houses was that the occupants could really enjoy their garden. The garden was seen as a place for recreation, and gardening a healthy and respectable hobby. Even architects like W.H. Bidlake conceded:

> Nor is the recent development of garden planning restricted to the homes of the wealthy, for a garden of reasonable size is now considered almost as essential to the small house and the cottage, as the various schemes for the formation of garden cities bear witness. There is, at last, a revolt — and it is one of the most inspiriting signs of the times — against the tyranny of the land speculator and jerry builder, a revolt against the dreariness of being confined in the long, unlovely street, the pretentious villa, or the slum court. There is a demand for pure air and the association of Nature's beauty with everyday life. The modern improvements in the means of locomotion have assisted this revolt, and emphasized this demand, and it is the privilege of the modern architect, as well as his gain, to play his part by designing small houses, not only economical in plan and in cost, but reticent in design.[4]

The less wealthy, especially those who owned their houses, took immense pride in their gardens and took advice on what to plant from the many available books and magazines.

THE BACK GARDEN BEAUTIFUL

In *The Back Garden Beautiful* (1909) the garden writer, Harry Havart, explained that the book

> was written with the idea of appealing to those people who, for perhaps the first time in their lives, find themselves happy in the tenancy or possession of a small house with a tiny garden attached thereto. Tens of thousands of such homes spring up every year in the suburbs of London and other great cities ... as fine old houses are pulled down and the sites and grounds developed for building purposes ...

Havart recommended a 'Quick Result Garden' for tenants of a 'migratory character'. This was based on hardy annuals and perennials like foxgloves, hollyhocks, larkspur, lupins and candy tuft. His other garden designs included roses, a herbaceous border and different boundary features.

OPPOSITE: *the coupled backs of a semi-detached pair in Worksop, (1905). The apple tree masks the lean-to rear extension which contained the ash-bins and outside WCs*

ABOVE: *the back gate of a semi-detached house, with a rear extension (1905)*

ABOVE: *a modern conservatory at the back of a terraced house built in 1910*

RIGHT: *watercolour of a
London garden by Beatrice
Parsons (1908)*

ABOVE & BELOW: *the pergola
and the trellis were popular
features in Edwardian gardens*

RIGHT: *garden designs
from* The Small Garden
Beautiful *(1906)*

ABOVE: *the back garden of
this suburban house (c.1901)
still has a central lawn,
flower beds and a curving
path like the designs in* The
Small Garden Beautiful

The back garden should be divided into distinct areas such as 'rock garden' and 'kitchen garden with herbaceous borders'. In *The Small Garden Beautiful* (1906) A.C. Curtis offered several designs for back gardens which each included a central lawn surrounded with borders on three sides and a gravel path running down the fourth. He also specified the position of the dustbin, 'which most municipal authorities insist upon ... one of those evils which have to be endured.'

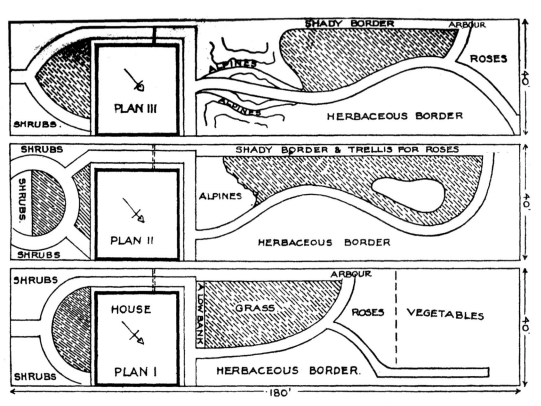

Hampstead Garden Suburb was limited to a maximum of eight houses per acre. The gardens were divided by trellis-work boundary fences with 'where possible a colour scheme with the hedges'. The natural individuality within the gardens of the Suburb was not so beneficial in Letchworth where a communal spirit was desirable.

Suburban gardens were seen as an easy, inexpensive place to entertain, and al fresco tea parties became popular. Manufacturers took advantage of the increasing number of householders with gardens and produced a great range of furniture and decorative items for them. Wooden and cast-iron garden furniture was produced on a large scale, as well as stoneware statues, urns and balustrades in a variety of sizes.

Pergolas and trellises were a distinctive item in Edwardian gardens. They were used to create a balance between the formal and natural elements in the garden. Rustic arches might also be combined with a trellis.

As part of the growing belief in the benefit of healthy exercise, the middle classes eagerly took up golf and tennis, which did not require the financial investment or social standing of the traditional sports of the upper classes such as hunting and shooting. The possession of a tennis court became such a social necessity that, as early as 1884, the *Spectator* had complained: 'every wretched little garden-plot is pressed into service, and courts are religiously traced out in half the meagre back-gardens of the suburbs of London, even though the available space is little bigger than a billiard table.'

ABOVE: *advertisement for fertiliser from* One and All Gardening *magazine (1905)*

ABOVE: *'Anyone for tennis?' (1913)*

LEFT: *urban gardens combined hard features such as pergolas, terraces and pots with soft ones such as climbing plants*

ABOVE: *terraced houses with coupled rear extensions (c.1901)*

6

Small Edwardian Town Houses

Small house designs proliferated as public money became available to build them. In addition, philanthropic schemes like the Garden City movement employed designers to solve the problems of workers' housing. However, the vast majority of small houses were still built speculatively, as the local authorities could build neither as cheaply nor in anything like the quantity required. In 1901 the MP and builder T.C.T. Warner boasted that he had built more houses than the LCC 'for profit and not for public purposes'.[1]

Some of the features of the large and medium-sized houses also appeared in the small house, giving the impression of a kind of family relationship between the designs which had not been apparent since the late Georgian period. Warm red brick, white rough-cast, casement windows, small window panes, hoods or porches over doorways, deep gables, eaves, brackets and even imposing chimney stacks could all be found on the LCC's cottage estates. Red-tiled roofs appeared in some designs at White Hart Lane but at Totterdown the roofs were slate.

Older types of small terraced houses with single storey bays continued to be speculatively built for as little as £150. An average rent in 1914 was 9s 3d per week, including rates.

Working mens' flats were another approach to housing the working classes. Two-storey medium-sized terraced houses were divided in half. Each 'half-house' was a two bedroom flat with parlour, kitchen and scullery. The front doors of each flat were either shared or placed side by side in the same porch. In 1905 a ground floor flat in Walthamstow cost 6s 6d a week. The floor above had slightly bigger rooms for 7s a week.

OPPOSITE TOP: *deep gables, white rough-cast with redbrick below, at Totterdown Fields (1903–11)*

OPPOSITE BELOW: *redbrick and tall chimney stacks at Totterdown Fields (1903–11)*

ABOVE: *speculatively built end of terrace house with single storey bay (c.1900)*

LEFT: *working mens' flats with paired front doors within a shared front porch (c.1901)*

ABOVE: *redbrick and tiles on the LCC's cottage estate at White Hart Lane (c.1904–15)*

RIGHT: 'Foundation
Cottages', the first houses
built in the 'Artisans quarter'
of Hampstead Garden Suburb
(1907)

RIGHT: artisan housing as
built in Hampstead Garden
Suburb (1911–12)

RIGHT: terraces of artisan
houses in Letchworth (1903-6)

MIXED DEVELOPMENTS

The model developments at Letchworth and Hampstead Garden Suburb were intended to be mixed developments for people of all social and income levels. In November 1903 a letter written by Henrietta Barnett appeared in the *Hampstead and Highgate Express*. It was headed 'A Garden Suburb for All Classes'. She expressed her hope for the development of housing for the industrial classes:

> The conditions of building are those which ensure the establishment of not a 'Garden City' but a 'Garden Suburb' in which every house, however humble, will be productive as well as pleasurable. The plan, however, will necessitate the provision of some shops, and some houses of a larger size and more extensive gardens.

In December 1903 she added that the 'garden suburb should be not for one class only but to include people of all degrees in which the houses of the industrial classes will be beautiful – as beautiful in the manner of cottages as villas can be in the manner of villas or mansions in the manner of mansions'.

Henrietta Barnett cut the first sod for the 'Artisans quarter' herself on 2 May 1907. The first buildings were a pair of cottages which became known as 'Foundation Cottages'. Henrietta Barnett had written on one of the earliest plans: 'This is the 70 acres for the houses of the industrial classes at 10 to an acre'. Unfortunately the Act of Parliament which exempted the suburb from the local by-laws fixed the average residential density at eight houses per acre which limited the Suburb's ability to provide houses for the industrial classes.

Hampstead Garden Suburb was planned by Barry Parker and Raymond Unwin. Parker and Unwin had been the architects of the first Garden City at Letchworth where they had addressed the problem of overcrowding by limiting the housing density to twelve houses per acre. They used a number of techniques to achieve this: short terraces, careful grouping of buildings and the provision of gardens and open spaces. Unwin published his ideas in a pamphlet entitled *Nothing Gained by Overcrowding* (1912) in which he compared garden city layouts with by-law terraces. The problem with garden city projects was that they tended to run out of funds. Consequently they had to sell or lease off plots which became medium or large houses. Even the small cottages might be taken up by middle-class 'week-enders'. The 'Cheap Cottages' exhibition at Letchworth had encouraged this (*see page 87*).

BELOW LEFT: by-law streets compared with Unwin's garden city layouts from Nothing Gained by Overcrowding (1912)

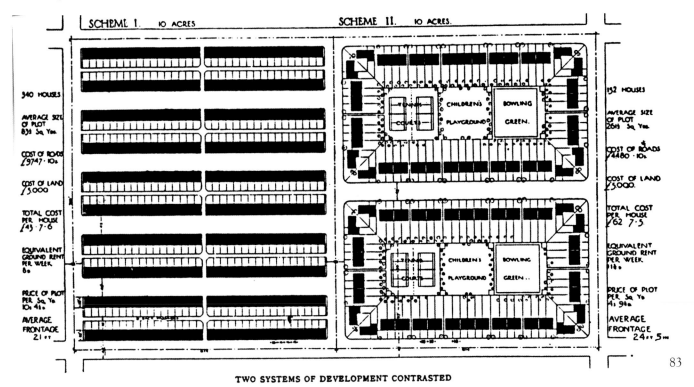

TWO SYSTEMS OF DEVELOPMENT CONTRASTED

RIGHT: *ground and first floor plans of small houses built by Corbett in Ilford (1903)*

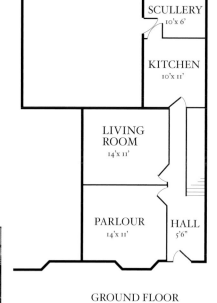

SCULLERY
10'x 6'

KITCHEN
10'x 11'

LIVING ROOM
14'x 11'

PARLOUR
14'x 11'

HALL
5'6"

GROUND FLOOR

BEDROOM
10'x 11'

BATH
7'x 6'

BEDROOM
14'x 11'

BEDROOM
13'x 11'

11'x 7'

BEDROOM

FIRST FLOOR

ABOVE: *a living room at Letchworth (1908)*

RIGHT: *plans of ground and first floors of pairs of 'workmen's cottages' designed by Geoffry Lucas at Letchworth (1906)*

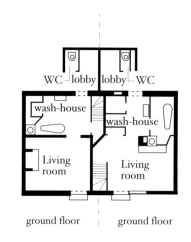

WC — lobby lobby — WC

wash-house

wash-house

Living room

Living room

ground floor | ground floor

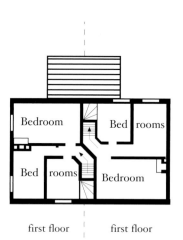

Bedroom

Bed rooms

Bed rooms

Bedroom

first floor | first floor

RIGHT: *layout of 'workmen's cottages' grouped around a green designed by Geoffry Lucas at Letchworth (1906)*

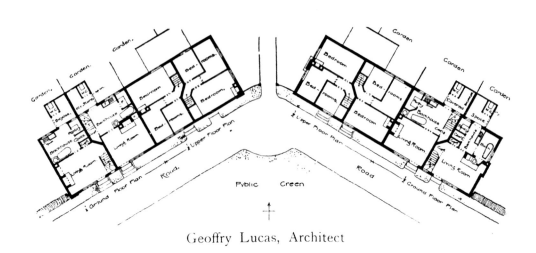

Geoffry Lucas, Architect

LEFT: 'workmen's cottages'
designed by Geoffry Lucas at
Letchworth (1906)

SMALL: PLAN

A debate began about whether or not the parlour was the best use of the available space in a small house. Designers such as Raymond Unwin thought that a single living-room was not only adequate but more spacious and healthy. This was despite the fact that Ruskin's definition of a house included both a kitchen and a parlour. Unwin had actually quoted this in *Cottage Plans & Cottage Sense* (a 1902 pamphlet which he wrote in support of a campaign against slum housing by the Fabian Society):

> not a compartment of a model lodging house, not the number so and so Paradise Row but a cottage all of our own, with its own little garden, its healthy air, its clean kitchen, parlour and bedrooms.

ABOVE: *small houses in Ilford (1901)*

But people still wanted a separate parlour for 'best', even if it was only 10 foot by 10 foot and scarcely large enough to hold the best pieces of furniture and all the family. The speculative builder Cameron Corbett's houses in Ilford gave the workers scaled-down versions of medium houses. These included a living room, kitchen and scullery in a rear extension and a parlour. The parlour and the living room were each 14 foot by 11 foot. On his Downshall estate of 1903, a three-bedroom house might be bought for £256 10s leasehold; plus ground rent of £5 1s, to be paid annually. Upstairs Corbett's houses had three or four bedrooms and a bathroom.

Geoffry Lucas's cottage designs at Letchworth placed a single kitchen–living room on the ground floor with a combined scullery and bath in a wash house behind. The wash house included a built-in pantry to store food. The hot water for bathing was heated in a set pot. There were three bedrooms upstairs. The cottages were built in terraces of four; each had its own garden. The terraces looked like individual houses and were carefully grouped around a public green. Each cottage had its own front door which opened into the kitchen–living room. A proper water-closet was placed in the rear extension which was reached through a lobby (under cover but open to the outside). Separate cupboards and built-in dressers were provided in the main living-room.

Newly built small houses usually had an effective boiler to heat water. As in Lucas's cottage designs, this was normally a 'set-pot' which might be augmented by a new but economical gas-ring for cooking.

Upstairs, built-in storage cupboards were also included in the house. Strenuous attempts were made to provide three bedrooms without having to enter one bedroom through another.

The LCC's council houses varied from 'three rooms' to 'five rooms'. 'Three rooms' had two bedrooms, a living room and a scullery within the main body of the house. 'Five rooms' had three bedrooms, a living room, a parlour and a scullery with a bath. The Peabody Donation Trust built 154 'five rooms' next to the LCC's White Hart Lane estate in 1907. Almost all the houses on the LCC's later estates at Norbury, White Hart Lane and Old Oak, Hammersmith (1912–13) had a bath.

ABOVE: *a mangle for drying clothes in the scullery or 'wash-house'* (Church Farmhouse Museum)

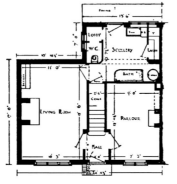

RIGHT: *ground and first
floors plans of a 'three room'
arrangement*

FAR RIGHT & BELOW
FAR RIGHT: *illustrations of
kitchen–living rooms from
c.1872*

RIGHT: *ground and first
floor plans of a 'five room'
arrangement*

RIGHT: *small front yards in
the LCC's White Hart Lane
estate (1904–15)*

FAR RIGHT: *one of the designs
in the 'Cheap Cottages'
exhibition (1905)*

SMALL: BACK

By 1900 many newly-built small houses had a scullery–wash-house in a modest rear extension. There might even have been space for a little room above, under the eaves if necessary. Further extensions were required for residual ash from the fires and the storage of coal. Those without rear extensions had portable ash-bins which could be placed anywhere in the yard.

The three and four-bedroom houses built by the councils now all had an inside water-closet. In some of the houses it was in the main building with an open lobby between it and the scullery for health reasons.

In other houses the water-closet was placed in a small rear extension and could only be reached from the outside. A small percentage of the houses were built with five rooms and in these the bathroom and a separate water closet were actually installed upstairs.

The larger council houses of the LCC Totterdown Fields estate had the wash house arrangement. Some were built with separate hot-water apparatus. Others stored the bath under the floor. Early local authority housing had similar arrangements to Geoffry Lucas's design at Letchworth with a lobby entrance to the WC from the wash-house.

In 1905 the *Country Gentleman* magazine organised a 'Cheap Cottages' exhibition at Letchworth, There were over 131 entries of varying designs, employing a wide range of materials and construction methods. Entries had to be built for a cost of no more than £150. The competition attracted over 60,000 visitors to the uncompleted Garden City. It was repeated in 1907 as an Urban Cottage Exhibition sponsored by the National Housing Reform Council. This time the cottages were designed in groups, each cottage to cost £175.

Despite the sponsors' intentions, the result of the exhibitions was that the public became aware that country cottages could be attractive week-end retreats.

ABOVE: *'five rooms'
– Peabody cottages near
White Hart Lane (1907)*

ABOVE: *the entries in the
Urban Cottage Exhibition of
1907 were designed in groups*

LEFT: *a design for an estate
of small houses showing fronts
and backs*

ABOVE: *re-creation of a
scullery sink* (Church
Farmhouse Museum)

87

FRONT AND BACK GARDENS

The plots of small houses still usually had only the minimum space for an effective back yard. At best, they might enjoy both front and back gardens. Front gardens were a status symbol for small houses. They showed their superiority to houses whose front doors opened directly onto the street. Harry Havart recommended that the front gate of a house with a front garden should not be directly opposite but at an angle. This would deter nosy neighbours whom Havart described as the 'misses Prigg who take such a keen interest in their neighbours' doings'. The houses in the LCC's original 'cottage estate' at Totterdown Fields (1903–11) had small front yards behind paling fences.

A.C. Curtis regretted that there was very little scope for anything more than a simple practical layout for front gardens:

> In the plan of front gardens very little originality is possible, the conditions are fixed, and near London the street urchins are such arrant lovers of other people's flowers. There is depth varying in different gardens of from fifteen to thirty feet, and through this little scrap of ground way must be made both to the back and front entrances. Hence, two paths, a belt of shrubs to form a screen between the house and road, and also between the house and 'next door' and some well-kept grass, form, almost inevitably, the basis of the composition.[2]

At the back of working men's flats, the flat above had access to the yard or garden down a flight of steps. At Letchworth, access to the back of the small terraced houses was through a passage in the terrace. A similar means was used in terraces of cottages in Hampstead Garden Suburb where they were called 'twitten passages'.

OPPOSITE: the back of a Peabody cottage near the White Hart Lane estate (1907)

ABOVE: working men's flats showing how the flat above had access to the garden down a flight of steps

LEFT: a design for storing the bath beneath the floor of the scullery (1910)

ABOVE: a terrace in Letchworth showing the passage through the terrace which gave access to the back (c.1905)

FAR LEFT: a small rear extension for the scullery– wash house, with a small room above, under the eaves (c.1900)

LEFT: plans for a pair of ground floor working men's flats

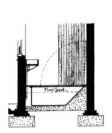
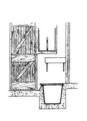
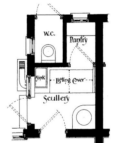

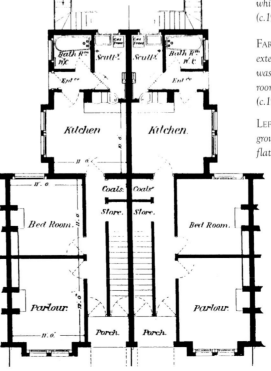

PART TWO:
EDWARDIAN
TOWN HOUSES

RIGHT & FAR RIGHT: *north and south elevations of a 'proposed house & Studio' at Studland Bay, Dorset, designed by C.F.A. Voysey (as published in 1906)*

RIGHT & FAR RIGHT: *the entrance and garden fronts of a house in Bromley, Kent, designed by Ernest Newton (c.1906)*

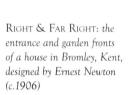

RIGHT: *entrance front of house at Norwood Hill designed by Halsey Ricardo with a 'motor-home' (c.1906)*

FAR RIGHT: *entrance front of a house at Edenbridge, Kent, designed by Robert Weir Schulz (c.1906)*

RIGHT: *the dining-room of Homewood, Knebworth, Hertfordshire, designed by Edwin Lutyens (1901)*

Edwardian Country Houses

 he majority of Edwardian country houses were relatively modest in size. The architect Ernest Newton stated: 'It is the day of the smallish house ... "country seats" and "noblemen's mansions" are no longer being built'.[1] These new country houses were houses in the country which did not derive their income from surrounding estates. They were built for a new clientele. These were what Ernest Newton called 'almost a new class – men who from small beginnings had made great fortunes and were fired with ambition to "found a family"'.[2] Often the first step towards the realisation of that ambition was the building of a country house, for, as G.K. Chesterton explained, the country house represented every Englishman's dream of domestic perfection:

ABOVE: *a design for a small country house by Gerald C. Horsley (c.1906)*

> Every man though he were born in the very belfry of Bow and spent his infancy climbing among the chimneys has waiting for him somewhere a country house that has never been built but which was built for him in the very shape of his soul. [3]

For most, of course, such dreams were no more than fantasies, at best they would have to be content with one of the new suburban houses. But those who did see their dream come true included the founders of Barkers, Harrods and Whiteleys who all built new country houses for themselves and their families while the Fenwicks, who owed their fortune to coal mining as well as the eponymous store, commissioned Lutyens to redesign Temple Dinsley in Hertfordshire. The trend was picked up in contemporary fiction where characters such as Soames Forsyte in Galsworthy's *Man of Property* (1906) and Henry Wilcox in E.M. Forster's *Howards End* (1910) aspired to set the seal upon their success by building a rural retreat.

Such patrons of the fashionable architects of the period were proud to see their names listed alongside those of their architects when the plans for their new homes appeared in the *Architectural Review* or *The Studio*. When work was completed the new house might well be photographed for the magazine *Country Life*, which had a seminal role in popularising the latest styles among those who owned, or aspired to own, a country house. Indeed the founder of *Country Life*, Edward Hudson, had himself set an example by commissioning Lutyens to build a house, Deanery Gardens, for him at Sonning in Berkshire.

Apart from their size, Edwardian country houses were also distinguished from their more palatial predecessors by the minute attention which their designers had paid to the smallest detail in order to ensure that each had its own individual character. As Ernest Newton explained, 'Every part of a building from start to finish is minutely designed ... mantelpieces, grates and panelling, door handles and hinges, even nails, are all drawn and made for our liking.' [4]

A very typical and influential example of a house of this kind was Homewood, Knebworth, Hertfordshire, built by Lutyens in 1901 as a retirement home for his mother-in-law, the Dowager Lady Lytton. Sir Lawrence Weaver, who included the house in his 1910 book *Small Country Houses*

ABOVE: *the entrance front of Homewood (1901). Photo by Stephen Pollock-Hill*

ABOVE: *the entrance front of a house at Rotherfield, designed by E. J. May (c.1906)*

RIGHT: *a house at Hurlingham designed by M. H. Baillie Scott (c.1906)*

of Today, described Homewood as 'beauty in gables' and from the front it is indeed the three deep gables fitted with elm weatherboards that are the most striking features of the building. The arch which spans the front entrance was something of an architectural joke on Lutyens' part since it does not enclose anything – the space beneath it is empty *(see plans opposite)*. The gable theme is continued on the west side with two further examples.

Homewood has that quality which Vita Sackville-West described as 'the peculiar genius of the English country house ... its knack of fitting in.'[5] Well captured by the architect's' daughter Elisabeth, who described approaching the house 'through hushed, mysterious woods' and finding it 'all white with sloped gables, small and intimate compared with the castle-like proportions of Knebworth House'.[6] Inside the house, Lutyens' attention to detail extended to making sure the stairs were shallow enough for an elderly lady and the door handles small enough for the hands of visiting grandchildren.

The features of Homewood were widely copied, particularly in houses in the same area, and M.H. Baillie Scott built a house with a roof design very similar to that of Homewood's garden front at Hurlingham around 1906. The same year, E.J. May designed a house at Rotherfield with a similar entrance front.

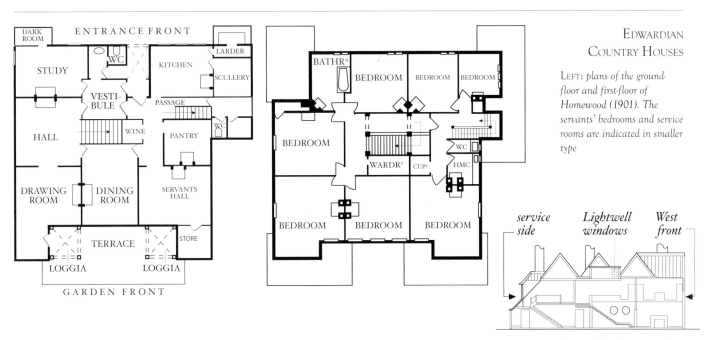

LEFT: *plans of the ground-floor and first-floor of Homewood (1901). The servants' bedrooms and service rooms are indicated in smaller type*

service side | Lightwell windows | West front

ABOVE: *through-section of Homewood, from the entrance front, showing the lightwell/lantern*

ABOVE: *a house at Reigate, designed in a late seventeenth-century style by Horace Field (c.1906)*

About 1906, the country house designs of architects such as Ernest Newton were leading the way towards a neo-Georgian revival. This took the form of a late seventeenth-century style with features such as symmetrical facades, sash windows, cornices and hooded porches as in his design for a house near Godstone Surrey; another example being Horace Field's design of that year for a house in Reigate, Surrey. However, Newton returned to the vernacular style when he felt it appropriate, for example at the Manor House, Upton Grey (1908). By 1909 Lutyens himself had abandoned the vernacular for the late seventeenth-century style which he called the 'Wrenaissance' after Sir Christopher Wren.

COUNTRY HOUSE PLAN

By the Edwardian period the plan was giving increasing prominence to the garden side. The most important rooms faced the garden: the drawing room and the dining room. Often only a study or a library faced the front of the house, as in E.J. May's design for a house at Rotherfield, Sussex. The windows of the servants' bedrooms were more likely to overlook the entrance front.

At Homewood, Lutyens addressed the problem of how to separate the private and service parts in a practical way. Both family and servants needed access to the front door. The servants needed to admit guests without trespassing onto the private side. Lutyens' solution was to place two front doors at the junction between the private and service sides. Servants could admit guests through one door and usher them into the vestibule. Members of the family could admit guests directly into the private side through the second front door. Rather than build a service wing, Lutyens placed the services on one side and the reception rooms on the other. The servants' bedrooms were upstairs on the service side. The dining room and the stairwell took up the centre. Another problem Lutyens solved was how to light the stairs and the landing. He built a lightwell into the pitched roof of the central gable; creating a flat roofed 'lantern'. Windows to light the stairs and landing were placed in the side walls of the 'lantern'. The main access to the terrace was through the French doors of the dining room. A door from the drawing room also opened onto the terrace through a loggia. The service side did not have access to the terrace although there was another loggia on that side to balance the garden front.

The other distinction in country houses was between male and female parts of the house. By the Edwardian period the principal male areas were the dining, billiard and smoking rooms. Traditionally the drawing room and the boudoir had been female preserves.

ABOVE: *Lutyens' design of
the roof allowed a 'lantern' to
light the stairs and landing at
Homewood*

RIGHT: *the hall showing the
staircase with doorways to
the private entrance and the
dining-room on either side.*
Photo by Stephen Pollock-
Hill

RIGHT: *a decorative scheme
for a boudoir with a frieze
of the 'water babies' (shown
above right) designed by
Winifred Horton (1901)*

ABOVE: *the drawing-room
fireplace at Homewood,
designed by Lutyens, made
from reconstituted stone*

The nineteenth century had seen the introduction to the country house of the smoking room and the revival of the great hall. The hall was useful for house parties as a mutual gathering place because of the division into male and female areas. Since 1864, it was understood that rooms were endowed with 'masculine importance and feminine delicacy'.[7] Halls with staircases which descended into them became popular because the party below could watch the descent of the ladies in their evening finery.

'Masculine importance and feminine delicacy' meant massive oak or mahogany and Turkey carpets in the dining room and spindly gilt or rosewood, silk or chintz in the drawing room. A dignified route between them was still of the greatest importance. Either the dining or the drawing room opened into the conservatory as at Flintham Hall in Nottinghamshire.

The drawing room had acquired several new functions during the reign of Queen Victoria, as a result of the practice of making 'morning calls'. These were carriage visits from one local hostess to another for a quarter-of-an-hour's polite conversation. They took place during the afternoon. The evening meal was taken later. The gap between luncheon at one-thirty and dinner at seven-thirty or eight o'clock had become so long that ladies had begun to take a meal of tea and cake in the afternoon. By 1900, afternoon tea had become an elaborate meal attended by both sexes. Tea was served in the drawing room in cold weather and outside when the weather was fine. It was one of the major features of life in a country house. Vita Sackville-West described: 'Those meals! Those endless extravagant meals, in which they indulged all year round ... how strange that eating should play so important a part in social life! They were eating quails and cracking jokes.'[8]

The drawing room had become a formal room dedicated to 'morning calls', afternoon tea and assembly both before and after dinner. The informal rooms were the morning room and the library. Morning rooms had first appeared in the early nineteenth century when they served as sitting rooms for the ladies. By 1900 it was normal for the men in a weekend house party to put on elaborate smoking jackets and retire to the smoking room after the ladies had gone to bed. Cigars and a tray of spirits were waiting for them. There was also the possibility of a game of billiards. Either the two rooms for this purpose were adjacent or they could be combined. A Voysey design for a house near Fairwater, Cardiff had a smoking room in an annex over a colonnaded porch. In some houses the male territory included a gunroom. The morning room, drawing room and the boudoir remained female preserves. The hall separated them as at Abbeystead Hall, Lancashire.

Judged by later standards, Edwardian country houses were far from luxorious. The fires in the bedrooms were seldom lit so the houses were chilly, 'bedrooms, often huge and many-windowed, could be as cold as churches'.[9] They seldom had more than one bathroom, even if they had as many as ten bedrooms. Some plans show a dressing-room adjacent to a bedroom which might have been fitted as a bathroom. But for many guests it was necessary to have hot water brought upstairs so that they could bathe in a hip bath, hopefully in front of a blazing fire. 'Private bathrooms? No!'[10] Upstairs plans often show service rooms such as a linen cupboard or a House Maid's Closet (HMC).

ABOVE: *the drawing room at Broad Leys, Windermere, designed by Voysey (c.1898)*

ABOVE: *billiard room at Blackwell, Windermere, designed by Baillie Scott (c.1900)*

ABOVE: *the staircase at Broad Leys, Windermere, designed by Voysey*

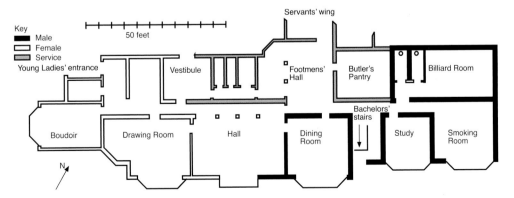

Key
■ Male
□ Female
▨ Service

50 feet

Servants' wing

Young Ladies' entrance   Vestibule   Footmens' Hall   Butler's Pantry   Billiard Room

Boudoir   Drawing Room   Hall   Dining Room   Bachelors' stairs   Study   Smoking Room

N

LEFT: *plan of the ground-floor of Abbeystead Hall (1886–88) showing the male and female parts, separated by the hall*

ENTRANCE FRONT

Muthesius observed that the forecourt should be on the road side because 'the whole development of the house is towards the garden side'.[11] A 'carriage drive' led to a forecourt which the house either faced or was placed around. Muthesius thought that the country house should be dislocated from the road, by a wall if necessary. The country house had an entrance front and a garden front but the former was becoming more sombre in comparison with the latter. In some country houses the dormer windows of the servants' bedrooms in the attic overlooked the forecourt of the entrance front.

Charles Holme was the owner and, later, the editor of *The Studio* magazine. In 1908, he commissioned the architect, Ernest Newton, to rebuild the Manor House, Upton Grey, Hampshire. This had been a Tudor farmhouse which was transformed into a country house. Newton chose the vernacular style as appropriate. The entrance front is on the road side but is separated from the road by a drive and a laurel hedge. The front door is timber-framed under a gabled porch with tile hung walls from the eaves down to the ground floor. The roof is tiled, with deep brick chimney stacks and dormer windows under hipped gables. The windows are casements with traditional diamond pattern leading. E.J. May had already designed a similar entrance front for a house on the Hindhead, Surrey (c.1906). But the columns of the entrance front of Monkton, Singleton, Sussex, showed that, by 1906, Lutyens was already inclining towards the 'Wrenaissance'.

E. Guy Dawber and R.S. Lorimer both designed entrance fronts with 'L' shaped layouts. Solom's Court, Surrey, had an 'L' shaped plan around an entrance forecourt. The two elevations facing the forecourt were less imposing than those facing the gardens.

R.S. Lorimer was described as the 'Scottish Lutyens'. His Peebleshire design had an 'L' shaped plan in which two low, central arches led to a covered entrance with the vestibule at the side.

The new Edwardian country houses had less need for outbuildings such as stables but there were new pieces of equipment such as generators for electricity which needed accommodation. Halsey Ricardo's design for a house on Norwood Hill, Charlwood, Surrey incorporated the latest requirement. It had a 'motor home' flanking the entrance (*see page* 90). The gardens were laid out to the side of the house furthest from the 'motor home'.

Robert Weir Schultz designed a house at Edenbridge, Kent. The gateway from the road led directly to the front door which was placed in the central feature of a symetrical facade which terminated in angled wings (*see page* 90).

OPPOSITE: *the entrance front of the Manor House, Upton Grey (1908)*

ABOVE: *the entrance front of a house on the Hindhead, Surrey, by E.J. May (c.1906)*

ABOVE: *the entrance front of Monkton, Singleton, Sussex, by Lutyens (c.1906)*

LEFT: *plan of Solom's Court, designed by E. Guy Dawber (c.1906)*

LEFT & ABOVE LEFT: *entrance front & plan of a house in Peebleshire designed by R.S. Lorimer (1906)*

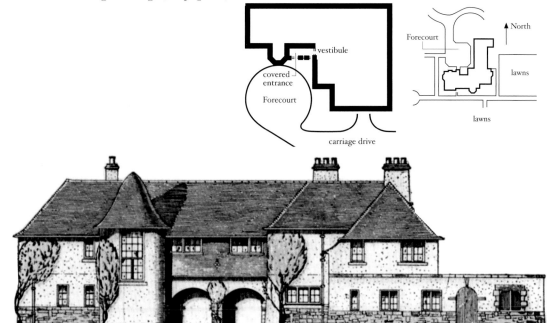

97

GARDEN FRONT

Muthesius proclaimed: 'love of the house is almost incomprehensible without love of the garden. A country house without a garden would in itself be an unimaginable idea, for it is mainly for the sake of having a house in its natural environment that people live far from the crowded conditions of the city.' [12]

The garden front had become the true front and it had also become the embodiment of the ideal: the house in its natural environment. According to Muthesius, gardens were divided into sections which were kept separate from one another. Each part of the garden should be placed adjacent to that part of the house to which it belonged: kitchen garden to service wing, flower garden to drawing room. The lawns should face the residential part of the house. 'Thus the garden extends the house into the midst of nature.'

Muthesius expressed the idea that the gardens should actually surround the house. Sir Lawrence Weaver agreed, referring to the 'encircling garden'. He continued that 'house and garden should be considered together as an architectural whole'. [13]

W.H. Bidlake suggested that the architect should impose order on the garden by 'building its terraces and walled courts, planning its rose pergolas and grass alleys, its herbaceous borders and its lily ponds, its retreats and arbours, all carefully studied in connection with the architectural lines of the house and the points of view from which the house makes the most agreeable pictures of gable and chimney.' [14]

A concept which was firmly established during the Edwardian period was that of hard and soft landscaping. Hard landscape was formed by buildings and architectural features like terraces. The terrace is softened by the plants being allowed to grow right up to the walls of the house. The garden front of the Eyot house at Sonning-on-Thames shows wooden trellises fixed to the walls to assist climbing plants and H. Tanner Jr's design for a house at Beckenham shows winding paths and flower-beds under the windows. Water features could also be used as hard and soft landscaping. A design for a house in Bromley (c.1901) allowed a pond as a soft feature close to the house.

OPPOSITE: *the garden front of the Manor House, Upton Grey*

ABOVE: *the garden front of Berrydown Court, Overton, Hampshire, designed by Edwin Lutyens (1898)*

ABOVE: *a design for a house in Beckenham, Kent, by H. Tanner Jr (c.1906)*

LEFT: *the Eyot house, Sonning-on-Thames, designed by Halsey Ricardo (c.1906)*

ABOVE: *a design for a house in Bromley, Kent (c.1901)*

ABOVE: *the garden front of Homewood, seen from the lower terrace. The hard landscaping is apparent from this view.* Photo by Stephen Pollock-Hill.

ABOVE: *Homewood, detail of the loggia on the private side which had direct access to the terrace. This view shows soft landscaping.*

On the garden front of Homewood, the roof extensions frame the dining room windows and those of the floor above. The colour of the roof tiles acts as a barrier between the house's natural surroundings and the man-made colour of the wall surfaces. Thus the house appears to be organic in the Arts & Crafts sense of not only being in the country but of the country. The wall surfaces of the garden front are considerably lighter than the elm-boarded gables of the entrance front. This accords with a trend which had been apparent since Philip Webb designed Standen in 1894. At Standen the garden front with its tile-hung gables, terrace and conservatory (*see pages 32 & 258*) is brighter than the entrance front.

Lutyens designed the gardens at Homewood himself. He used hard and soft landscaping. On the terrace, plants and pots were allowed to come right up to the walls of the house. Herbs and creeping plants could grow in the paving and in beds around the base of the walls. In other country houses climbers were encouraged to grow on vertical surfaces such as walls and posts. They were also allowed to grow through gaps. Climbing plants like the Mexican daisy might be planted along the steps with lavenders, thymes and other herbs.

The lower terrace hosts ornamental features such as pots and urns to achieve hard and soft effects in the garden away from the house. This could also be done with water features such as formal ponds with water lilies or shrubs billowing through benches or balustrades and plants cascading down rockeries. R.A. Briggs' design for the garden front of a house at Hambledon also shows hard and soft landscaping: the beds have been placed around the base of the walls and

LEFT: *garden front of a house
at Northwood, with a frieze of
decorated plaster, designed by
Arnold Mitchell (c.1906)*

there is a terrace with topiary. Formal steps negotiate the slope down to the lawns below. The design was published the same year that Homewood was built.

ABOVE: *a design for the
garden front of a house at
Hambledon (c.1901)*

Arnold Mitchell's design for the garden front of a house at Northwood combined a frieze of decorated plaster with segmental bay windows. Climbers and shrubs were allowed to grow almost up against the plasterwork. By contrast, Lutyens designed the garden front of Monkton, Singleton, in a more formal 'Wrenaissance' manner with loggias under semi-circular brick arches which supported balconies at first-floor level and columns up to the roof between them.

LEFT: *the garden front of
Monkton, Singleton, designed
by Lutyens (c.1906)*

ABOVE: *the formal garden at the Manor House, Upton Grey – looking up from the bowling lawn towards the Rose lawn and the house*

RIGHT: *part of the Rose lawn with the tennis lawn beyond on the lowest terrace*

Country House Gardens

ABOVE: *Wayford Manor,
Somerset – the terrace and
gardens were redesigned by
Harold Peto in 1902*

ccording to Muthesius, the three common elements of the Edwardian country house garden were 'terrace, flower-beds and lawns'. The terrace was important because it enabled one to step into the garden in a dignified way. If the ground did not assist construction of a terrace by sloping away from the house, it would be necessary to excavate the ground in front of the chosen area.

The lawn was next in importance, especially for games. Muthesius: 'The commonest of these games-lawns is the lawn-tennis court.' Bowling and croquet lawns might also be laid out.

The commonest form of flower garden was the rose garden which was often laid out as a sunk garden; lily gardens and specialised gardens containing particular collections of flowers, such as rock or alpine gardens, were also popular.

Clipped hedges were the walls which the garden designer used to delimit the different areas of the garden. In 1906, W.H. Bidlake explained that gardens were often laid out as a formal garden closest to the house, becoming more natural further away. The gardens of the Manor House, Upton Grey demonstrate this approach.

ABOVE: *the rose garden
of the Croft, Winchfield,
Hampshire, designed by R.W.
Schultz (c.1906)*

In 1908 Charles Holme commissioned Gertrude Jekyll to design the gardens at the Manor House, Upton Grey. Gertrude Jekyll liked both formal and wild gardens. On one side of the house, she designed a cottage-style formal garden and, on the other, a wild garden. Both gardens have been restored to her original plans by the owners (*see plan on page 104*).

The formal garden consists of an ornamental flower garden, or rose lawn, set on terraces above a bowling green and a tennis lawn. The formal garden is bordered by yew hedges which separate the formal garden from the kitchen garden and orchard on one side and a nuttery on the other. Jekyll had the grass slopes that ran down from the garden front converted into terraces. These terraces are supported by dry-stone walls which give the effect of vertical flower beds. A heavy oak pergola leads away from the house towards shallow stone steps which run down from the terrace to the rose lawn. The formal stone beds are planted in a cottage style with soft colours of pink and grey. A contemporary, the architect Reginald Blomfield, described the rose lawn as 'colourful tarts set out on a pastry cook's tray'. The main borders, at the sides, are planted in Jekyll's 'drifts of colour' (*see page 107*). These become most dramatic in late summer.

Below the rose lawn, further flights of steps lead down to the bowling and tennis lawns. Beyond the tennis lawn the yew hedge is formed into an arbour crowned with climbing roses. The nuttery to the south is planted with hazelnut trees which are coppiced to provide supports for the tall herbaceous plants in the borders. Bluebells and primroses grow beneath the trees. Old apple, plum, damson, greengage and pear trees grow in the orchard on the other side. The kitchen garden is laid out in practical grids where cuttings, seedlings and rare plants are nurtured. These are then used to restock the gardens. The kitchen garden is also used to grow a good supply of fruit and vegetables. On the other side of the house, opposite the entrance front, Jekyll designed and created a 'wild garden'.

ABOVE: *an arbour at one end
of the bowling green of the
Manor house, Upton Grey
(1908)*

PART THREE:
COUNTRY HOUSES
& GARDENS

RIGHT: *plan of the gardens of the Manor House, Upton Grey*

ABOVE: *detail of the Wild Garden (see plan, right)*

BELOW: *the pond in the Wild Garden*

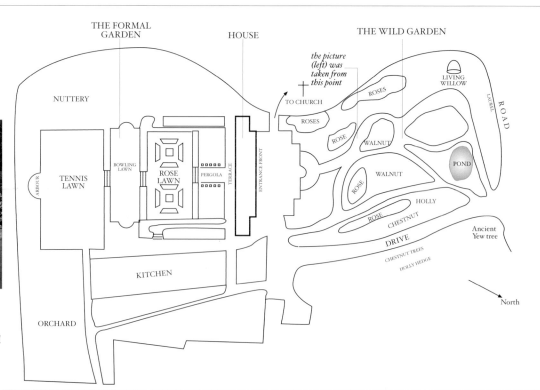

THE FORMAL GARDEN

HOUSE

THE WILD GARDEN

NUTTERY

TENNIS LAWN

ARBOUR

BOWLING LAWN

ROSE LAWN

PERGOLA

TERRACE

ENTRANCE FRONT

the picture (left) was taken from this point

TO CHURCH

ROSES

ROSES

ROSE

WALNUT

ROSE

WALNUT

LIVING WILLOW

LAUREL

ROAD

POND

HOLLY

ROSE

CHESTNUT

KITCHEN

DRIVE

CHESTNUT TREES

HOLLY HEDGE

Ancient Yew tree

North

ORCHARD

The famous and influential garden designer William Robinson conceived the idea of the 'Wild Garden' as a reaction against the formal Victorian garden. This featured topiary, hedges, geometric designs and mass carpets of colourful bedding. He stated: 'To make a flower-bed to imitate a bad carpet, and by throwing aside all grace of form and loveliness of bloom, was indeed a dismal mistake ...' Instead, he suggested that hardy plants should be planted in natural-looking groups alongside more tender indigenous plants to provide cover for them. In *Gleanings from French Gardens* (1868) he stated: 'We have no doubt whatsoever that in many places as good an effect as any yet seen in an English garden from tender plants, may be obtained by planting hardy ones only!'

The hardy plants might include foreign imports such as pampas grass, Yuccas, bamboos, crambe and rheum. As he later wrote in *The Wild Garden*, 'I was led to think of the enormous number of beautiful hardy plants from other countries which might be naturalised, with a very slight amount of trouble.' In his popular book *The English Flower Garden* (1883) he explained:

> The term Wild Garden is applied to the placing of perfectly hardy exotic plants in places where they will take care of themselves. It has nothing to do with 'the Wilderness', though it may be carried out in it. What it does mean is best explained by the winter Aconite flowering under a grove of naked trees in February; by the Snowflake abundant in meadows by the Thames ...

ABOVE: *the formal entrance to the Wild Garden, Upton Grey*

The Wild Garden at Upton Grey develops from formality nearest the house to naturalness furthest away from it, sloping down from the drive towards the nearby church. Grass paths lead through iron gates and urns at the entrance. Mown paths wind around banks of roses, stands of walnut trees and the hardy bamboos. Snowdrops, primroses, oxlips, cowslips, wood anemones, scilla, muscari and fritillaria have survived in the Wild Garden since Jekyll's original planting. Eventually the paths arrive at the pond which is surrounded by rocks and planted with indigenous and water-loving plants. It is screened from the drive by chestnut trees and holly. The far end is masked from the road by laurels.

ABOVE: *the wild willow arbour in the Wild Garden, Upton Grey*

Robinson became involved in a fundamental debate about garden design with Blomfield. As an architect, Blomfield insisted on an architectural approach which favoured formal gardens; Robinson maintained that plants should be the basis. 'There has always been war to the knife between the landscape gardeners and believers in formal gardens.'[1] Gertrude Jekyll carefully steered a path between the two. She was helped by her fruitful relationship with the architect Lutyens with whom she designed a hundred gardens. She favoured woodland planting and her own home, Munstead Wood, near Godalming, Surrey, was sited among trees. At Munstead Wood, Lutyens demonstrated that architectural features and plants could co-exist by setting a wooden gate in the break of a hedge. About 1906, they co-operated at Hestercombe, near Taunton, Somerset. Lutyens used architectural features to create the spaces within the garden which Jekyll planted. To an existing terrace, Lutyens added two long stone water features known as rills, on either side of a sunken garden,. At the far end he introduced a pergola walk. The parterre garden formed by all these features is called the Great Plat.

ABOVE: *one of the rills at Hestercombe, designed by Lutyens (1906)*

In *Colour Schemes for the Flower Garden* (1921) Jekyll explained that just stocking an area with plants only made a collection rather than a garden. The idea should be to create beautiful pictures. What made gardening into an art was integrating everything into a harmonious whole: 'a dream of beauty, a place of perfect rest and refreshment of mind and body – a series of well-set jewels.' In her opinion, the fine art was to:

> place every group of plants with such thoughtful care and definite intention that they shall form part of a harmonious whole, and that successive portions, or in some cases details, shall show a series of pictures. It is to so regulate the trees and undergrowth of the wood that their lines and masses come into beautiful form and harmonious proportion; it is to be always watching, noting and doing, and putting oneself into closest acquaintance and sympathy with the growing things ... In this spirit the garden and woodland, such as they are, have been formed.

ABOVE: *terrace, flower-beds and lawns at Hestercombe, Somerset, designed by Lutyens and Gertrude Jekyll (c.1906)*

RIGHT: *part of the rose lawn
at Upton Grey adjacent to the
nuttery and the orchard*

RIGHT: *one of the main
borders of the formal garden
at Upton Grey, in May, with
the yew hedges which divide it
from the kitchen garden*

LEFT: *a hardy flower border at Munstead Wood, Surrey, in 1907: red geraniums, dahlia 'fire king' with salvias backed by hollyhocks*

ABOVE: *white roses and lavender on the terrace at Munstead Wood*

She took a great deal of trouble over 'methods of arranging growing flowers, especially in ways of colour combination'.

'DRIFTS OF COLOUR'

Jekyll abandoned carpet-bedding, topiary work and box edging in favour of an informal approach, laying out cottage-style gardens of old-fashioned flowers. She made the herbaceous border famous. Her 'drifts of colour' were spectacular. These were planting arrangements in which the colours of the plants in season blended into each other. For example, at Upton Grey, from cool blues and yellows at the ends to hot oranges and reds in the centre.

Herbaceous borders and 'drifts of colour' were highly labour intensive. Kitchen gardens and yards of clipped hedges also required considerable maintenance. Labour was both available and relatively cheap. Edwardian country house gardens created considerable employment. Jekyll employed seventeen gardeners in her own garden at Munstead Wood; Ellen Willmott of Warley Place, Essex employed more than eighty gardeners.

ABOVE: *a herbaceous border at Hestercombe, originally planted by Gertrude Jekyll*

Jekyll advocated seasonal planting. In *Colour Schemes for the Flower Garden* (1921) she explained: 'To plant and maintain a flower border, with a good scheme for colour, is by no means the easy thing that is commonly supposed. I believe that the only way in which it can be made successful is to devote certain borders to certain times of year; each border or garden region to be bright for from one to three months'. Her spring garden had Morello cherries on the high walls and drifts of white arabis and yellow and white tulips. The June garden had a double border of lupins and irises and a blaze of salvias. During September her garden featured pale yellow snapdragons, blue heliotropes and asters.

Another contemporary technique was the training of beech, lime or hornbeam into 'pleached' screens. Young trees were trained, pruned and encouraged to grow so that their branches formed a screen which masked off the area beyond.

ABOVE: *the fountain court at Iford Manor, with bronze deer on plinths*

ABOVE: *the Italianate terrace at Iford Manor, designed by Harold Peto*

ABOVE: *the outdoor dining-room at Iford Manor*

ITALIANATE GARDENS

After 1900, the growing taste for neo-classical design included Italian gardens. These were formal gardens which featured structures such as pergolas, rotundas, loggias and balustraded or colonnaded terraces with statuary, columns, fountains and pools. Italian gardens had first been introduced to England during the seventeenth century 'in the time of the English Renaissance', as at Powis Castle, Welshpool, Powys. Gertrude Jekyll exclaimed: 'The garden was more lavishly treated with architectural enrichment than the house itself', but she warned, 'there can be little doubt that the true Italian garden cannot be rightly transplanted into our climate' because it needed brighter light, a warmer temperature and 'an endless abundance of rushing water'. [2] She added that even genuine Italian sculptures often had the 'appearance of unhappy exiles'. But she admitted that there were some fine examples of Italian gardens in England. She frequently expressed her admiration for the garden design of Harold Peto which was culturally diverse but predominantly Italianate.

The most popular feature of Edwardian gardens of many different sizes was an Italianate one, the pergola. This became a term applied to any walk-through structure suitable for flowering climbing plants. In 1902 Peto designed an Italian garden for Daisy, Countess of Warwick, at Easton Lodge in Essex. Here, the pergola had rounded arches and a central dome. When he finally designed his own garden at Iford Manor, Bradford-on-Avon, Wiltshire, it, too, was demonstrably Italianate. The existing garden included a steep hillside with a grassy terrace at the top. Peto made the terrace the main feature. He paved it in York stone with gravel borders for potted plants and sculptures. He built an articulated colonnade and flights of steps up to the terrace which he gave retaining walls like those of the hillside gardens around Rome, Tuscany and the Italian lakes. Below the terrace a double flight of steps descended to a lily pool. At the Western end of the terrace he placed a semi-circular stone seat he described as 'apse like'. At the entrance to the gardens a Pompeiian doorway gave access to a fountain court with two large plinths which supported bronze deer copied from Herculaneum. Between them water streamed into a pool through a lion's head mask. Peto designed an outdoor dining-room in one of the enclosed courts.

LEFT: *the terrace and lily pool
at Iford Manor, designed by
Harold Peto (1902-14)*

ABOVE: *Homewood, divided
into different areas by hedges
and changes in level*

ABOVE: *Hidcote Manor
Garden – an interwar
development of the garden as
rooms*

A contemporary on a weekend house party remembered that on Sunday mornings while the men 'would drift ... to the smoking room[, t]he women would idle in the saloon watching the rain descend upon the Italian garden.'³ The author Edith Wharton (1861–1937) agreed with Jekyll; in *Italian Villas and their Gardens* (1904) she suggested that rather than trying to create an Italian garden 'in the literal sense,' it would be preferable to plan 'a garden as well adapted to its surroundings as were the models which inspired it'. This was consistent with Jekyll's preference for lead rather than marble, as she stated in *Garden Ornament* (1918):

> The busts of the Caesars and other ornaments and sculptures in white marble are not quite at home in our gardens ... we have more suitable material in our home quarries ... There can scarcely be any doubt that the happiest material for our garden sculpture and ornament is lead ... the surface of the metal, with age and exposure, acquires a patina of silvery grey that harmonizes well with our garden evergreens.

THE GARDEN AS ROOMS

The garden could be subdivided into rooms by means of yew or low box hedges. In addition to yew hedges, Lutyens used changes of level to break up the garden of Homewood into different areas. His fellow architect, Sir Lawrence Weaver, described the garden at Homewood as 'rich with colour and rich with quick scents'. Lutyens used similar techniques to re-order the gardens of his wife's family seat, Knebworth House. He simplified the flower-beds and statuary of the Victorian gardens into lawns and avenues of pollarded lime trees and yew hedges.

Hidcote Manor, Chipping Campden, Gloucestershire was a further development of the concept of outdoor garden rooms. The project began in 1907 and continued into the interwar years. Its creator, Lawrence Johnstone (1871–1948) arranged the gardens as a series of rooms, not just separated by hedges and different levels but each with a different character. This was accentuated by the dramatic treatment of the topiary of the walls and hedges. The garden is also famous for its rare shrubs and trees and outstanding colour-coordinated herbaceous borders. Johnstone was an exotic plant-hunter. Exotica featured in several interwar gardens.

ABOVE: *Hidcote Manor
Garden – dramatic topiary*

PART THREE:
COUNTRY HOUSES
& GARDENS

RIGHT: *the lime walk,*
Sissinghurst Castle Garden

ABOVE: *the yew walk,*
Sissinghurst Castle Garden

RIGHT: *the moat at*
Sissinghurst Castle Garden

ABOVE: *a lead flower pot at*
Sissinghurst Castle Garden

Vita Sackville-West and her husband, Harold Nicolson, took the garden as rooms concept even further when they made Sissinghurst Castle Garden their home. From 1930 onwards their family actually lived in separate buildings within the garden. It was the ultimate development of the traditional concept of extending the house 'into the midst of nature'. They planted the rose 'Madame Alfred Carrière' alongside the South Cottage the day they moved in. The South Cottage was the first building they made habitable. Their sons slept upstairs in the Priest's House. The family dining room was downstairs. They converted part of the old manor house into a library. Vita used the Elizabethan Tower as her study. So the dwelling rooms were connected by the gardens. Harold added several new walls and hedges to the existing walls and buildings. This transformed the six acres around the buildings into separate gardens enclosed by hedges of yew, box, rose and hornbeam. He described it as 'ramshackle farm tumble'.

He also linked the gardens by vistas or lines of sight along walks and through openings. He later claimed: 'we have got what we wanted to get – between the classic and the romantic, between the element of expectation and the element of surprise.'

Vita filled the enclosures with beds and plants. Harold added paths, pots and statuary. Originally all the paths were grass. Vita remained an adherent of Edwardian gardening techniques such as seasonal planting and colour in the flower garden.

She created a purple border along the north wall of the courtyard. The cottage garden was conceived as the personification of cottage gardens. The colours were restricted to yellows, reds and oranges. Four large yew trees tower over it. It was personal to both Vita and Harold. She came down early to work on it. Harold gathered flowers from it for his London flat where he stayed during the week.

The lime walk was Harold's particular project. The lime trees are pleached. He planned it and clipped the limes himself. He referred to it as the 'spring garden' or 'my life's work'. There are statues at each end in the Italianate style and Tuscan pots in the intervals.

Harold added a yew walk to separate the orchard from the tower lawn and the white garden. The two remaining 'arms' of the medieval moat enclose the orchard. At the end of the moat they

ABOVE: *the rose garden with the South Cottage in the background, Sissinghurst Castle Garden*

ABOVE: *the Elizabethan tower from the tower lawn, Sissinghurst Castle Garden*

LEFT: *the purple border on the north wall of the courtyard, Sissinghurst Castle Garden*

111

ABOVE: *the herb garden,
Sissinghurst Castle Garden*

ABOVE: *the 'rondel' at
Sissinghurst Castle Garden*

ABOVE: *rosa mulliganii,
in flower, on the central
canopy of the white garden at
Sissinghurst Castle Garden*

RIGHT: *the Wall Garden
at Nymans, with its Italian
marble fountain and topiary
globes*

both created a herb garden, enclosed by buttressed yews. The herb garden was a special delight to Vita who had an acute sense of smell. It contained over one hundred varieties which she could identify with her eyes closed. Beside the herb garden there is a thyme lawn. The rose garden contains Harold's 'rondel', a disc of mown lawn surrounded by a circle of yew hedges, with gaps in each quadrant leading to formal beds edged with box.

The white garden was created as a conventional rose garden but Vita changed it to white flowers and pale grey foliage after the Second World War. Harold designed the crossing paths and a pattern of low box hedges. It was a showpiece of seasonal planting but the roses on the central canopy, *Rosa mulliganii*, only flower in early July. Family weddings had to be on the second Saturday of July so that the bride and groom were able to receive their guests under the central canopy when it was in full flower.

She described the progress of the gardens in her weekly gardening column for the *Observer*. The gardens became famous and were opened to the public in 1938. Vita called the visitors 'shillingses' because the admission price was one shilling (5p).

The gardens at Nymans, Handcross, West Sussex had been developed by the Messel family since 1895. The Messels continued their development through both the Edwardian and interwar periods. From the start the Messels were willing to experiment. They created a Pinetum with no less than fifteen varieties of Pinus, other conifers and dwarf rhododendrons. They also transformed an old orchard into a Wall Garden with an Italian marble fountain and topiary yew globes on either side. The Wall Garden was suitable for tender exotics because of its mild

FAR LEFT: *the house and gardens at Coleton Fishacre (1925)* (National Trust Picture Library)

LEFT: *exotic planting along a path at Coleton Fishacre* (National Trust Picture

ABOVE: *the stone arch over the inlet to the upper pond, with white water lilies, at Coleton Fishacre* (National Trust Picture Library)

ABOVE: *the rill garden at Coleton Fishacre (1925)* (National Trust Picture Library)

ABOVE: *Echium Pininana – interwar exotica at Coleton Fishacre (1925)* (National Trust Picture Library)

microclimate and highly fertile soil. These included plants from Chile and Argentina which were grown from seed that the head gardener's son, Harold Comber, brought back from his travels in Tasmania and the Andes during the 1920s. The Heather Garden was one of the first of its kind. It combined ericas with dwarf rhododendrons; many of them were grown from seed collected by the plant hunters George Forrest, Frank Kingdon-Ward and Joseph Rock. These were sheltered by Pinus montana. In 1903, they built a pergola beside the croquet lawn. It supported Wisteria sinensis and Wisteria multijuga which was imported from Japan in 1904.

As well as magnolia and cherry trees along the drive, they planted other discoveries of exotic plant hunters including Davidia involucrata (the handkerchief tree, from 1908) and Alsatroemeria ligtu angustifolia 'Vivid' (from 1937). The Messels created a rock garden of local sandstone which they planted with helianthemums and dwarf shrubs such as cotoneaster. The gardens reached their peak about 1930 when they were opened to the public on a regular basis.

Coleton Fishacre, Kingswear, Devon, had both conventional and unconventional features for an interwar house and garden. In 1924 Rupert and Lady Dorothy D'Oyly Carte commissioned Oswald Milne, a pupil of Edwin Lutyens, to design a house and gardens for their family to use as a holiday home. The garden is traditional in its use of hard and soft landscaping – as well as formal terraces, a pool garden and a Rill, it also had a bluebell wood. But it is unusual in that it is a garden by the sea. The D'Oyly Cartes chose the site for their house and garden after seeing it from the sea while sailing their yacht between Brixham and Dartmouth. The microclimate in the narrow valley at Coleton allows many rare and tender plants to flourish. Bamboos, mimosas, myrtle and other moisture-loving plants grow profusely around the pool and streams. A stone arch spans the inlet to the upper pond where white water lilies bloom. Thickly planted rhododendrons, magnolia and camellias create a stunning display of colour in the spring. A gazebo overlooks the sea below. Paths wind through clumps of bamboo, groves of mimosa, magnolias and other shrubs down to a small sea cove.

Like the Messels, the D'Oyly Cartes experimented with trees and shrubs from around the world, including exotic plants, such as Echium Pininana, and unusual climbers such as the Coral Plant (Berberidopsis corallina) and Chilean Mitre Flower (Mitraria coccinea).

9

Interwar Front

s building resumed after the end of the First World War, both architects and builders carried on in the way they had before the war: in either the vernacular 'cottage' style or neo-Georgian. Architects were inclined towards neo-Georgian but they were not unanimous. But there was one major difference for the speculative builders. Houses were no longer speculatively built for rent but for sale. In 1914 between six and ten per cent of the population were owner-occupiers. By 1938 the proportion had risen to 34 per cent.[1] Another significant development was the large scale publicly-funded building of small houses for the working classes. The Addison Act of 1919 made it compulsory for local authorities to build houses for rent by the working classes. As the *City of Manchester Plan* (1945) later noted, terraced houses were more economical in terms of use of land and neo-Georgian was a logical choice for the new council houses.

Those who bought their own homes wished them to be clearly different to local authority housing. So a pattern developed with small houses being built in neo-Georgian terraces and medium-sized in vernacular style semi-detached. The owner-occupied medium-sized houses had to have a bay window to distinguish them further from the council houses.

LARGE

Activity resumed in many of the places where it had been interrupted in 1915. The development of the Sloane Stanley estate at the former Camera Square continued gradually in its new form as Chelsea Park Gardens. In style, it was the mixture of vernacular and neo-Georgian in which it had been begun before the war. Red brick walls and round-headed door arches with fanlights were combined with casement windows, gables and hanging tiles. The successful artist, Alfred Munnings, already an ARA, moved into a house built there on a corner site in 1920.

Suburban building also resumed in places like Golders Green and Gerrards Cross. The Tudors, Gerrards Cross, Buckinghamshire was designed in 1920–21 by Baillie-Scott for Harold William Sanderson, a director of Wallpaper Manufacturers Ltd. The building contractor was Jordans Village Industries of Beaconsfield. The cost of building was, reputedly, £30,000. Later, during the 1920s, The Tudors became the home of Austin Reed, the men's outfitter who had opened his shop in Regent Street in 1926. Baillie-Scott chose a vernacular, timber-framed style with brick or plaster infills. Like his pre-war design in Hampstead Garden Suburb, which is known as Baillie-Scott Corner, the timber framing of The Tudors was structural. The entrance front has a jetty construction with an oriel window over the porch. The infill between the frames was smoothly finished in plaster. The pitch of the clay tiled roof extends in a catslide right down to first-floor level in cottage style. The line of the eaves is maintained on the end wall, facing the road, by hanging tiles on either side of the massive chimney stack. The pair of chimney stacks are angled in mock Tudor style.

On the service wing the dormers have hipped gables and the brick infill of the timber frames is set in a herringbone pattern. At the lower levels the bricks are laid in Flemish bond. The windows are all casements with lead glazing bars.

OPPOSITE: *front entrance of The Tudors, Gerrards Cross, designed by M.H. Baillie-Scott (1921)*

ABOVE: *Alfred Munnings' house in Chelsea Park Gardens*

ABOVE: *Chelsea Park Gardens' mixture of vernacular and neo-Georgian*

ABOVE: *the service wing of The Tudors, Gerrards Cross (1921)*

ABOVE: *suburban detached house in North Sheen (1924) – with overhanging eaves, roughcast finish, hipped roofs and bay*

PART FOUR:
INTERWAR HOUSES

RIGHT: *Welwyn Garden City, detached house lived in by the architect, Louis de Soissons (1920)*

ABOVE: *Welwyn Garden City (c.1921)*

RIGHT: *Chelsea Square, terraced house with mansard roof and dormers over segmental bay (1928)*

ABOVE: *neo-Georgian large terraced houses (1925)*

By 1920 the majority of fashionable opinion had swung in favour of 'Georgian' as opposed to vernacular forms or 'cottage style':

> 'Georgian' has flourished greatly during recent years, and has been much exploited for the numerous garden suburbs that have sprung into existence.[2]

Because the Welwyn Garden City project was underfunded, it had to sell off plots. The large houses built on these plots had to be similar in style to the rest of the development because they all came under the planning jurisdiction of the Garden City's designer, Louis de Soissons. Welwyn's style became the standard for interwar neo-Georgian. This was flat-fronted, red brick under a pitched roof with projecting eaves. The front entrance was emphasised by a porch or doorcase. The windows could be either casement or sash with the lights evenly divided into small panes by the glazing bars.

Between 1928 and 1932 the former Trafalgar Square in Chelsea was rebuilt as Chelsea Square in neo-Georgian style by the architects Darcy Braddell and Humphry Deane. They designed various roof configurations including mansard roofs with dormer windows as well as conventional pitched roofs. The most striking designs had mansard roofs with green pantiles, dormers and eaves overhanging segmental bays.

MEDIUM

Speculative builders resumed building medium-sized houses in suburban areas as land and materials became available. In some cases this resulted in medium-sized detached houses as in Wentworth Road, Golders Green. In the suburbs, neo-Georgian was associated with council houses. Therefore speculative builders preferred to build in a variety of vernacular styles including the Edwardian version of 'Old English'. They tried to emulate the work of architects such as Baillie-Scott. These attempts developed into the half-timbered style which would become known as Tudorbethan. The houses built by the speculative builders were intended to appeal to mature married men. But by the mid-1930s builders were diversifying to appeal to others such as the elderly and single. They began to build different types such as bungalows or chalets which were both cheaper and suitable for smaller households. The *Daily Mail* Ideal Home Exhibition of 1923 had featured an entire 'Bungalow Town' of 'labour -saving bungalows'.

ABOVE: *the half-timbered style known as Tudorbethan in Hendon (c.1924)*

ABOVE: *the 'Rochester' bungalow (1939)*

ABOVE: *semi-detached chalets built by New Ideal Homesteads in Montrose Park, Kent (1933)*

LEFT: *detached, medium-sized house in Golders Green (1922)*

ABOVE: *a semi-detached suburban house built during a brief fashion for external shutters (1925)*

RIGHT: *semi-detached houses in Golders Green with overhanging eaves above gable wings (1914–15)*

ABOVE: *E.J. May's design with overhanging eaves and a 'gable wing' (1920)*

ABOVE: *semi-detached houses in Chaucer Road, Cambridge, designed by T.H. Lyon (1920)*

ABOVE: *semi-detached house in Edgware with overhanging eaves above bay (c.1924)*

TOOTH AND GAP

The speculative builders also copied other forms which had been developed by architects. Overhanging eaves had been used by architects such as the Palsers in their pre-war designs in Hampstead Garden Suburb. Before building ceased during the First World War, similar designs were speculatively built in Golders Green and other developing areas like Gerrards Cross. After the war such features were widely used by the speculative builders. E.J. May's design for a house in Chislehurst featured overhanging eaves above bay windows which formed a gable wing. This projected forward from the main body of the house. By 1920, when May's designs were published in *The Architectural Review* in the 'gable wing' was becoming a popular feature. The plan of the house was asymmetrical but, built as a semi-detached pair, it developed into the pattern which would become known as 'tooth and gap'. The finish of the 'gable wing' could be a fusion of traditional and more contemporary features: for example, the bay might be half-timbered with rough-cast infill and the additional embellishment of a rectangle with stepped corners (an Art Deco motif). By the 1930s the gable was hipped, as was the main roof. This made the overhanging eaves, which were no longer supported by brackets, more prominent.

T.H. Lyon designed semi-detached houses for a development in Chaucer Road, Cambridge which were also published in *The Architectural Review*. They were finished in roughcast at first floor level with red brick below.

In suburbs such as Edgware or Victoria Park in Manchester, the semi-detached became the predominant type. The Northern line of the London Underground arrived in Edgware during 1924. Speculative builders began to build a more modest form of 'tooth and gap'. This consisted of semi-detached houses with 'half-timbered' gables over bay windows. Similar development took place around the extension of the Piccadilly Line from Finsbury Park to Cockfosters. In Manchester, the Corporation reported 'a steady movement of population from inner city areas to new suburban housing estates on the outskirts took place accompanied by an acceleration of wealthier families to new residential districts, mostly in Cheshire'.[3]

LEFT: 'tooth and gap'
suburban semi-detached pair
(1934)

DIFFERENT IN STYLE

The interwar norm was that medium-sized houses should be different in style to small (council) houses. Bays were essential to further distinguish the owner-occupiers' homes from council houses. Welwyn Garden City was an exception to the interwar pattern because large, medium and small houses were built in the same style, a local version of neo-Georgian. The second attempt to build a garden city at Welwyn in Hertfordshire was more successful at becoming a mixed development than any of the pre-war schemes. This happened because the local authority co-ordinated their council house efforts with those of the garden city project. It was so admired that 41 houses in neo-Georgian style formed the village at the 1920 *Daily Mail* Ideal Home Exhibition.

ABOVE: *a house in a semi-detached pair in Victoria Park, Manchester, with front doors at opposite ends (c.1928)*

The speculative builders soon realised that potential owner-occupiers valued their privacy, so the front doors were placed at opposite ends of semi-detached pairs. This became a characteristic of many interwar houses. There were alternatives (*see plan on page 131*). Publicity material frequently proclaimed the variety of design: 'semi-detached, but each pair of a different design' or 'No pair of houses alike in road'. Some builders gave their types names such as 'the Honeymoon Cottage' (£950), 'the Monk's House' (£1,050) or 'the Sunshine House' (£1,100), from Rayner's Lane, Harrow, in 1933.

LEFT: *a cul de sac in Welwyn Garden City (1920)*

119

OPPOSITE: *lightly built bay on a semi-detached house in Northenden, part of the Wythenshawe development, outside Manchester (1931 onwards)*

LEFT: *the compromise design – a semi-detached pair with 'sun-trap' windows and flow-curved walls under a pitched roof in Edgware (1934)*

ABOVE: *a semi-detached pair with tile-hung bays in Cockfosters (c.1931)*

LIGHTER BAYS

Bay windows were more lightly built during the interwar period than they had been before 1914. Instead of rectangular stone lintels and mullions, tiles were hung from posts erected over a brick base. Clay tiles hanging on a bay at first floor level are a characteristic feature of interwar houses. Interwar bays were usually segmental.

MODERNISM REJECTED

Speculative builders tried Modernism around 1932, while there was a fashionable 'sun-cult'. A small number of flat-roofed houses with plain walls began to appear in both angular and flow-curved styles. This culminated at the *Daily Mail* Ideal Home Exhibition of 1934 where they were grouped into a 'Village of Tomorrow'. But the public were unimpressed and a compromise design appeared in Edgware. It had smooth walls and metal framed 'sun-trap' windows under a conventional pitched roof. This design was copied elsewhere by other builders.

The Modernist architect, Erno Goldfinger, designed three houses, one of which was to be his own home, in Hampstead. He tactfully concealed their modern construction and plan behind a red brick exterior which was sympathetic to the older properties of his neighbours.

LEFT: *three houses designed by the architect Erno Goldfinger (1938). The central house was his own home. The plate glass windows indicate the Modernist design which is concealed behind brick-facing in sympathy with the older houses nearby*

121

OPPOSITE & BELOW:
*Neo-Georgian council
housing (1923)*

LEFT: *small, red-brick neo-Georgian terraced houses with mansard roofs at Welwyn Garden City (1922)*

SMALL

The choice of the local version of red brick neo-Georgian rather than rough-cast vernacular was made by Welwyn Garden City's designer, Louis de Soissons. This version of neo-Georgian included features like mansard roofs and the occasional bay window to enliven the terraces. Other local authorities followed this example in building neo-Georgian terraced houses.

Local authorities such as the Derby Corporation responded to the Addison Act by passing motions to build houses by the thousand. In 1920 Derby was planning one thousand flat-fronted, rendered semis with sash windows, a hooded porch and a hipped roof. They continued to build even after central government withdrew its subsidies. Derby Corporation even tried out some steel prefabricated houses in 1925. They were semi-detached, built twelve to an acre, close to the Rolls-Royce works. Dudley tried some cast-iron houses but they were more expensive than brick.

ABOVE: *steel pre-fabricated house built for Derby Corporation (1925)*

LEFT: *terrace at Welwyn Garden City with pantile roofs (1922)*

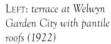

ABOVE: *a pair of experimental cast-iron houses built in Dudley (1925)*

ABOVE: *council houses in vernacular terraces with gambrel roofs, Wythenshawe (1931–34)*

ABOVE: *semi-detached house in Northenden, part of Manchester's 'municipal satellite' (c.1934)*

A MUNICIPALLY OWNED SATELLITE

At the end of the First World War it was estimated that Manchester needed 52,000 new houses. The only suitable land was in Cheshire. By 1926 the right kind of land had finally been purchased around Wythenshawe but the state subsidies had been withdrawn. It took a further five years before Manchester Corporation was able to wrest control from the local Rural District Council (Bucklow RDC).

Wythenshawe was remarkable for several reasons. First, it was a municipally owned satellite rather than a suburb. Second: 'the majority of working class housing was built by the corporation. Of 52,000 houses built between 1919 and 1939 approximately 30,000 were built by local authorities.'[4] Third: the council houses were built in a vernacular style, in short terraces with gambrel roofs. As a contrast, many of the nearby privately built semi-detached houses were neo-Georgian. Of course, they were also distinguished by their bay windows. Manchester's corporation allowed 'a proportion of private development at an average of twelve houses per acre'. This was justified by the principle that 'unused land was idle capital'.[5]

A fourth feature was that the main road, Princess Parkway, was designed to bypass the residential areas. The development was further enhanced by the preservation of existing trees and schools, set in ample playing fields.

Elsewhere private enterprise had taken over the task of housing the working classes. Between 1919 and 1939, 3,998,000 new homes were built, 1,112,000 by local authorities and 2,886,000 by private enterprise. In 1921 the programme of central government subsidised house building was terminated when only 214,000 of the proposed 500,000 homes had been built. In 1922 the Health Minister hoped 'that future state intervention will not be required and that the building industry will return to its pre-war economic basis'.

During the 1930s big building companies, such as Laing, Costain and New Ideal Homesteads, were able to build houses which even semi-skilled workers could afford to buy. For example, in 1937, a carpenter who earned £3 17s 6d per week plus some overtime was able to buy a house in Hurstfield Crescent, Hayes, Middlesex from T.F. Nash (Builders) Limited for £515. The carpenter's wife earned about £2 per week working in a biscuit factory. The builders recommended their application for a mortgage from the Leicester Building Society, Harrow branch. They received an offer from the building society of a mortgage of £465; this represented 90 per cent of the total cost of the house including all fees, to be repaid over twenty-five years at £2 16s 6d per month. The deposit was £50. The carpenter had savings of £25, and borrowed £25 from his best man which was repaid at 2s 6d per week. The house was a semi-detached with two bedrooms and a garage space. It was brick-built and cheaply rendered with stone chippings to the first-floor elevations over a ground-floor brick finish.

Some of the big building companies such as Wimpey, Taylor Woodrow, Costain and New Ideal Homesteads were so successful that, during the 1930s, they were floated on the stock exchange. Taylor Woodrow had started house building in 1930, using borrowed money. By 1935 they were brought to the Stock Market with annual profits of £75,000.

Some early attempts to provide small houses for the working classes were publicised as 'garden cities', such as the one in Edgware. (At least one earlier observer, Muthesius, had been under the impression that the LCC's 'cottage estate' in Tooting was part of the Garden City movement). The Edgware 'garden city' was a development of small houses built in pairs. The entrance to one was at the front with the other at the side. Like Letchworth the houses were vernacular in style with roughcast finish and casement windows.

ABOVE: *brochure for New Ideal Homesteads (1931)*

ABOVE: *advertisement for Davis estates (c.1934)*

LEFT: *Edgware 'garden city', a pair of small houses in vernacular style; the entrance to the house on the right is at the side*

RIGHT: *re-creation of a Moderne interior (c.1934) with 'sun-trap' window and radiator visible behind the dining table* (Geffrye Museum)

ABOVE: *a bentwood armchair designed by Alvar Aalto (1931–32)*

ABOVE: *tubular steel chair designed by Mies van der Rohe (1927)*

RIGHT: *traditional or 'cottage style' in a Drages catalogue (c.1934). The Savoy range of furnishings illustrated cost £33 10s*

10

Interwar Plan

he interiors of interwar houses differed from those of pre-war houses in that all newly built homes had a choice of gas and/or electricity. They were more hygienic with WCs inside and bathrooms upstairs. A pattern emerged: once land became available for building, a developer would buy it. Then he would lay the roads and services before selling off the plots for building. The electricity companies were very eager for sales and imposed few conditions before laying their mains. Gas companies sometimes required developers to specify that a number of rooms would be 'carcassed' for gas. If this cost was met by the builder, mains and water services might be provided at the utilities company's expense.

Depending on their owners' resources, new homes might be furnished from department stores like Drages in Birmingham or Baxendale's in Manchester. Pre-war, Edwardian style became traditional and even conservative when compared with the alternatives. These were Art Deco during the 1920s and Modernism during the 1930s. Innovations such as the new plastics and wireless sets found their way into even the most traditional homes. Telephones and door handles might be made of Bakelite or Erinoid, the trade name for casein-formaldehyde. The grille of a wireless set might display an Art Deco motif such as the sunrise or sunray. These might also be found in stained glass on the front door.

ABOVE: *1930s plastic door handle*

The new styles definitely affected décor, particularly wallpapers. During the second half of the 1920s, traditional floral patterns faced the challenge of geometric patterns and stepped borders. During the 1930s the Modern influence advocated plain walls. Coal-fired fireplaces remained the focal point of the room. This continued to emphasise the hearth rug which was available in a full range of styles. In fact the rug became even more prominent, as it could be the most strikingly patterned item in the room. Furniture also varied from avant garde bentwood or steel to traditional dark wood. Finnish bentwood designs, such as those of Alvar Aalto were reasonably priced. But Aalto's plywood furniture and Mies van der Rohe's tubular steel chairs were more likely to be found in city flats than suburban homes.

ABOVE: *Pye Model 'K' wireless set with 'sunray' grille (1932)*

Enthusiasts for the Modern movement were known as Modernists. They favoured picture windows like those of Goldfinger's houses in Hampstead. Porthole windows were an alternative but they could be regarded as a compromise because they resembled traditional features such as the bull's eye window. Compromises between Modernism and traditional were known as 'Moderne' or 'Modernistic'.

Three piece suites in living rooms were fully covered in furnishing fabrics. Much furniture was scaled down in size because rooms were smaller The new furniture was substantial, solid looking and square. Fewer pieces were required but small, low, occasional tables were useful additions. The overall emphasis was lower and more horizontal, with stepped corners to fireplaces and bookcases.

ABOVE: *re-creation of 'sunrise' motif in stained glass on a front door*

Lighting was another area where innovation could enter the home. Wall-mounted and pendant lights created shadows which broke up the integrity of the architectural space. This appalled the Modernists, who preferred uplighters. Functionalism was also a principle of modernism: Goldfinger chose some wall mountings which he had noticed at a local cinema.

RIGHT: *a Westminster drawing-room, decorated in neo-classical style (1920)*

ABOVE: *interwar upholstery from Liberty's 1936 spring catalogue*

ABOVE: *Baillie-Scott decorated the dining-room of The Tudors in neo-classical style (1921)*

ABOVE: *the vestibule of The Tudors, flagstones and oak framing (1921)*

RIGHT: *the drawing-room of The Tudors (1921)*

LARGE

During the early 1920s the drawing rooms of large houses were panelled in neo-classical style with architectural features such as columns or dentilled cornices; loose rugs on the floor, upholstered armchairs and china on display in glass-fronted cabinets, either fitted or free standing. Electric lighting might be pendants in the form of a chandelier, or electrolier, supplemented by china lamps which would be placed on pedestal occasional tables.

Its suburban location allowed THE TUDORS, Gerrards Cross (1921) to retain both a service wing and the orientation of private quarters towards the gardens which were at both the side and the back. True to the Arts & Crafts tradition, the architect M.H. Baillie-Scott designed many of the interior details including the fireplaces and staircases. His attention extended as far as the window sash levers. The oak framing is clearly displayed in the vestibule, which is paved with flagstones. Large fireplaces continued to be the focal point of the reception rooms. The dining room was decorated in a neo-classical style with plasterwork swags on the fireplace surround and plaster corner details on the ceiling.

Upstairs, the oak framing is also evident on the landing and the passage between the bedrooms, one of which has a loggia overlooking the garden. When Austin Reed lived in The Tudors he had a fitted wardrobe built to his particular requirements with customised drawers for items such as his starched collars and studs. The house had its own central heating boiler. Large houses always had electricity, if necessary, from their own generator.

The houses in Chelsea Square, built between 1928 and 1932, had three reception rooms, five to eight bed and dressing rooms, two or three bathrooms, service lifts and self-contained servants' quarters. Their orientation was towards the communal garden in the square. The houses on the east and west sides faced the square across a road but the houses on the south side actually connected with the gardens.

ABOVE: *the passage between the bedrooms, showing the oak framing*

ABOVE: *the loggia overlooking the garden – access is from one of the bedrooms*

LEFT: *the landing at The Tudors (1921)*

ABOVE: *Austin Reed's fitted wardrobe (c.1928)*

ABOVE: *the original heating boiler (1921)*

129

PART FOUR:
INTERWAR HOUSES

RIGHT: *Lyndhurst bedroom suite from a Drages catalogue*

Upper floor

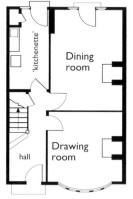

Ground floor

ABOVE: *ground and first floor plans of a three-bedroom semi detached house (c.1936)*

RIGHT: *Oxford suite from a Drages catalogue*

ABOVE: *a 1920s fitted cocktail cabinet*

130

Advances in technology and a comparative shortage of craft skills together with the increased scale of house building led to the standardisation and mass production of building components, for example, Hope's metal casement windows. Moderne 'sun-trap' windows were mass produced by Crittall Ltd. At the Ideal Home Exhibition of 1934 a brochure claimed: 'the wide bay window gives the sun no chance of escape'. They were fitted to the Moderne houses at Edgware.

Houses sold for less than £1,000 seldom had more than two or three 'power' points and the same number of five amp points for wireless sets or table lamps. Use of electricity was mostly limited to lights, irons and small fires such as might be used in bedrooms. Builders' brochures gave an estimate of four and a half pence per unit for electricity in 1935.

Rear extensions had almost disappeared. This reduced the size of both the kitchen and the bathroom. In some cases the kitchen was reduced to a 'kitchenette' which was little more than a passage through to the back door, fitted with a cooker, worktop and sink. It could be as small as nine by six feet. The builders tried to present it as 'labour-saving'. Chalet type houses had a small rear extension which accommodated the kitchen and a larder.

More expensive houses had features like fitted cocktail cabinets or double-height halls with 'cathedral windows'. These were stained glass windows which lit the stairs as they ran up to the first floor. Kitchen and scullery might be combined, leaving the former kitchen as a living room where informal meals might be taken and the wireless set located. There might still be a step down to the scullery where the cooking and washing up would be done.

Most semi-detached houses had three bedrooms. There were numerous variations to the plan including the 'gable wing' type which was more likely to have four bedrooms with additional features such as an entrance loggia. The most modern-looking items in traditional style homes might be ceramics produced by Shelley's or designed by either Susie Cooper or Clarice Cliff. The new smaller furniture came in suites which were box-like and entirely fabric-covered (*see Chapter 26, Patterns*). Art Deco items such as circular tables or 'hostess trolleys' also featured. Hot water in the upstairs bathroom would have been supplied by an improved gas-fired geyser apparatus such as an Ascot.

ABOVE: *a drawing room with the smaller box-like furniture (1925)*

ABOVE: *an Art Deco circular hostess trolley*

ground floor

first floor

LEFT: *ground and first floor plans of a four bedroom 'tooth and gap' semi-detached house (c.1915)*

ABOVE: *plan of the ground floor of a semi-detached chalet (1933)*

RIGHT: *ground plans of
two-bedroom (non-parlour)
and four-bedroom (with
parlour) council housing*

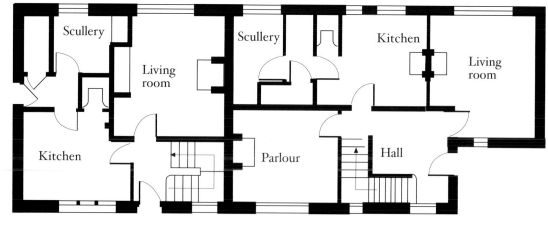

RIGHT: *first floor plans of
two-bedroom (non-parlour)
and four-bedroom (with
parlour) council housing*

ABOVE: *a drainer such as
might have been fitted in a
scullery*

RIGHT: *interior of a house in
Dagenham*

ABOVE: *re-creation of an
interwar kitchen–scullery*

SMALL

After the government's post-war housing programme ended, in July 1921, various other measures were taken centrally to help to house the lower paid. These included subsidies to builders and local authorities. Low interest rates and the low cost of building materials were the most significant factors which helped the provision of houses for the working classes. This lasted until the re-armament programme began to push costs up during the 1930s.

The debate about the merits of a single living room versus living room and parlour continued into the interwar period. Architects working for local authorities were inclined to follow Unwin's advice that a single living room was all that was necessary. His ideas about planning and housing density had become orthodox. By 1918 he was holding an influential position at the Ministry of Health. However, local authority housing was frequently made available in both parlour and non-parlour types; as two- or four-bedroom plans with a corresponding difference in rent. When the speculative builders began to build small houses for sale there was never a question: by 1925 they were able to offer potential buyers a parlour (or 'lounge'), with dining room, kitchen, three bedrooms, WC and upstairs bathroom for £695.

Speculative builders engaged in erecting the low-priced homes were able to reduce the costs by the use of unskilled labour, extended lines of credit from suppliers and widespread piece work. This brought the purchase price of a house down to less than £500. These houses incorporated many items which the working classes wanted but which were often missing in municipal dwellings, such as a parlour or 'lounge' as well as a dining-room and bay windows.

The evidence of *Mass Observation* (1943) and the *Dudley Report* (1944)[1] showed that the debate had finally been settled. According to the *City of Manchester Plan* (1945) familes tended to use the scullery as a kitchen and reserve the living room for special occasions, as if it was a parlour, with the result that:

> inadequate living space gave rise to a greater number of complaints; the strongest was that scullery or kitchen was too small because there was nowhere for many ordinary family activities. Unanimous that scullery in this type of house is far too small

The kitchen-sculleries which the *City of Manchester Plan* criticised were about eighty square feet in size. The design was based on the earlier practice of cooking on the coal-fired range in the living-room. When the gas cooker replaced the range as the means of cooking, it was placed in the scullery and all the other kitchen equipment followed it; consequently most meals were eaten there 'to meet these needs we consider that municipal house of future should provide two good rooms on ground floor so that meals should not interfere with other activities such as the children's homework.[2]

The rent for non-parlour types at Wythenshawe varied from 5s 3d to 7s 3d per week. Parlour types were 8s 6d to 8s 9d per week. All the houses had basic electricity for 9d per week.

ABOVE & BELOW: *details of a modest interwar kitchen (c.1932)*

BELOW LEFT: *ground & first floor plans of a speculatively built small house priced at £595 (1925)*

ABOVE: *re-creation of an interwar 'kitchenette'*

FAR LEFT: *a gas cooker such as might have been fitted in a 'kitchenette' (1929)*

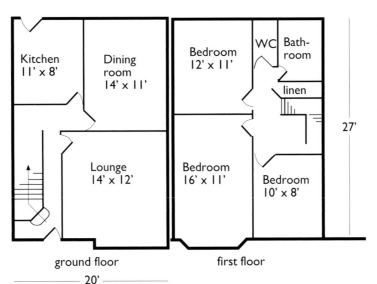

Kitchen 11' x 8'

Dining room 14' x 11'

Lounge 14' x 12'

Bedroom 12' x 11'

WC

Bathroom

linen

Bedroom 16' x 11'

Bedroom 10' x 8'

27'

ground floor

first floor

20'

ABOVE: *Chelsea Square
– looking towards the houses
on the south side which have
direct access to the gardens
(1928–32)*

RIGHT: *Chelsea Square
– the houses on the east side
which face the square and
have garages behind. Access
is through several arched
passages (1928–32)*

Interwar Back

The treatment of the backs of large houses during the 1920s, not only picked up directly from pre-war practice but also drew on some far older, Georgian, traditions.

The houses on the east side of Chelsea Square faced towards the communal gardens in the Square. This was a direct revival of the eighteenth-century urban layout in which a square should have gardens and a pleasing view or 'prospect'. The backs of the houses on the south side of Chelsea Square had direct access to the gardens in the Square.

By the time Chelsea Square was designed it was clear that facilities for motor cars should be incorporated into a large house. The architects updated another old tradition – the mews. Mews were an arrangement in which stabling for horses and carriages was located near the rear of the house. On the east side of Chelsea Square, the garages were placed behind the houses with access via passages through the terrace itself. The distinctive doors of the interwar garages may be glimpsed through the passages which are decorated with semi circular arches in red brick.

The nearby development at Chelsea Park Gardens is divided by the main road, Beaufort Street. The development began before the First World War on one side of Beaufort Street. The opposite side of the street was built after the war. There, the occupants had direct access to the communal garden which they could also enjoy from their rear-facing terraces, balconies and windows.

ABOVE: *Chelsea Square – looking across towards the houses on the east side which overlook the gardens (1928–32)*

LEFT: *Chelsea Park Gardens – rear-facing terraces overlooking the communal garden (1922–36)*

RIGHT: *garden front of The
Tudors, Gerrards Cross
(1921). Note the loggia and
detailed brickwork*

RIGHT: *steps down to another
level of the gardens at The
Tudors, Gerrards Cross
(1921)*

In suburban locations such as Gerrards Cross, large houses such as The Tudors had considerable space for gardens. The Tudors' gardens are unusually extensive but they are consistent with the pre-war tradition of having an imposing garden front. Located on the opposite side to the entrance front, the garden front also has a loggia overlooking the gardens which may be entered from the house through a discreet door on the side of the bay window. The infill of the timber-framed walls is enlivened with some detailed, herringbone brickwork.

The French doors of the dining room open through another side of the house onto an extensive terrace. There is hard and soft landscaping with steps leading down to lawns and flower beds. The gardens are divided into rooms by changes of level, hedges and borders.

In 1920 the garden front of a house in Roehampton was 'improved' by the addition of a large loggia which extended the full width of the front. French casements opened into it from the principal reception rooms. This provided views of the gardens and the heath beyond. A house at Shepherd's Green, Chislehurst was more typical with a garden front from which the terrace opened onto a lawn tennis court.

FAR LEFT: *French doors from the dining room opening onto the terrace of The Tudors, Gerrards Cross (1921)*

LEFT: *loggia of a house at Roehampton (1920)*

ABOVE: *the door at the side of the bay window at The Tudors (1921)*

LEFT: *rear-facing terrace of a house at Shepherd's Green, Chislehurst (1920)*

MEDIUM

The plots in which suburban houses were laid out allowed for a small garden at the front and a larger one at the back. It was the first time that most of the occupants of suburbia had ever owned any property. Traditionally property had meant land. Their garden was the embodiment of land. Gardens also linked the suburbs with the country.

There was still a practical side to the back. Semi-detached houses allowed access to the back via a narrow passage on the open side. This was necessary for services such as coal deliveries and the collection of dustbins.

The builders and estate developers knew that the promise of front and back gardens was even more attractive to potential buyers than the previous history of the land on which the new development was being built. Laing's 1937 publicity brochure for their estate near Enfield West stressed the park, gardens and the three minute walk to the station. These elements acted as complementary attractions: private suburban gardens set in what had formerly been a historic estate could indeed be represented as idyllic and they frequently were – for example, a 1932 promotion for Petts Wood, near Orpington, Kent, which described:

> ... a fairyland of birch and gorse, all assuring one that Petts Wood is, and must remain, a country home ... Houses of distinctive design, pleasant half-timbering, overhanging bays, sweeping gables, timbered porches, all set well away from the road, bright and sunny in their white dress. No fences but little crazy stone walls, where iris and rock plants grow, crazy paths, flower laden beds, and bright, green lawns, while at the back nod the health-laden pines.

The reception rooms of suburban houses opened onto the garden, possibly down a flight of steps. The simplified plan made this easier than it had been with coupled rear extensions. The area nearest the house might be paved as a terrace or patio. Then came a lawn with flower beds on either side. A.W. Curton's 1935 houses had gardens which were 'Good size, enclosed with close-boarded wooden fences with oak posts. Front gardens turved; crazy patterned concrete path to house.'

OPPOSITE: *the back of a detached house in Golders Green with steps down to a terrace immediately outside (1922)*

ABOVE: *the front gardens of interwar suburban houses in Hendon*

ABOVE: *semi-detached house showing access to the back at the side and the coalbunker (c.1932)*

ABOVE: *catalogue featuring types of houses available on Laing's Enfield West estate (1937)*

LEFT: *the back of an interwar suburban house in Hendon*

ABOVE: *re-creation of Walter Straw's 'glasshouse' in Blyth Grove, Worksop (c.1930)*

ABOVE: *re-creation of the interior of Walter Straw's 'glasshouse' where he grew cacti*

RIGHT: *the backs of semi-detached houses in Cambridge (1920)*

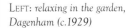

LEFT: *relaxing in the garden, Dagenham (c.1929)*

ABOVE: *front cover of* Good Gardening *magazine (1937)*

A plot for growing vegetables might be situated at the far end where there could also be a garden shed or even a 'glasshouse'. Here one could indulge in a hobby such as growing cacti. Walter Straw's interwar 'glasshouse' has been recreated in the back garden of the Straws' house in Blyth Grove, Worksop (see *'places to visit', page 259*).

Gardens were a place of escape and relaxation. They also became the subject of an entire leisure industry with publications such as *Good Gardening* magazine and *Foulsham's New Gardening Book* which offered 'expert instructions & suggestions for Quick Results for both flowers and vegetables'. Products such as seeds were available through catalogues and the post.

ABOVE: Ideal Home Book of Garden Plans (1930s)

ABOVE: *Foulsham's New Gardening Book (c.1929)*

LEFT: *illustration of a back garden from an advertisement for Atco's lightweight lawn mower (1930)*

FAR LEFT: *London garden by R. Kirkland Jamieson (1937)*

PART FIVE: DETAILS

RIGHT: *montage of exterior details – see chapters on roofs, brick and stone, windows, doors and chimneys*

Key to Exterior Details
1 *1923 terraced*
2 *1911–12 terraced*
3 *semi-detached (c.1934)*
4 *semi-detached pair (c.1934)*
5 *semi-detached (c.1934)*
6 *neo-Georgian semi-detached (1924)*
7 *neo-Georgian terraced (1921)*
8 *semi-detached (c.1934)*
9 *neo-Georgian doorcase (c.1930)*

*Key to Interior Details – see
chapters on Doors, Fireplaces,
Kitchens & Cooking,
Bathrooms, WCs, Lighting
& Electrical Appliances,
Patterns, Tiles, and Stained
& Coloured Glass*
1 Silver Studio textile design
(1933)
2 wall-mounted light (c.1900)
3 Minton tiles
4 Hawkweed wallpaper
(1902)
5 electrolier (c.1910)
6 drainer
7 'new art' tile (c.1905)
8 oak table (1910)
9 Silver Studio textile (1935)
10 anglepoise light (1932)
11 sunrise stained glass design
(c.1932)
12 Voysey carpet design
(c.1898)
13 art nouveau glazed
internal door (c.1904)
14 1920s glazed brick
fireplace surround
15 furnishing fabric designed
by L. Butterfield (1903)
16 art deco clock (c.1930))
17 No 2 'Standard' gas cooker
(1927)
18 C.R. Mackintosh fabric
design (1918)
19 1930s internal door
20 tulip tree furnishing fabric
(1903)
21 lavatory (1921)
22 Unitas ceramic WC by
Twyfords (1883)
23 graining: root of oak

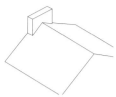

ABOVE: *basic pitched*

TOP RIGHT: *pitched, tiled (c.1903–10)*

TOP FAR RIGHT: *pitched (1922)*

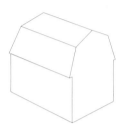

ABOVE: *mansard*

RIGHT: *mansard (1928–32)*

ABOVE FAR RIGHT: *dentils (c.1925)*

BELOW FAR RIGHT: *gambrel, tiled (c.1934)*

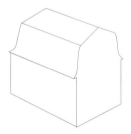

ABOVE: *gambrel roof*

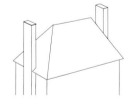

ABOVE: *hipped roof*

RIGHT: *hipped roof with transverse gables over bays (c.1934)*

FAR RIGHT: *hipped roof of a moderne semi-detached pair (1933)*

Roofs

oofs themselves were an important element in Edwardian domestic architecture. Architects designed houses whose roofs were made into features with emphatic roof slopes or gables. Speculative builders copied deep gables and catslide roofs. On a gable the roof required a transverse pitch. Low eaves were an integral part of cottage style. Roof designs included the basic pitched and many variations.

The basic pitched roof was simple to construct, and had a functional slope to keep out the weather. Vernacular style houses continued the slope of the roof down to the eaves to achieve the cottage look. The junctions between different slopes were originally fitted with specially shaped tiles.

Neo-Georgian houses also had pitched roofs. The structural timbers were strong enough to take the weight of the covering and its supporting rafters but had very little extra weight-bearing capacity. A significant neo-Georgian variation of the pitched roof had exposed supporting pieces (known as dentils) beneath the eaves.

Some of the variations in roof design had been developed to counter problems such as spanning deep plots.

ABOVE: *cottage style – slate continued down slope to eaves at first-floor level (c.1909)*

VARIATIONS

The mansard was a roof with a steep slope below a shallower slope. It could accommodate rooms and be lit by dormer windows. Projecting eaves allowed water to run off but also allowed a shallower pitch.

The gambrel was a vernacular variation of the mansard in which the steep slope flared outwards near the eaves. The catslide was a continuous pitch from the ridge down to the eaves at ground floor level.

Hips, or hipped roofs, were a traditional form which had additional slopes rising to the roof ridge from the end walls. Some end-of-terrace houses with pitched roofs were hipped. Hips became most apparent in the suburbs, where pairs of semi-detached houses were frequently built with hips on their main roofs. Before 1900 the roofs of bay windows were hipped.

The Edwardian period and interwar periods utilised gables particularly over bay windows. This required a transverse pitch. The neo-Georgian revival rehabilitated tiles and pantiles as popular alternatives to slate which had been an almost universal choice of roofing material.

ABOVE: *pitched, tiled (c.1907)*

ROOF COVERINGS

Slate, mostly from Wales, became the most common roofing material in the late eighteenth century. Slate is thinly sliced, impermeable stone and is lighter than brick-based tiles. It had the advantage of allowing the pitch of the roof to be slightly shallower. The alternatives were clay-based tiles or curved pantiles. The vernacular and neo-Georgian revivals both favoured tiles.

PART FIVE: DETAILS

ABOVE: *transverse pitch over bay window*

ABOVE RIGHT: *deep gable – tiled with low eaves and transverse pitch, in front of a hipped roof (c.1909)*

ABOVE FAR RIGHT: *gable – slate with transverse pitch (1913)*

RIGHT: *slate roof with tiles over bays (c.1924)*

FAR RIGHT: *overhanging eaves above bay (1934)*

RIGHT: *flat roof over a composite bay – segmental at first-floor level, lean-to over ground floor and porch (1923)*

FAR RIGHT ABOVE: *hipped dormers in Golders Green (1914–15)*

FAR RIGHT BELOW: *flat roof over dormers, on Sir Alfred Munnings house, in Chelsea Park Gardens (1920)*

146

By 1900 plain clay tiles were becoming more popular than Welsh slate as the covering for pitched roofs. Just as with bricks, the architect W.H. Bidlake was still yearning for handmade tiles:

> Our modern roof tiles are open to the same objection as the bricks, with this difference, that if the bricks are made too thick, the tiles are made too thin, but in both alike there is the same want of surface texture, the same want of individuality between one tile and another, the same hardness of colour and shape. It is very remarkable that while in so many other matters which concern the house of to-day the movement for the revival of the crafts has exercised a beneficent influence, the brick and tile manufacturers are still behind in the dark mid-Victorian days. It may be advanced that bricks and tiles made by the old methods would cost more ...[1]

ABOVE: *overhanging eaves and hipped gable (c.1914)*

On the transverse pitch of a roof with deep gables, the roof ran down the gable from the ridge to the eaves at first-floor level.

But it was the less spectacular hipped roof which became the most common form of the interwar period. It became the norm for pairs of semi-detached houses.

A feature which developed in the years just before the First World War was the overhanging eave. This became a characteristic feature of semi-detached houses during the interwar period. Between 1908 and 1910 the architects, Edwin and James Palser, used it in Hampstead Garden Suburb. By 1914–15 speculative builders were using it in nearby roads for four-bedroom, semi-detached houses. These houses had the projecting gable wing which became the archetypal, interwar, 'tooth and gap' design.

Different parts of roofs could have different coverings; the bay of an interwar terraced house might be roofed with plain, clay tiles while the main roof was of Welsh slate. Segmental, or curved, bays were a characteristic of interwar houses. Often the segmental bay of an interwar house was covered by the overhanging eaves. Alternatively the bays of Edwardian and interwar houses might have hipped or even flat roofs. The latter were finished in asphalt or sheet metal where protected by a parapet, or clad in metal where there was a projecting eave.

DORMER WINDOWS

Dormer windows were a means of lighting rooms within the pitch of the roof itself. During the Edwardian and interwar periods dormers might have either pitched, hipped or even flat roofs: the dormer windows of 7 St James's Square have pitched roofs (1911); semi-detached houses in Golders Green have dormers with hipped roofs (1914–15); the dormers of Sir Alfred Munnings house in Chelsea Park Gardens have flat roofs (1920). At Wythenshaw, dormer windows fit neatly into the gambrel roofs of the terraced houses (c.1934).

FLAT ROOFS

Flat roofs covering the entire building were built during a brief period in the 1930s. One builder tried some flat-roofed semi-detached houses at the Upper Farm estate, West Molesey, Surrey. Large span roofs were usually constructed from reinforced concrete. But the public preferred their homes to have conventional hipped roofs. This had already been demonstrated in the successful Moderne compromise at Old Rectory Gardens, Edgware in 1933.

ABOVE: *flat roof (1939)*

In 1934 the Modern movement staged an entire 'Village of Tomorrow' at the Ideal Home Exhibition. But it failed to catch the interest of the general public.

PART FIVE: DETAILS

RIGHT: *map of England and Wales, showing brick and stone areas*

ABOVE: *older bricks which Edwardian architects preferred (from top) – seventeenth-century Sussex; late eighteenth-century London stock; late eighteenth-century Sussex*

ABOVE: *stock bricks (from top) – London, which gets its yellow colour from chalk which is added to the clay; Wealden (from Kent and Sussex), which gets its colour from sand which is added to the mould; clamp fired, in which additional fuel is added to burn the bricks during firing.*

ABOVE RIGHT: *English bond – alternating courses of headers and stretchers*

RIGHT: *Flemish bond – alternating headers and stretchers on each course*

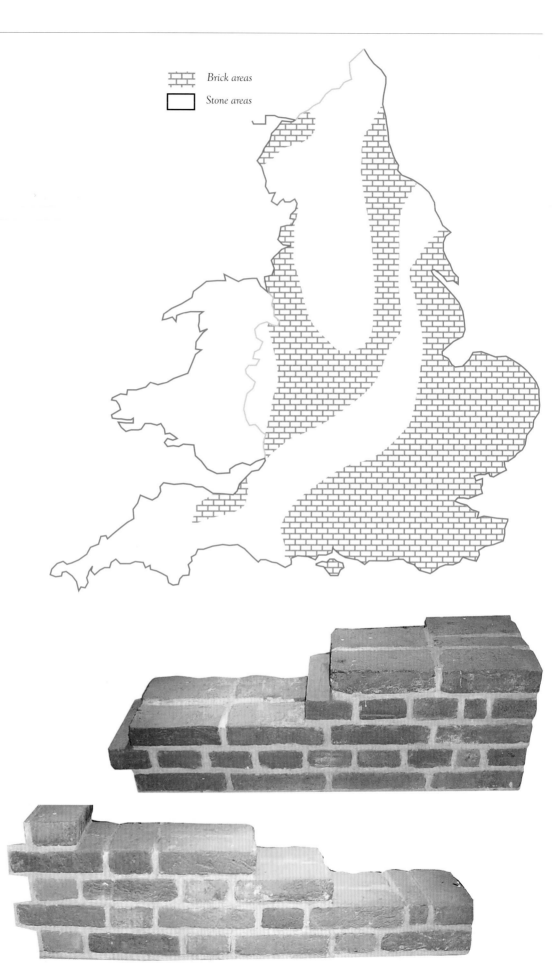

▦ Brick areas

☐ Stone areas

13

Brick & Stone

S ince the late seventeenth century brick had been the principal building material. The alternative was stone, but only in areas where it was available locally. By the Edwardian period brick was available everywhere. Brick had been widely adopted for its fire-resistant qualities. Its use in polite architecture during the Georgian period also helped to popularise it. Originally, bricks were made locally, sometimes even on site. The colour varied according to the local 'earths'. There was a definite pecking order: 'best', 'good' and 'common'.

'Stock' brick usually implied good quality and stocks were used as 'face' bricks on the exposed outer surfaces. Inferior 'place' bricks were used on the inside and party walls. The best bricklayers did the face work; apprentices took care of the place work. Expensive coloured brick was often used only on the façade, particularily for medium-sized houses.

ABOVE: *early Georgian brickwork (1700–24) with more expensive bricks used for window arches*

The structure of a brick wall demands that the various layers be locked, or 'bonded', together for strength. Various patterns were developed for this purpose. English bond was one of the earliest. It consisted of alternating courses of 'headers' and 'stretchers'. The headers, laid across the course, were meant to ensure face and place bricks were locked to each other. Another pattern, Flemish bond was, for a long time, almost universal. This bond comprised alternating headers and stretchers in each course, which in turn overlapped those of the course below.

Mortar was used to fill any gaps which might have allowed the weather to penetrate. Friction and adhesion between mortar and brick prevented dislocation of the components and enhanced the load-bearing properties of the wall. The mortars used during the nineteenth century were lime based but during the Edwardian and interwar periods cement-based mortars steadily took over. These were made from limestone and clay, mixed in the proportion 2:1. The mixture was ground together, burnt at high temperature. The clinker was then ground to a fine powder which is the finished cement. When mixed with water, it crystallises into a stone-like structure.

Builders often adopted a penny-pinching attitude to their work. The results were bad building which was referred to as 'jerry-building'. Frequently this meant bad brickwork – such as the most notorious form of 'jerry-building' which was 'snapped' headers. Broken half-bricks were used in the outer course of a wall: consequently there was no bond – all for the sake of saving a few half-bricks. This had been so rife in the Georgian building industry that even the experts condoned it. It was still frequent in the second half of the nineteenth century.

Bricks were taxed with varying degrees of severity until 1850. The tax was levied per thousand. Larger bricks went further and cost the manufacturer less in tax. Customs and Excise officials had to inspect the moulds. As a result, bricks became standardised to three-and-three-quarters to four-and-a-half inches in width and from eight to nine inches in length. The depth varied from two to three-and-a-quarter inches.

Edwardian architects such as W.H. Bidlake were critical of the mass-produced bricks which were used by cost-conscious builders. They regarded them as being of 'soulless uniformity':

> The aim of every brick manufacturer nowadays is to produce bricks as exact in shape, as sharp in arris, as smooth in surface, as uniform in colour, and as bright a red as it is possible to make them, and every bricklayer is taught that the best face-work is the most accurately laid and the most perfectly uniform in colour; and to attain this ideal the bricks will often be carefully picked over and those rejected which vary in only a slight degree from the standard red. Consider also the detestable method of tuck-pointing in white, or even in black mortar, which consists in outlining the brick

ABOVE: *herringbone brickwork on a house designed by Baillie-Scott (1921)*

RIGHT: *herringbone brickwork on the bay of a speculatively built medium sized house (c.1914)*

ABOVE: *terracotta moulded ornament around a front door (c.1900)*

joints by applying thin strips of mortar over the surface first made uniformly red by rubbing over it a soft brick. This is a still more reprehensible means of securing that soulless uniformity which is the delight of the modern bricklayer. And to the further detriment of modern brickwork, the bricks themselves are of very clumsy proportion, having (as a result of the brick tax) a thickness of three inches, exceeding that of the old bricks by half. Surely the atmosphere of the smokiest town is not enough excuse for brickwork such as this, and it is absolutely certain that a cottage or a country house is ruined by it.[1]

Some architects re-used old bricks but, true to the Arts & Crafts tradition, Bidlake wanted hand-made bricks and tiles:

Undoubtedly they would cost more than the common wire-cut, machine-made bricks, but they would not be as costly as the special facing-bricks; and, were they even more so, who would not be willing to allow the extra expense if the alternative were the spoiling of an otherwise beautiful home by the artistic inferiority of its materials for the roofs and walls.[2]

Much of the half-timbered work of the Edwardian and interwar periods was false because local by-laws usually stipulated that half-timbered work should be backed by brick. Bidlake:

In many districts the bye-laws prohibit half-timber work, unless it is backed by a brick wall. This does not deter the half-timber enthusiast, for he nails his half-timber inch deal boarding to the wall, puts plaster in between, and lo! a timber house of the old style.[3]

During the later part of the interwar period cavity walls became an increasingly popular form of construction. To keep down costs stretcher bond was used; header bricks were only used where necessary at corners, window or door apertures.

PATTERN & COLOUR

Decorative effects were made by using different coloured bricks. Bricks could also be cut or mouded in imitation of classical details and string courses. Patterns such as herringbone were used by architects such as Baillie-Scott. They were not beyond the reach of speculative builders either. Window arches were an important structural and decorative feature and a guide to the quality of the building. Tapering bricks for arches were created by 'rubbing' – skilled and, therefore, expensive work. Terracotta moulded ornament became widely available during the second half of the nineteenth century.

Colour was subject to fashion. During the second half of the nineteenth century the choice had become ever wider as catalogues advertised local varieties of brick nationally. These were distributed by rail and finally delivered by carrier. Previously only locally available colours – reds, blues, yellows and browns, were used as detail and surface decoration. Polychromy became a real possibility, even for small houses, after the middle of the nineteenth century.

STONE

Stone was more expensive and usually more prestigious. If it wasn't available locally it was too expensive except for limited use in details such as lintels or doorsteps. In stone areas houses of all sizes were still being built of stone during the interwar period. The best stone work was 'ashlar', smoothly finished blocks which fitted tightly and neatly together. A cheaper alternative was to use ashlar for facing but to fill in behind with roughly dressed stone, rubble or brick.

Stone also varied in colour from locality to locality. Portland was grey but Bath was sandy. Hopton Wood, a limestone from Derbyshire, was used by Edwardian architects. Classically influenced architecture inclined towards stone if affordable. Stucco had been an alternative if the appearance of stone was wanted.

The vernacular revival encouraged the use of external rendering in the form of rough-cast plaster. This was convenient for cost-cutting builders because it could conceal poor brickwork. Smooth rendered walls also presented a more modern appearance during the interwar period.

ABOVE: *a traditional brick mould used for hand-made bricks*

ABOVE: *window arches were made from tapering bricks* (Weald & Downland Museum)

ABOVE: *Bolton Wood buff, a sandstone*

ABOVE: *Crosland Hill, a York sandstone*

ABOVE: *Hopton Wood, a limestone from Derbyshire*

ABOVE: *dormer window; note the low eaves (1905)*

ABOVE RIGHT: *casement windows (c.1909)*

ABOVE FAR RIGHT: *casement windows with leaded panes (c.1905)*

RIGHT: *leaded first-floor casement windows (c.1905)*

FAR RIGHT: *casement windows with top-hung top lights and leaded panes on a ground-floor bay (c.1911)*

RIGHT: *original Queen Anne sash window with segmental arch (c.1704)*

FAR RIGHT: *sash windows with relieving arches (1911)*

ABOVE: *leaded oval window (c.1905)*

14

Windows

From the late eighteenth century until the 1840s sash windows became standard for town houses. Eight or twelve panes were common with substantial glazing bars. Local building regulations remained stringent against the risk of fire. Consequently windows, because they were made of wood, had to be fully recessed behind a reveal which was eight inches or two courses of brickwork deep. These regulations were finally relaxed in 1895. Windows no longer had to be so deeply recessed and surrounds were allowed to project.

In large and medium houses the sashes were 'hung' from cords. In small houses, where they were often unhung, they had to be chocked open or closed.

Plate glass had arrived in 1832. With plate glass came French doors allowing easy access to balconies and verandahs. For the next fifty years windows were subdivided into only two or, at most, four panes. Glazing bars became thinner. Bay windows became popular after the taxes on windows and glass were abolished in 1851. It became possible to align windows above the bay, as pairs or windows with margin lights fitted neatly above.

The vernacular revival from 1875 onwards had a profound effect on window design by re-introducing the casement. Glazing bars and small panes, known as quarries, came back into fashion. Cames, the traditional form of lead glazing bars, were also re-introduced.

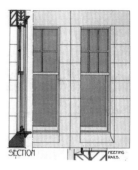

ABOVE: *an economical compromise design – detailed upper light with single pane in lower light (c.1909)*

EDWARDIAN WINDOWS

By 1904 it was observed that 'The old fixed light leaded window has become the favourite in English houses'.[1] The emphasis on individuality resulted in as much variation as possible. As an economy, the top light might be subdivided into several panes by glazing bars and the lower light left as a single pane.

Vernacular forms such as the oriel were revived, and every other existing form was employed, including dormers and various shapes of 'bull's eye'. Above all, the casement, hinged at the side or top hung, was also re-introduced.

ABOVE: *oriel window (c.1904)*

During the Edwardian period items such as casement windows could be bought in bulk from the growing number of builders' merchants. Due to reduced import duties foreign timber was flowing in from Russia, Sweden and Canada. Around 1900 the *Timber Trades Journal* was full of new and improved designs for planes, lathes and turning machines.

To achieve the horizontal cottage look windows were set lower in walls, and eaves were extended downwards so upper storey rooms could project into the roof space, where they were lit by dormer windows. Ground-floor windows were tucked in under the eaves. Margin lights and fanlights around the front door were given particular attention. Muthesius commented: 'coloured lights are put into halls and other prominent spots such as front-doors, ends of passages etc.'[2]

Naturally, sash windows formed part of the neo-Georgian revival. After 1910 sashes were modelled on early Georgian or Queen Anne examples. This emulation of early classicism was further enhanced by a return to thicker glazing bars, small panes and projecting surrounds. The shallow segmental arch belonged to both vernacular and classic traditions; it was a cheap and easy way to build a window arch, especially over sash windows.

ABOVE: *margin lights and fanlight (c.1901)*

INTERWAR WINDOWS

During the interwar period there were considerable advances in technology. These coincided with a comparative shortage of craft skills and the increased scale of house building. The results were standardisation and the mass production of building components. Hope's Metal Casements and Crittall Ltd of Braintree, Essex, were among the first to standardise and mass produce windows. They manufactured windows from mild steel of angle-iron section. Crittall became well known for their curved metal 'sun-trap' windows. They also made windows with lattice-work leading. When combined with half-timbering, their lattice-work windows created the 'mock Tudor' look. There was a brief fashion for a 'continental' look during the mid-1920s. This was responsible for external shutters being fitted to suburban homes.

Bay windows were an essential feature of speculatively built medium-sized, interwar houses. These usually emulated vernacular style, making leaded casement windows popular. This was a further contrast with the neo-Georgian council houses, which, naturally, were fitted with sashes.

Metal-framed windows gave a Modernistic look which could be incorporated into semi-detached houses under a conventional hipped roof. The double doors of garages, or 'motor-homes' were usually each fitted with six square windows.

OPPOSITE: *mock Tudor with Crittall lattice windows (1936)*

ABOVE: *Bull's eye window (1920)*

LEFT: *advertisement for Hope's casements (1920)*

FAR LEFT: *Crittall's 'sun-trap' windows (1933)*

ABOVE: *external shutters (1925)*

BELOW LEFT: *interwar neo-Georgian sash windows (1921)*

ABOVE: *garage doors (1925)*

Part Five: Details

Top Right: *Victorian front door (c.1898)*
Top Middle Right: *Edwardian front door (1901)*
Top Far Right: *ledged front door (c.1904)*

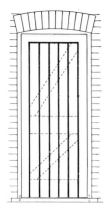

Above: *outside of a ledged door*

Right: *neo-Georgian doorcase (1911)*
Middle Right: *design for detailed glazing (c.1909)*
Far Right: *front door (c.1911)*

Above: *period illustration of the construction of a door*
Right: *four-panel door*
Next Right: *six-panel door*
Middle Right: *mahogany six-panel door*
Far Right: *glazed Art Nouveau internal door*

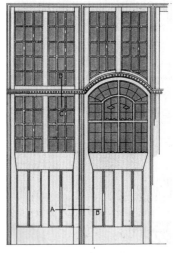

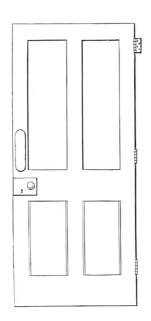
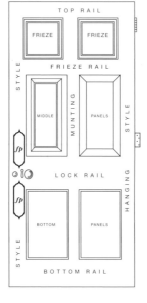

15

Doors

Victorian front doors had been four-panelled since 1840. After the basement began to disappear during the 1860s, the front door was inset within the body of the house. This formed a porch. Around 1900 the porch began to be tiled up to waist height. At the same time the panelling of the doors themselves began to change to a solid panel, subdivided vertically, surmounted by six small panes of glass. The mid-rail was was raised to reinforce it because the insertion of the lock case had weakened it. After 1910 the neo-Georgian revival brought a return to six panels. The front door was brought forward in line with the walls but was sheltered by a projecting porch, hood or canopy. Doorcases or hoods also made a comeback. Throughout the Edwardian era margin lights and fanlights were decorated with stained glass.

Ledged doors were an alternative to the panelled door. Some examples of ledged front doors may be found at Letchworth. More often they were used for external entrances to the kitchen or scullery. Paired front doors appeared in working men's flats or small council houses.

Glazed panels were almost as common as solid wooden infills. Clear glazing or translucent glazing in 'obscure glass' was fitted into fanlights above front doors. Upper panels around the door were also fitted with detailed glazing.

In large and medium houses external doors were made of hardwood. Internal doors were of softwood and therefore painted. Small houses were less likely to possess hardwood front doors unless they faced the street, although as small dwellings improved they too benefited from stronger, smarter hardwood doors.

ABOVE: *Around 1900 porches began to be tiled up to waist height*

INTERNAL DOORS

Internal doors followed the same development as external. Six panels were typical until the 1840s, thereafter four. Towards the end of the nineteenth century light woods such as yew or ash were used and left unpainted in step with the trend towards a lighter look. After 1900 there was a great deal more variation in the number and proportion of the panels. The junction of the frame and panels was decorated with a moulding. There was a huge range of mouldings available from the many local joinery works of the time. Glazed panels were almost as common as solid wooden infills. Internal doors might have fanlights to borrow daylight from better illuminated main rooms. During the Edwardian period there were occasional examples of Art Nouveau extravagance. The door frame was always concealed behind a moulded wooden architrave which matched that of the skirting at floor level.

ABOVE: *door fittings – brass handle and finger plate with sliding bolt (c.1903)*

Small houses often only had ledged doors internally and perhaps for the rear entrance, WC or privy. They would have been made from softwoods, usually pine and painted.

DOOR FITTINGS

As usual the grandest rooms had the best fittings, which consisted of handles, escutcheons and finger plates. These were usually made of brass although porcelain and china were also popular. Edwardian door furniture included elaborate lever type handles and finger plates.

The variety of designs available increased with the advent of mass production during the nineteenth century. Once again choice was assisted both by the increasing circulation of catalogues and the development of builders' merchants and retailers.

ABOVE: *door fittings – brass lever handle and lock (c.1903)*

RIGHT: *front door of detached house (1933–36)*

FAR RIGHT: *front door of a small house (c.1925)*

RIGHT: *front door of semi-detached house (c.1932)*

FAR RIGHT: *interwar neo-Georgian doorcase (c.1930)*

INTERWAR DOORS

During the 1920s front doors continued to be either vernacular or neo-Georgian in style. Heavy mouldings continued to be applied to the panels of prestigious doors, particularly the front door. The upper panel of front doors was usually glazed. The lower panels continued to be sub-divided vertically. Semi-detached houses were more likely to have their front door recessed.

The frame was formed of solid stiles and rails joined together by mortice and tenon. The thickness of the infilling panels could be as little as five sixteenths of an inch. During the interwar years solid panels began to be replaced by plywood. There were occasional examples of extravagance such as the oak-panelled doors of The Tudors, designed by Baillie-Scott, but Modernists preferred their doors to have plain flush surfaces over a conventional frame as, for example, in Goldfinger's houses in Hampstead. This approach was not widely adopted until after the Second World War.

BELOW LEFT: *oak panelled door, designed by M.H. Baillie-Scott (1921)*

ABOVE: *1930s panelled door*

ABOVE: *Modernist plain surface door (1939)*

16

Chimneys

himneys had been a strong feature of domestic architecture especially during the Queen Anne and early Georgian periods. Even speculative builders gave the chimney special treatment. In 1901 coal burned in fireplaces and ranges was still the main fuel for both heating and cooking. Coal-burning fireplaces remained popular throughout the interwar years.

Fireplaces and chimneys were essential in all homes. Each fireplace had its own flue to carry the smoke up through the house to the roof where it escaped through the open chimneypot. Terraced and semi-detached houses gathered flues from their neighbours. Fireplaces serving the same storey were often placed back to back so that their separate flues could be carried up together. A well-designed flue was not only curved to avoid fireplaces on other levels but also to prevent rain and draughts of cold air reaching the fire. No daylight should be visible at the top.

By the Edwardian period the layout of the flues had become standardised throughout all the building styles. The flues were gathered together to leave the roof at the same place. This simplified both roof construction and weather-proofing. Gathering flues together made them more efficient, because the updraught in one flue induced a similar effect in adjoining ones. This phenomenon could be used for ventilation by fitting a ventilator high up in the room to be ventilated. A vent duct rose alongside the chimney flue. When a fire was lit the combustion gases in the flue heated the surrounding brickwork and as the air in the ventilation duct rose it drew the stale air out of the room.

ABOVE: *chimney stacks of timber-framed houses in East Grinstead (c.1599)*

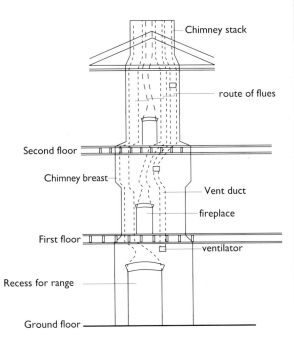

Chimney stack

route of flues

Second floor

Chimney breast

Vent duct

fireplace

First floor

ventilator

Recess for range

Ground floor

ABOVE: *early Georgian terraced houses (c. 1725)*

FAR LEFT: *the gathering of chimney flues with a ventilation duct*

LEFT: *even speculative builders gave chimneys special treatment: this stack rose from an inglenook in the front reception room (c.1915)*

The correct placement of the chimney stacks on the roof was also essential to an efficient fireplace because the direction of the wind or air current affected the escape of the chimney gases. The stack finished in a fireclay pot. The chimneypot's lower rim had to be built in behind special courses of bricks to make it strong enough to withstand strong winds. These 'oversailing' courses might be corbelled which made the top of a chimney stack look even more like a box.

SMOKE DOCTORS

Down draughts could force smoke back down the chimney. Cowls known as smoke doctors were fitted to chimneys which suffered from down draughts. Conical cowls protected the chimney from downdraughts but prevented the escape of the flue gases. Circular deflectors allowed the wind to bounce off the windward side while the smoke escaped to leeward. Medium-sized houses like Mr Straw's house in Worksop (1905) could feature an impressive display of chimney stacks and cowls. The Tudors, Gerrards' Cross (1921), did not have the problems which required smoke doctors. Another solution was to make the chimneypots taller, as at Peabody Cottages next to the LCC's White Hart Lane estate.

OPPOSITE: the chimney stack of The Tudors, Gerrards' Cross, designed by M.H. Baillie Scott (1921).

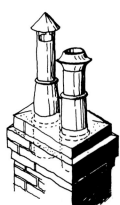

ABOVE: smoke doctors: the one on the left has a conical cowl. the one on the right a circular deflector. Oversailing courses around the base of the pots helped them withstand strong winds

ABOVE: tall chimney pots at Peabody Cottages (1907)

LEFT: an impressive array of chimneys in these semi-detached houses in Worksop (1905)

163

17

Fireplaces

ireplaces were the most important functional items in reception rooms or bedrooms, even after the introduction of central heating. The fireplace was also the decorative focus of the room. The treatment of the fireplace revealed the importance of a room. Muthesius stated: 'By far the most important feature in the English room is the fireplace.'[1]

Traditionally, fireplaces had been built of brick to burn wood. On upper floors, the brick hearth had to be integrated into the timber floor construction. A solid brick base was extended about two feet from the wall. This was supported underneath by a brick arch. It was covered by slate or cement up to the level of the floor. The timber floor joists formed an aperture around this brick base with the floor joists connecting with the wall on either side. The floor joists in between terminated in a hardwood cross-piece known as a trimmer.

The original fittings of the fireplace were intended to hold logs. Wood-burning fireplaces were wasteful of both heat and fuel. From the seventeenth century, coal became the standard fuel in all large towns. Gas fires had been available since the 1860s but were unpopular because gas was about four times more expensive than coal. Before the First World War gas fires consisted of cast-iron grates containing a mat of asbestos fibres. Electric fires first appeared in 1912, but the elements had to be sealed in glass tubes which severely limited their effectiveness (*see Chapter 23, Lighting & Electrical Appliances*).

The hob grate, designed for coal, became the norm. Instead of standing freely in the centre, the fire was enclosed by cheeks or 'hobs' which fitted into each side of the fireplace. The hobs were made of cast iron with wrought-iron bars. They were also useful for cooking and keeping food and drink warm.

Both the grate and fireplace were redesigned several times. A number of innovations threw more heat back into the room and reduced the amount of fuel used. The most important innovation was the register grate. This reduced heat loss straight up the chimney by the introduction of a metal back and sides. The 'register' itself was an adjustable flap which allowed more or less heat to escape as desired. The addition of fireclay retained yet more of the heat. A model of the register grate with a semicircular arched fireback remained popular throughout the latter part of the nineteenth century.

SURROUNDS

Decorative tiles were an important feature of fireplaces which had a register grate. They filled the space between the surround and the grate. By the end of the nineteenth century such tiles were being mass produced (*see Chapter 30, Tiles*).

OPPOSITE: *an Edwardian fireplace with tiled surround and a wooden mantel, designed by C.F.A. Voysey*

ABOVE: *a bedroom fireplace (c.1901)*

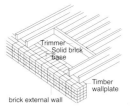

ABOVE: *construction of a hearth on an upper floor*

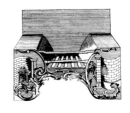

ABOVE: *A hob grate*

FAR LEFT: *a traditional wood burning open fireplace in use in an early seventeenth century farmhouse. Both recess and hearth are brick. Metal fire dogs support the wooden logs* (Weald & Downland Museum)

LEFT: *a register grate with a semicircular arched fireback* (Geffrye Museum)

RIGHT: *a typical Edwardian fireplace with smoke hood, fireclay back, splayed sides with tiles and marble surround*

MIDDLE RIGHT: *a fireplace from an Edwardian terraced house (c.1901)*

FAR RIGHT: *'Swindon' fireplace with Solus electric fire (1921)*

ABOVE: *a hall with an inglenook designed by W. H. Bidlake (c.1901)*

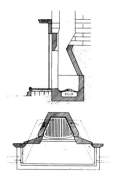

ABOVE: *cross-section and plan of an improved Edwardian fireplace (1911)*

ABOVE: *a simple pine fireplace surround*

By 1900 wooden mantels rivalled marble as the most desirable form. Overmantels with many shelves and bevelled mirrors had become fashionable, replacing the single large mirror in middle-class homes. The new mantles gave people a place to display bronze and brass. They were most likely to be found in 'Tudorbethan' style homes. Muthesius commented that the fireplace had become so important it even made the hearth rug into a showpiece.

He explained that recent attempts had been made

to improve the rate of fuel consumption by making the fire burn more slowly... The fire can be regulated and the iron jacket (hob cheeks) replaced by ones made of fireclay, which when heated supplements the radiation of the fire by giving out an even greater warmth over a longer period, so having the effect of a stove. The sloping sides of the fireplace between the opening and the jambs, which was formerly made of iron, is now faced with tiles. [2]

In larger houses, the Arts & Crafts taste for medieval features produced bigger, more open fireplaces. But, in modest homes, fireplaces actually became smaller. This was because the addition of more fireclay made the grate even more heat efficient. The fireback was shaped and also made of fireclay. The grate was gradually moved further forward so a metal smoke hood became necessary to keep the smoke rising into the flue. The ash pan below was at floor level. The smoke hood and the angled or 'splayed' tile surround became the characteristic features of the Edwardian fireplace.

The Edwardians had a deeply emotional attitude to the fireplace as the heart of the home. Fireplaces in country houses might even be wood-burning. Others were designed with 'inglenooks' or cosy corners with built-in seating. Many fireplace surrounds became simpler. They were often made of wood and even pine was acceptable.

INTERWAR FIREPLACES

During the interwar period the fireplace remained the focal point of the room. Radiators might be added to warm draughty passages but the emotional appeal of the open fire ensured its continued popularity. In large houses fireplaces could still be imposing. The surrounds might be made from different marbles. A 1920s example has a coral marble frieze, with green Connemara marble around it, a chamfered metal hearth and jet black Belgian marble for the fireplace edge detail.

During the 1930s fireplace surrounds were influenced by Modernism on one extreme and Art Deco on the other. Those influenced by Modernism had a simple functional appearance. Those influenced by Art Deco might have stepped shoulders and elaborate marble surrounds.

The first electric fire had appeared in 1912 with a nickel heating element. By 1921 imitation coal effect models had been introduced. Surrounds for electric fires were manufactured, such as the 'Swindon' fireplace for the Solus electric fire by West Electrics. After the First World War, gas fires were fitted with ceramic honeycomb burners. Electric and gas fires were used in bedrooms rather than reception rooms.

FAR LEFT: *a large fireplace with brick-built recess designed by Baillie-Scott (1920)*

ABOVE LEFT: *an elaborate 1920s fireplace surround*

LEFT: *an Art Deco 1930s marble surround*

LEFT: *detail of a 1920s glazed brick fireplace (shown below)*

ABOVE: *a 1920s glazed brick fireplace*

LEFT: *a Modernistic 1930s fireplace*

ABOVE: *a state of the art kitchen range (c.1900)*

TOP RIGHT: *a well equipped kitchen with a smaller range (c.1900)*

ABOVE: *promotional illustration of an Edwardian gas cooker with a grill and a rack above for warming plates*

RIGHT: *Radiation 'New World' H16 gas cooker (1923)*

FAR RIGHT: *No 2 'Standard' gas cooker (1927)*

Kitchens & Cooking

Until the eighteenth century, all domestic cooking was done over an open fire using solid fuel. Ranges began to appear during the 1780s. The fire was still open but a 'slider' was introduced to vary the width of the fire according to necessity. The food was either heated in a pan, boiled or roasted using a spit. If less heat was required the hob or 'cheeks' at the side of the grate were used. By the 1840s completely closed ranges or 'kitcheners' were being used in large houses. Kitchens were still equipped with cast-iron solid-fuel ranges during the Edwardian period. They were hefty items made by iron-founders, with a black lead finish. The kitchen range at Standen, Sussex, was representative of the best turn-of-the-century kitchen equipment. By this time most ranges had fully enclosed fires but even small houses might have a cast-iron fitting which contained an oven and a hotplate arranged around a coal fire. More sophisticated types of range had a boiler at the rear and additional ovens for roasting and baking at the sides. In addition there might be hotplates over the ovens and a plate rack above it. The heat of the fire could be concentrated on particular ovens by adjusting various flues by means of dampers. There were alternatives to solid fuel: gas cookers first appeared during the mid-nineteenth century. By 1901 smaller appliances such as gas rings and electric kettles were available.

ABOVE: 'Trident' range with boiler and oven on either side of the fire (1906)

GAS COOKERS

During the interwar period gas cookers largely replaced ranges in medium-sized houses. By the early 1920s they had developed sufficiently to ensure that they became a standard fitting in newly built homes in the developing suburbs. By comparison with the heavy ranges, they were cheaper, lighter, free-standing and made of pressed steel panels. They had an enamelled finish which was coloured black and white or a mottled grey. The gas rings could be adjusted through three-position taps. The greatest single advance in gas cooker design since their introduction was the thermostat-controlled flue oven. This allowed cooking to become precise, as the oven could maintain a constant temperature without regular supervision. In 1923 the Radiation 'New World' H16 gas cooker was one of the first gas cookers to be fitted with a thermostatically controlled oven. The Radiation group of manufacturers called their version of the thermostat the 'Regulo'.

In 1927 the No 2 'Standard' gas cooker was an early attempt by the National Gas Council to produce a standard design throughout the industry. It incorporated white enamelled panels on the door and two sides, with an enamelled back plate and oven linings. It also had a lagged oven, double grill, two burners and a plate rack.

Replacing a range with a gas cooker opened up a considerable amount of space in the kitchen, because the new gas cooker was usually placed in the scullery. The kitchen could become a family room, but the scullery was likely to become very cramped because all the other kitchen equipment for washing-up and laundry would follow the cooker. Solid-fuel ranges made a comeback during

PART FIVE: DETAILS

FAR RIGHT TOP:
kitchen sink (c.1900)
FAR RIGHT BELOW:
butler's sink (c.1921)

RIGHT: *re-creation of a
set-pot* (Church Farmhouse
Museum)

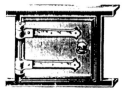

ABOVE: *copper and soot door
for set-pot (from an 1883
catalogue)*

RIGHT: *advertisement for a
gas refrigerator (1937)*

This
GAS REFRIGERATOR

• is absolutely silent

• has no
moving parts

• has nothing to
wear out or
go wrong

• can't interfere
with the wireless

AND IT'S YOURS FOR ONLY **2/6** A WEEK

IT'S THE ELECTROLUX FAMILY MODEL!

An Electrolux *gas* refrigerator is easily the most convenient way of keeping your food safe and appetising—of stopping the waste of those "left-overs"—of keeping butter firm and salads crisp and milk sweet and safe—of making possible a whole lot of exciting new ices and iced dishes and cold drinks.

An Electrolux *gas* refrigerator is absolutely silent, cheap to run, and so reliable that it is *guaranteed* for five years. And the model illustrated is big enough for an ordinary family, yet costs only 2/6 a week, charged on your gas bill.

Go round to your local gas showrooms, and see what a lot of room there is in it—but how little space it takes up!

ISSUED BY THE BRITISH COMMERCIAL GAS ASSOCIATION
1, Grosvenor Place, London, S.W.1

Advertised Goods are Good Goods. 185

FAR RIGHT: *Creda electric
cooker (1933)*

the 1920s with the first appearance of the Aga and its rival the Esse. The new ranges were enamelled and might be supplemented by an enamelled coke boiler for hot water and heating. Magazines such as *The Studio* represented them as suitable for a 'farmhouse' kitchen.

ABOVE: *a large Aga solid fuel range (1938)*

Electric cookers were available from companies like Creda but, in the rivalry between gas and electricity, cooking was an activity which was dominated by gas. The Creda electric cooker was patented by the Credenda Conduit Co and made by the Simplex Electric Company, both of Birmingham. It was one of the first electric cookers to be fitted with an automatic oven thermostat to control oven temperatures. Like all cookers of the 1930s it was fully enamelled with two hotplates – the heating element of the square plate also heated the grill beneath; the round plate included a newly-introduced spiral tube element which glowed when hot.

Poor households might cook on a gas ring. Their gas was supplied through a coin-operated meter. In 1903 Jack London described a poor family who cooked on a single gas ring. They paid for the gas 'by dropping a penny in the slot':

> They possessed no stove, managing their cooking on a single gas ring in the fireplace ... When the penny's worth of gas was drawn, the supply shut off; 'a penny gawn in no time, an' the cooking not 'alf done!' [1]

The absence of servants in middle-class homes meant that the lady of the house was obliged to spend more time in the kitchen. This provided an incentive to ensure its design made it light, clean and convenient. The builders' solution was to place cooker, sink and worktop in the same room for the sake of efficiency in food preparation. Although builders represented the 'kitchenette' as a labour-saving arrangement, it was really a way keeping the floor space to a minimum so that they could erect the maximum number of houses on an estate. Kitchenettes might be as small as ten feet by six feet.

ABOVE: *a kitchen 'planned to save steps and avoid expenditure of needless energy' as featured in* Good Housekeeping *magazine (1937)*

SET-POTS

Gas cookers were much cleaner than coal-fired ranges but something else was needed to heat water. If no boiler was available, water was heated in a copper or a set-pot. A set-pot was an enclosed fire with a flue. The fire was enclosed in a brick structure which was either open or fitted with a cast iron 'soot-door'. A removable metal pot with a wooden lid was set over the fire. This could be lifted out when the water was ready. They were often placed in a corner towards the back of the house. Designers of houses for the working classes tended to include set pots in their wash-house designs as an economical use of space.

A copper was a separate boiler which could be either coal or gas-fired. Kitchen sinks were installed in the scullery or wash house. Large houses might have sinks installed on landings outside the bedrooms or nearby in the service wing. These were usually shallow sinks known as slop sinks or housemaids sinks. A slop sink was equipped for the disposal of the contents of chamber pots. Larger deeper sinks were known as butler's sinks or scullery sinks. Dressers and a table were standard furnishings in a kitchen. Open dressers began to be replaced by more hygienic fitments. In rented houses, dressers were itemised among the fixtures and fittings.

ABOVE: *a pine kitchen dresser (c.1900)*

REFRIGERATORS

The refrigerator was one of the innovations of the interwar period but it was an expensive luxury. In most homes the normal arrangement for keeping food fresh was the larder. This was a small room off the kitchen or scullery. Ideally a larder should have been north facing. They normally had a gauze window to keep food cool while preventing insects from reaching it.

Both gas and electricity companies produced refrigerators. Gas refrigerators were promoted as 'silent' and unable 'to interfere with the wireless'. In 1937, they were available on hire purchase for 2s 6d a week. They were not superseded by electric models until later.

Right: *a re-creation of an Edwardian bathroom with tiling up to the level of the dado rail and discreetly glazed window. The hand basin is panelled which was old fashioned by the Edwardian period*

Above: *bathroom with a tiled section around a basin and free standing iron bath with clawed feet, showing a heated towel rail and a luxurious crocodile-skin travelling toilet case* (National Trust Picture Library)

Above: *some Edwardian baths had elaborate systems for unplugging and draining them*

Above: *a hip bath in a bedroom* (National Trust Picture Library)

19

Bathrooms

ince 1871, public awareness of hygiene had grown so much that 'sanitary' had become the buzzword. The Prince of Wales had nearly died of typhus which had been attributed to 'bad plumbing'. Large and medium-sized houses had been built with bathrooms as part of their original plan from around that time onwards. By the Edwardian period, large houses even had en suite bathrooms for the most important bedrooms. Virtually all medium-sized houses were built with bathrooms conveniently near the bedrooms. Medium-sized houses had been using geysers to heat water for baths since 1869. Geysers created clouds of steam which meant that bathrooms had to be decorated with impermeable materials such as tiles. The geyser, invented by Benjamin Maughan in 1868, was a gas-fired device which heated water as it flowed into the bath. The early geysers could be quite dangerous, as they had no flue, but they provided hot water as and when required. They were gradually improved and became safer and more reliable. The Ascot models, from 1932, were more efficient, with features such as automatic lighting from a pilot light.

Edwardian bathrooms were tiled to a height beyond which water could not reach. Windows were designed and glazed to maintain privacy. Hand basins, or lavatories as they were known, were fully exposed and often mounted on wall brackets to ensure they were kept clean. They were fully ceramic, often had a mirror above them and even fittings for toothbrushes and glasses. Baths were free-standing with separate feet. They were made of cast iron and fully enamelled with roll tops. Some were fitted as shower baths. Others had elaborate systems for unplugging and draining them. Floors might be tiled or covered with linoleum. A WC completed the bathroom suite, although this might be situated in an adjoining room. Fully plumbed-in showers were expensive and usually combined with the bath.

But most new small houses still had to manage with the wash house, kitchen or scullery arrangements. This involved heating water in a set-pot or copper then filling a bathtub. This might have been the utilitarian type with handles whch would have been hung on the wall when not in use for either bathing or washing. Alternatively it might have been a hip bath.

ABOVE: *an Ascot geyser (1932)*

ABOVE: *Shank's combined shower and 'canopy' bath (c.1910)*

LEFT: *an Edwardian bathroom with handbasin, shower and towel rail from a Hamptons catalogue (1910)*

ABOVE: *a bath tub such as might have been hung on the back of the door while not in use. It would have been used in a 'wash-house'* (Church Farmhouse Museum)

FAR RIGHT: *a Twyfords advertisement for a full bathroom suite (1920)*

RIGHT: *1920s bathroom taps* (National Trust Picture Library)

ABOVE: *combined hot and cold taps in a Modernist bathroom (1938)* (National Trust Picture Library)

RIGHT: *a tiled 1920s bathroom with roll-top bath and towel rail from Stockport, Cheshire* (National Trust Picture Library)

ABOVE: *an illustration from a Wates brochure which claimed their houses offered 'hot water without restriction' (1939)*

ABOVE: *a bath with shower unit (c.1930)*

INTERWAR BATHROOMS

By the 1920s baths were being boxed in, as shown in a Twyfords advertisement of 1920, featuring 'matching easy to clean panels'. By the 1930s baths could be tiled up to the rim (*see page 219*). Tiling went as high as possible up the walls, perhaps with a border design. The hand basin was usually placed near the bath so that they could share plumbing and drain pipes. Pedestal types were top of the range. Hand basins might also be fitted in bedrooms, perhaps with a splashback unit. Ceramic bathroom suites were available in a variety of colours. Twyfords offered a choice between lavender blue, celadon green, old ivory and black. The coloured baths and basins distinguished them from the plain white bathrooms of those in state housing or many suburban homes. However, Modernists preferred plain white tiles.

Bathroom accessories, such as soap holders and towel rails, were chromed. Taps were also of polished chrome. Their design was more streamlined than earlier. They were sometimes combined, with hot and cold taps sharing a single spigot. Showers were more widely available. They were almost always incorporated into the bath, for example in hand-held shower-heads either in combination with the taps or as separate items. Well-fitted bathrooms were among the attractions of newly built houses as sales brochures from companies such as Wates proclaimed.

ABOVE: *tin bathroom cabinet with mirrored door (c.1930)*

ABOVE: *coloured sanitary appliances (from a 1935 catalogue)*

FAR LEFT: *a bathroom with many of its original 1930s fittings including the wall tiles, mirrored cabinet and airing cupboard* (National Trust Picture Library)

ABOVE LEFT: *a modernist bathroom lit by a circular skylight. The curved wall carries a curved towel rail.* (National Trust Picture Library)

LEFT: *a modest bathroom, with walls finished in enamel paint, as fitted in 1923.* (National Trust Picture Library)

ABOVE: *a 1920s handbasin with chromed fittings and enamelled mirror* (National Trust Picture Library)

RIGHT: *WC 'washdown' basins and lavatories (hand basins) from Twyfords catalogue (1883)*

ABOVE: *Twyfords 'Unitas' – the first one-piece ceramic pedestal closet (1883)*

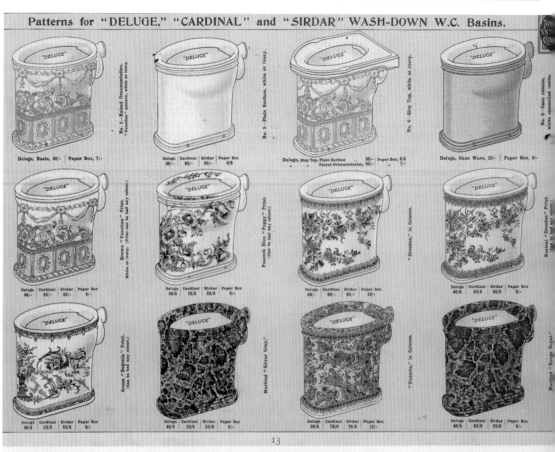

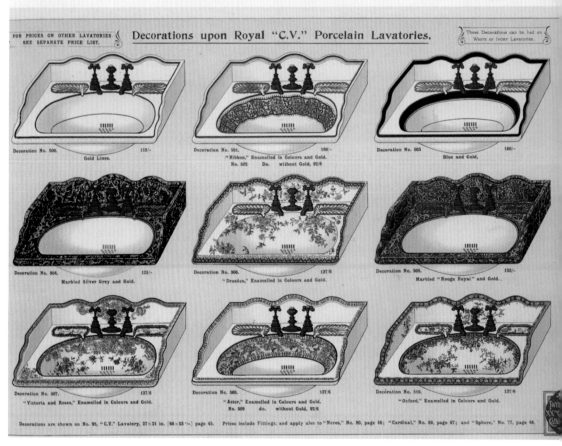

WCs

ABOVE: *the pedestal wash-out was complicated but it had a ceramic 'S' trap (1851)*

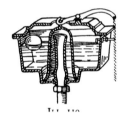

ABOVE: *the syphonic cistern (1872)*

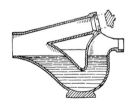

ABOVE: *the disconnecting trap: note the inspection cover (1872)*

ublic health acts had obliged new or newly furbished households to have a fixed sanitary arrangement since 1848. This meant a 'water closet, privy, or ash pit, furnished with proper doors and coverings'. Further legislation, in 1875, obliged builders to submit simple plans showing how sewage was to be disposed of before they could begin work on a new house. Builders were able to comply with the public health acts because they had easy access to ready-made components. These were supplied by companies which were becoming household names for their sanitary ware including Doulton, Twyfords and Thomas Crapper.

The water closet (WC) was developed from designs patented in the 1770s. These early designs were originally intended to eliminate the foul smell which came back up the open pipe from the sewer or cess-pit below. They were pan or valve types which were complicated, liable to become dirty and needed constant maintenance. As companies such as Doulton and Twyfords became involved there were considerable improvements.

Doulton decided to mass-produce glazed stoneware pipes for sewers and drains after the publication in 1842 of a *Report on Sanitary Conditions of the Labouring Classes of Great Britain*. By 1848 twenty per cent of Great Britain's sewers were made of Doulton's pipes. In 1849 Twyfords switched their production from domestic wares such as teapots to sanitary ware. In 1851 George Jennings continued the development of the WC with the 'wash-out' design of bowl. It was still complicated but used a ceramic 'S' trap. The next major development was Thomas Crapper's invention of the syphonic cistern or 'Valveless Waste Water Preventer' in 1872. A single pull emptied the entire cistern. Before, the cistern emptied only while the chain was being pulled. By the Edwardian period cisterns were still of a great variety. They were not yet standardised but they were nearly all syphonic – one flush drained the tank – but each type of tank required a different pull: fast, slow, even or jerky. Crapper's new cisterns had a characteristic domed top which accommodated the top of the flush pipe. This was enclosed in a cylinder which was raised by pulling the chain. The water was drawn up above the level of the flush pipe and this started the siphonage which emptied the cistern. The ball valve then allowed the cistern to be refilled to a level just below the top of the flush pipe.

Crapper is also credited with the next significant development: the intercepting, or disconnecting, trap. This prevented the smell and gases from the main sewer coming back up into the house (the original reason for the WC itself). This had been at its worst in terraced houses in which the connection to the sewer ran beneath the dwelling.

The intercepting trap placed an effective waterseal between the house and the main sewer. It also provided a means of inspecting and clearing blocked drains and prevented the build up of potentially explosive gases.

Even followers of the Arts & Crafts movement failed to object to mass production when it came to sanitary fittings. About 1910 the architect John Cash stated: 'On sanitary grounds there can be no doubt that the type of water-closet pan known as the "pedestal" is to be preferred, the whole apparatus is in view, and there are no secret hiding places for filth.'[1] Twyfords' catalogue of 1883 showed a range of WCs of the pedestal wash-down type. The WC basins were entitled: Deluge, Cardinal and Sirdar. They cost from forty-six shillings and sixpence to fifty-five shillings each but they were cheaper than the lavatories (hand basins) on the same page.

RIGHT: *an outside WC (1923)*

ABOVE: *close-up of a high-level cistern (1923)*

ABOVE: *polished high-level cistern*

ABOVE: *enamelled high-level cistern*

ABOVE: *low-level cistern with oak tank*

PERFECTION OF CLEANLINESS

In 1883 Twyfords produced the 'Unitas': this was the first one-piece ceramic pedestal closet. It was hygienic and cheap. The 'Unitas' was free-standing and the entire appliance was fully exposed. Twyfords proclaimed: 'No filth, nor anything causing offensive smells could accumulate or escape detection' and that it was a 'Perfection of Cleanliness'. In response Doulton produced their own version, the 'Combination'. In 1899 Twyfords produced the 'Twycliffe': the first 'syphonic' WC.

By 1908 the casting process was developed so that it included two firings. This was further improved during the interwar period with a double-trap syphonic WC from Twyfords which appeared in 1930.

Large houses were most likely to be fitted with the latest models but the large building companies also wanted up-to-date models. They were able to order on a large scale. Medium-sized Edwardian houses might have more than one WC. The second would be outside for use by servants. By the interwar period an outside WC might have older fittings such as a wooden seat. New WCs had seats and lids made from the new plastics which were considered more hygienic than wood. They were usually made from Bakelite. This required added carbon to prevent it being brittle so it was often black. Pipes and other accessories were often chromed.

Edwardian cisterns might be wooden and lined with sheet metal or cast iron and wall-mounted at a high level. At first the height was necessary to ensure the flush was strong enough to wash out the waste. Typical cisterns released three gallons of water per flush. The high wall mounting made a long chain necessary.

By the late 1880s sanitaryware manufacturers had improved the WC basin so that it was more efficient at pushing waste out of the bowl. This made low-level tanks possible. Lever-operated low-level cisterns were top of the range during the Edwardian period but became more popular during the 1930s, although high-level cisterns remained common.

ABOVE: *high-level version of Twyfords 'Centaur' syphonic WC, from an Edwardian showcard*

ABOVE: *low-level version of Twyfords 'Centaur' syphonic WC, from an Edwardian showcard*

FAR LEFT: *a similar WC basin to the 'Unitas' shown in Twyfords 1883 catalogue*

LEFT: *a 1930s low-level cistern*

RIGHT: *Edwardian electrolier at the Grand, Folkestone; the shades are upturned, like a gas fitting*

FAR RIGHT: *pendant light fitting (c.1900)*

RIGHT: *a counterweight pendant light fitting designed by Lutyens*

FAR RIGHT: *counterweight pendant light fitting*

Lighting & Electrical Appliances

ABOVE: *re-creation of a gasolier* (Geffrye Museum)

At the top of the market, the owners of Edwardian country houses could choose how they wished to light their homes. Gas had gained acceptance after its adoption in the House of Commons in 1852. It then faced a serious challenge from mineral oil lamps, which it overcame due to the introduction of the 'incandescent' gas mantle in the 1890s. This gave twice as much light as the earlier 'fish-tail' burners. It was also more efficient, which meant it could be turned down and consequently gave off less smoke. Unfortunately it produced a rather green light.

But in 1911 Maurice Hird was asking: 'electricity, air-gas or acetylene?'[1] He decided that 'The rich man with a very large establishment will almost certainly decide in favour of electricity which in his case will give the lowest working costs, while his less wealthy neighbour will most likely instal air-gas or acetylene.' Air-gas was a mixture of petrol vapour and air with a higher proportion of air than petrol. Acetylene, produced by a mixture of calcium carbide, was the simplest mechanically. Coal gas was the cheapest but it fouled the air and the decorations when used with incandescent mantles. Finally Hird concluded:

> Electricity however has the great advantage of giving a light which neither vitiates the air nor fouls the decorations and which can be disposed of in such a manner as not to jar with the various historical styles of decoration found in so many country houses.[2]

ABOVE: *advertisement for electricity generators for country houses*

Architects integrated the new form of lighting into their designs for country houses which had their own generators. These usually ran on paraffin. In 1901 the architect W.H. Bidlake wrote:

> The increase in domestic luxury is indeed one of the characteristics of our time, and the architect must be alert to supply the demand. What more remarkable example of the increased comfort of modern living could be cited than the lighting of our houses? In the early Victorian days it was still necessary to stand shivering on a cold winter's morning, vainly striving to light the sulphur-tipped splint from the tinder ignited by a flint spark. The invention of the lucifer match for ever abolished those good old days. Still lamps had to be filled and candles snuffed, until, with the introduction of gas, it was necessary only to light a match and turn a tap to find one's self in a well-lighted room. At present, if one lies awake at night one has only to thrust one's hand under the pillow and press a button, and lo! a brilliant electric lamp, pendant over the bed, shines forth as if by magic. We take a novel from the bedside, read a chapter, turn over to sleep, and in turning, almost unconsciously, we extinguish the light.[3]

ABOVE: *an oil lamp*

Consistent with the Arts & Crafts tradition, many architects designed the electric light fittings for their houses themselves. Lutyens was an early exponent of electric light fittings. His pendants incorporated counterweights so the height of the light could be adjusted. The adoption of electric light by country houses soon encouraged the occupants of town houses to follow their example.

For the occupants of town houses it was a question of availability. Electricity had first become available at the same time as the 'incandescent' gas burners. But the earliest public supplies were consumed by the new form of public transport, the electric tram. By 1900 electricity was ready to become a rival to gas. It had gained the approval of the experts for its clean, odourless and efficient qualities. It also had the advantage that, unlike gas, it did not flicker. These qualities

ABOVE & RIGHT: *light fittings designed by W.A.S. Benson*

FAR RIGHT: *electrolier pendant light fitting with ceiling rose at the Grand, Folkestone*

RIGHT: *Edwardian standard lamp with silk shade*

FAR RIGHT: *wall mounted light fitting at the Grand, Folkestone*

appealed especially as the price came down. Speculatively built houses in new suburbs such as Ilford or Golders Green were likely to have been provided with electric lighting. But they were unlikely to have any power points until the interwar years, when electrical household appliances became available. Houses in the inner suburbs continued to be lit by gas until after the First World War.

Until the arrival of the incandescent light bulb in 1907, electric light was no brighter than gas. The new light bulbs were the brightest to date, giving out the equivalent of a 25 watt bulb today. Electricity companies canvassed older properties street by street, hoping to gain enough subscribers to 'lay on' supplies. Electricity became a prominent feature of advertising for new housing, increasing its association with a better class of home: an association reinforced by its choice for prestigious developments such as Hampstead Garden Suburb.

By 1914 most new large and medium houses were being fitted with electricity but there was still fierce competition. Electricity was at a disadvantage because it was more expensive than gas.

The cleaner, brighter light resulted in lighter, more delicate décor and colours. Led by designers like W.A.S. Benson, electric appliances eventually began to acquire their own character rather than resembling gas fittings. Pendant light fittings were called electroliers, like gasoliers and the original chandeliers. Muthesius:

ABOVE: *Edwardian electric light bulb*

> the architect W.A.S. Benson was the first to solve the problem of design in metal in the more modern spirit when he created the lamps that were later to have a revolutionary effect on all our metalware. Benson was the first to develop his design directly out of the purpose and the character of the metal as material. Form was paramount to him. He abandoned ornament at a time when, generally speaking, even the new movement was fond of ornament. In so doing he opened up new ground. It is probably typical of the English dislike of gas that he worked relatively little for gas-lighting. But when electric light appeared on the scene, he saw his true field open before him. If one looks at electric lamps as a whole, one can see how much further the artistic means of the time had developed already, in a way that does not apply to gas-lamps; for as the problems posed by electric lighting arose, so the right forms were found in the shortest possible time. Benson was the leading spirit in electric lighting-appliances in England, on the continent he was the fruitful instigator. He developed not only the most pleasing lines and forms but also many surprising ideas about lighting. Thus he was the first to illumine dining-room tables with light reflected from a shiny metal surface while keeping the actual source of illumination hidden, thus eliminating unpleasant dazzle.[4]

ABOVE: *wall mounted light fitting*

During the Edwardian period electric lighting followed the example of gas lighting by being mounted on brackets fixed to the wall. This was supplemented by table lamps and 'standard' lamps 'that stand free in the room and are the height of a man'. These lamps were fitted with silk light shades which often featured flounces. Liberty's silks were especially suitable for this. They were regarded as particularly English compared with alternatives such as American mosaic glass-shades, of which Tiffany's became the most famous.

During the 1920s electricity captured the lighting market. Developers of new estates opened negotiations with electricity, gas and water companies before laying out the roads and services of the new estates. The Central Electricity Board and the National Grid were both established in 1926 to bring some order to the pricing policies and supply arrangements of the electricity companies. There was, however, still a problem with the different forms of electricity: alternating current (AC) and direct current (DC). Appliances made for one would not work on the other, so a change of location might mean that expensive appliances, such as vacuum cleaners, would not work in the new home.

ABOVE: *Edwardian switches and fuse boxes*

ABOVE: *Magnet electric iron (1929)*

RIGHT: *Bestlite (1930)*

FAR RIGHT: *Modernist pendant light fitting*

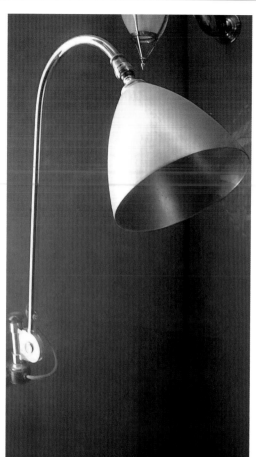

ABOVE: *uplighter designed by Siegfreid Giedion for Bronzenfabrik AG (1932)*

RIGHT: *1930s electric strip light*

FAR RIGHT: *Anglepoise light (1934)*

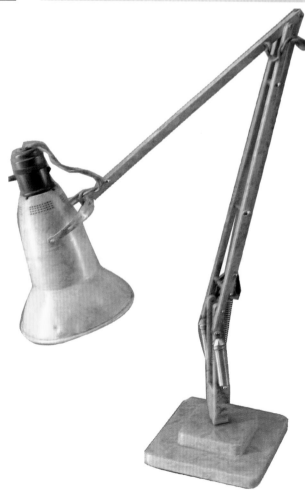

The most useful 'labour saving' device was the electric iron which became the cheapest and most popular of all the new domestic appliances. By 1939, it was estimated that 77 per cent of homes wired for electricity owned an electric iron. Irons cost 15s each. Vacuum cleaners fell in both price and weight during the 1930s. They had the added appeal that the housewife did not have to wear an apron while using them. She particularly wished to avoid being mistaken for a domestic servant.

Modernism, with its emphasis on functionalism, had a considerable effect on light fittings. Modernists preferred uplighters because their indirect light did not break up the architectural space as a central rose would have done. Strip lights with their diffused light were also acceptable. Functional designs like the Bestlite (1930) and the Anglepoise (1934), designed by George Cawardine, were also influenced by Modernism.

As builders worked with developers on an increasing scale they laid out the services before even dividing their newly acquired estates into building plots. This meant that even modest three-bedroom houses could have electricity from the outset. But some areas still did not have electric light during the 1930s, for example parts of Sunderland. Houses in these areas still used gas mantles, oil lamps or even candles.

ELECTRICAL APPLIANCES

Other electrical appliances included vacuum cleaners, kettles, toasters and clocks. They had to be fitted with plugs, an item which had to be designed from scratch. Interwar plugs were made from Phenol-Formaldehyde, one of the new plastics which had to be mixed with resins to prevent it from becoming brittle. This meant that they were only available in black or brown. Electrical flex was braided and intertwined down the chain from which pendant lights were suspended. There were three-pin 'power' plugs for the more powerful appliances and lighter, two-pin 5 amp plugs for lamps and wireless sets.

The Magnet range were British-made electrical goods. In 1929, their vacuum cleaner cost £2 12s; their electric irons 15s or 22s 6d; a range of electric kettles varied in capacity and power from 26s to 52s. Their toaster cost 25s and an electric towel rail £7 15s.

ABOVE: *Magnet electric toaster (1929)*

ABOVE: *Magnet electric kettle (1929)*

ABOVE: *three pin plug made from Phenol-Formaldehyde (c.1930)*

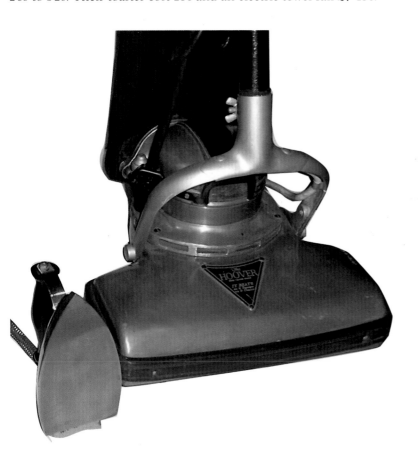

ABOVE: *Magnet vacuum cleaner (1929)*

LEFT: *Smoothwell iron and Hoover vacuum cleaner*

RIGHT: *a* Punch *cartoon about attitudes to the telephone (1913)*

GENTILITY IN OUR GARDEN SUBURB.
"JUST THINK OF IT, MRS. BROWN HAS GOT THE TELEPHONE FIXED. I WOULDN'T HAVE ONE."
"WHY NOT?"   "YOU HAVE TO ASSOCIATE WITH ANYBODY."

RIGHT: *telephone No. 150, a candlestick model with a dial (1924)*

FAR RIGHT: *a Danish 'jydysk' model, the type of handset preferred in Europe*

Telephone & Wireless

The telephone first became part of the house and its equipment during the Edwardian period. It had been invented and patented by Alexander Graham Bell in 1876. The telephone had been preceded by the telegraph, which had been widely adopted by the railway companies. In 1879 telephone calls were classified as telegraphs, which came under the authority of the Post Office.

ABOVE: *women operators at the London telephone exchange in 1883*

Bell demonstrated his telephone to Queen Victoria, who ordered a line from Osbourne House in the Isle of Wight to Buckingham Palace in London. Another line was installed for the Press between the House of Commons and Fleet Street. These first lines were 'point to point'. As more telephones were provided, telephone exchanges became necessary to allow interconnection to other lines on the network. Customers, or 'subscribers', called the exchange, which connected them, manually, to the person with whom they wished to talk.

The first networks were operated by independent telephone companies such as the National Telephone Company. They had to obtain 31-year licences to operate from the Postmaster-General. In 1881 the Post Office began to convert some of its telegraph service exchanges for use as telephone exchanges. The first was Swansea, followed by Newcastle-upon-Tyne, Bradford and Middlesbrough. The first telephone exchange opened in London in 1883. The operators were all women; boys were employed initially but proved too liable to distraction. Separate receivers were used and the transmitters were mounted on the face of the switchboard. The operator made temporary connections by plugging and unplugging flexible wires, known as 'cords', into the switchboard in front of her.

A network of lines grew between exchanges in the larger cities. These were called 'Trunks' or junctions. Many of the Trunk lines used existing telegraph wires, some in underground cables and many on overhead routes. By March 1914, exchanges in London, Birmingham, Liverpool, Leeds, Guildford, Canterbury, Sheffield, Hull, Swansea, Newport and Fenny Stratford were connected to each other.

Mrs C.S. Peel installed a telephone in her refurbished house in Brompton Square as part of its modernisation. The telephone, she later remarked in 1931, was 'not (then) as usual a piece of domestic equipment as it now is'.[1] A 1913 Punch cartoon entitled 'Gentility in our garden suburb' showed that attitudes towards the telephone included a certain amount of social difficulty – despite the fact that Queen Victoria had been a 'subscriber'. Candlestick models based on the Western Electric pattern were popular in Great Britain but not in Europe where combined receiver and microphone handsets were preferred. The most popular model was the type 2, a candlestick. Early telephones consisted of a (Bell) receiver, a microphone (transmitter) and a bell set, which also contained the impedance matching transformer (in those days known as an Induction Coil). The Induction Coil kept long distance calls from fading out.

ABOVE: *early wall-mounted payphones*

ABOVE: *Model No. 162 (1929 onwards)*

ABOVE: *the dial (1922 onwards)*

RIGHT: *a manual exchange switchboard*

The first Post Office exchange in London was opened on 1 March 1902; this 'Central Exchange' had a capacity for 14,000 subscribers. A second 'City' exchange (capacity 18,000) was followed by 'Mayfair' to serve the West End, 'Western' for Kensington and 'Victoria' for Westminster in the same year. Several other Post Office exchanges were also opened in the London suburbs. In 1906 the Post Office's first coin-operated call box was installed by the Western Electric Company at Ludgate Circus, London.

In 1911 Maurice Hird observed: 'The telephone is now one of the usual modern conveniences found in the country house.'[2] At first telephones were used as much for 'intercommunication' within the house as for external calls. Designers saw their potential as an alternative to bells and speaking tubes for summoning the staff or locating guests. These 'intercommunication' telephones were usually wall-mounted.

By 1912 a unified telephone system was available throughout most of Britain. From this date the Post Office became the monopoly supplier of telephone services. The first experimental public automatic telephone exchange was opened for service at Epsom, Surrey. It used the Strowger automatic switching system.

From 1922 the Post Office adopted the Strowger switching system as standard. An additional system was adopted to direct telephone calls through the complex network of circuits linking exchanges in large cities. This was known as the 'Director' system.

In 1924 the Telephone No. 150 was launched. It was a candlestick model which introduced most subscribers to the dial for the first time. The dial operated the automatic exchange switching mechanism by sending out a series of electrical impulses corresponding to the number being dialled. It was no longer necessary for the operator to connect all calls. Where a No. 150 was still connected to a manual exchange, the space in the base of the telephone for the dial was covered by a dummy insert (used as a number label holder) which could be replaced by a dial when the exchange went automatic.

In 1929 the development of the immersed electrode principle in transmitter design made it possible for the Post Office to introduce two new innovative telephone designs (numbers 162 and 232). These were the first instruments to successfully incorporate a 'hand combination' (a handset with combined receiver and transmitter) which could be used with central battery lines. By 1930 the GPO had ceased production of candlestick telephones in favour of the 162 and 232 types. These models had pyramid shaped bodies which supported the handset.

ABOVE: *Model No. 232*
(1929 onwards)

Early telephones had required their own magneto generator and primary battery to receive and transmit calls. A central battery, which provided the power for making calls, had been invented in 1882 but the first Central Battery exchange (Telephone Avenue, Bristol) did not open until 1900. In the Central Battery System, all the energy required for signalling and speaking was drawn from one large battery at the exchange. The battery was common to all circuits requiring current and supplied all the needs of the exchange. The subscriber's magneto generator and primary battery became unnecessary. Provision was made in the circuit to reduce sidetone. The new designs were some of the first large-scale production items to be made of plastic. They were produced in 'Bakelite', and there was a limited choice of colours.

The telephone system was developed and refined rapidly during the 1930s. In 1930 automatic metering up to 3d was introduced on director exchanges. The Directory Enquiry Bureau was opened in August 1932. In 1934 the transfer charge system was introduced. This enabled callers to have a call made through an operator charged to the person receiving that call. In 1936 the speaking clock and the 332 type were introduced. Telephone No. 332 was an improved version of the innovative No. 162 as it was less liable to breakage and provided extra facilities controlled by press buttons. Like the 232, the 332 incorporated a drawer in its base. In 1937 the 999 emergency telephone service was made available to London subscribers and was later extended throughout the country. When 999 was dialled a buzzer sounded in the exchange and a red light flashed to draw an operator's immediate attention.

ABOVE: *Model No. 332*
(1936 onwards)

WIRELESS

Developments in radio communications, or wireless telegraphy, were among the first achievements of the twentieth century. Wireless telegraphy was involved in two of the most notorious incidents of the Edwardian period: the case of Doctor Crippen (1910) and the sinking of the *Titanic* (1912). Marconi wireless telegraphy sets were capable of sending and receiving transmissions of the 'Spark-Gap' kind which could carry Morse code but neither voice nor music.

In 1906 Flemming and De Forest invented the thermionic valve. This produced a reliable 'carrier wave' that could carry voice and music. Wireless sets with a thermionic valve could amplify the signals enough to enable loudspeaker operation. But wireless activity was prohibited during the First World War by the Defence of the Realm Act (1914). When the act lapsed in 1921, the manufacture and sale of wireless sets was once again allowed. Instrument makers like W.G. Pye had manufactured military equipment during the war. After the war they had to look for new products. In the case of Pye, their wireless sets would make them a household name. At first, wireless sets were traditional in style with wooden cabinets. These early models were known as 'receiving sets'. Some were domed and were referred to as cathedral sets. Others began to display contemporary Art Deco features like the sunrise motif. During the 1930s models became more modernistic with plastic casings, such as the Ekco AD36.

ABOVE: *Marconi crystal set*

In 1934 J.B. Priestley described 'post war England' as 'miles of semi-detached bungalows, all with their little garages … their wireless sets, their periodicals about film stars, their swimming costumes and tennis rackets and dancing shoes.'[3]

RIGHT: *advertisement for the Pye Two Valve 'receiving set' (1924)*

ABOVE: *Marconi 'receiving set' (1922). This was the first mass produced commercial wireless set from the Marconi company*

RIGHT: *Jackson Bell 62 'Swan' model (1931)*
FAR RIGHT: *GEK 43 (1933)*

ABOVE: *Philco 89 (1935)*

RIGHT: *Philips 930A (1930)*
FAR RIGHT: *Ekco AD36 (1935)*

ABOVE: *Atwater Kent 165 (1933)*

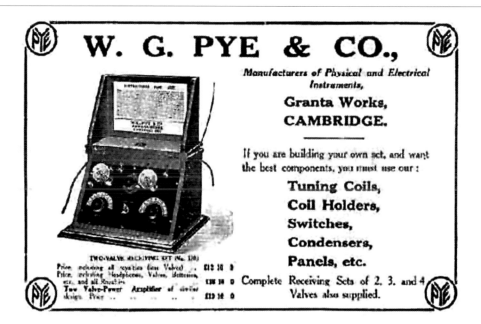

EARLY WIRELESS & CRYSTAL SETS

Wireless broadcasting in Great Britain began in 1920 on an experimental basis. Marconi set up a station, 2MT, in a former army hut near Chelmsford, Essex. For nearly three years, the experimental station broadcast daily half hour programmes of news and entertainment. Listeners could tune in using crystal sets. These were the simplest form of wireless receiver and required neither external power nor batteries. The headphones of a crystal set were powered by the energy collected from the aerial. This came from the radio waves sent by the transmitter of the radio station to which the set was tuned. The Cosmos (1925) was a top-of-the-range crystal set. It featured separate plug-in coils for receiving different wavelengths and a knob for fine tuning.

ABOVE: *Cosmos crystal set (1925)*

Marconi's company became convinced of the commercial potential of radio broadcasting. By May 1922 they were negotiating with wireless set manufacturers and other interested organisations to set up more broadcasting stations around the country. They agreed to work under an umbrella organisation called the British Broadcasting Company (BBC). They guaranteed its finances for an initial period of two years.

In October 1922 the government granted the BBC a licence to operate. The BBC would aim to provide quality programmes consisting of variety entertainment, concerts and plays funded by a tax collected from the sale of wireless sets and from a licence fee administered by the Post Office. Additional experimental stations were set up in London, Manchester, Birmingham and Newcastle. In 1923 more BBC stations were established in Cardiff, Glasgow, Aberdeen, Bournemouth and Sheffield – but the original station, 2MT, was closed. 1924 saw more local stations at Plymouth, Liverpool, Leeds/Bradford and Belfast. Relay stations were opened in Edinburgh, Hull, Nottingham, Dundee, Stoke-on-Trent and Swansea.

ABOVE: *the first issue of the Radio Times (1923)*

The first radio receiving licences cost 10s. The quality of the programmes transmitted was sufficient to sell 500,000 licences. On 14 November, John Reith became Managing Director of the BBC and declared that the BBC must bring the best broadcasting to the widest possible number of homes.

By 1924 there were over 1.5 million wireless sets in use; many were still crystal sets, but valve sets were gradually becoming popular. They were more expensive, and they needed both low voltage and high voltage batteries to work. A valve set might cost about £7.

The BBC's original licence expired on 31 December 1926. A government committee recommended that the BBC should be replaced by a public authority. In 1927 the British Broadcasting Company was nationalised and became the British Broadcasting Corporation. It was granted a ten year Royal Charter to keep it independent of interference from central government. It began to publish the *Radio Times* which included programme listings.

On 21 August 1927 the BBC began to replace the original pioneering local stations, such as BBC London (2LO) and BBC Birmingham (5IT). More powerful transmitting stations were required to carry both the National Programme and the Regional Programme services to the whole country. A purpose-built station at Brookmans Park in Hertfordshire opened in 1929. Additional high power regional transmitting stations were also established to cover Northern Ireland, Scotland and Wales.

An experimental overseas service was set up in 1926 to transmit programmes from Britain to the Empire. In December 1932 a permanent Empire Station began to broadcast from Daventry.

During the mid 1920s wireless sets were sold in appealing cabinets of walnut, mahogany and oak which were regarded as furniture. By the early 1930s most suburban homes had a wireless of some sort. They received their signal from an aerial strung from the roof to a tall pole at the end of the garden. The wire ran through a switch which had to be opened during a thunderstorm. Wireless sets became less expensive as mass production brought prices down. A three-valve all-mains set had cost £15–£17 in 1931. By 1934 the price of a model such as the circular Ekco 'superhet.' with its four valves and integral speaker had fallen to £8 8s.

ABOVE: *a modernistic front cover of the Radio Times (1929)*

Wireless sets were a characteristic feature of suburban homes, where they were prominently displayed in living rooms on mantlepieces or sideboards. 'Listening in' to the wireless was a popular indoor leisure occupation. New wireless sets such as 'superhet.' models would be proudly demonstrated to visitors. 'Superhet.' was the term for a set with a superheterodyne receiver which improved reception by mixing and multiplying the signal before it was passed to the amplifier.

From 1931, commercial stations such as Radio Normandie provided alternative broadcasts. English programmes were broadcast after the French programmes had gone off the air. On Sundays, when the BBC was concentrating on religious output, Radio Normandie was said to command 80 per cent of the British radio audience. Roy Plomley, the founder of *Desert Island Discs*, was heard on Radio Normandie. Gracie Fields voiced commercials. The programmes were financed by advertisers such as Philco and Henleys, a car sales company.

In May 1932 the BBC moved to new headquarters at Broadcasting House in Portland Place, London. In 1933 another commercial station, Radio Luxembourg, began to broadcast on long wave from 5pm to midnight. The programmes were less formal in nature than those provided by the BBC. They were also funded by advertising and sponsorship. Radio Luxembourg was sufficiently popular with the British listening public to expand. By 1933 their programmes ran from 3.30pm to midnight.

J.B. Priestley stated his approval of the wireless because it was both modern and democratic:

> the very modern things, like the films and the wireless and sixpenny stores, are absolutely democratic, making no distinction between their patrons ...[4]

PYE: A HOUSEHOLD NAME

In 1896 William George Pye, a trained instrument maker, set up his own company to design and manufacture high precision scientific instruments. Pye benefited from the enormous demand for military equipment during the First World War, but by 1921 this market had disappeared. The management decided to try the new field of domestic wireless receivers and planned their first wireless set to receive the experimental signals then being broadcast.

After William Pye's son, Harold, joined the company in 1924, Pye produced a successful wireless, the '700 Series'. By 1933 it was producing 40,000 sets a year; by 1939 it was set up for full scale production of television sets.

It was a wireless broadcast by the Prime Minister, Neville Chamberlain, that brought the interwar years to an end. On the morning of Sunday 3 September 1939, the Prime minister told the nation that it was at war with Germany. The film director, John Boorman, was six years old at the time. He was playing in the back garden of his suburban home. He remembered the broadcast as 'the moment when all the Sunday morning lawnmowers stopped'.[5]

Companies like Pye switched from making wireless and television sets to military equipment.

OPPOSITE: *Broadcasting House (1932)*

ABOVE: *Bell 2033A (1934)*

ABOVE: *front covers of the* Radio Times *– left 1931, right 1934*

ABOVE: *an Exco set with bakelite casing (1932)*

ABOVE: *Philco 'tombstone' set (1935)*

LEFT: *Pye 'Invicta' television (1939)*

CENTRE LEFT: *Pye wireless set (1933)*

FAR LEFT: *Pye set with sunrise motif (c.1928)*

PART FIVE: DETAILS

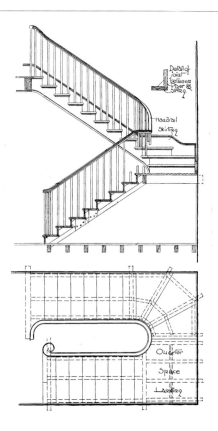

FAR RIGHT: *dog-leg staircase of a medium-sized house (1901)*

RIGHT & BELOW RIGHT: *elevations and plans of open newel or well staircase (c.1910)*

RIGHT: *staircase of a medium-sized house, with newel post extending up to arch over stairs at ceiling height (1910)*

FAR RIGHT: *elevations and plans of winder and dog-leg staircases (c.1910)*

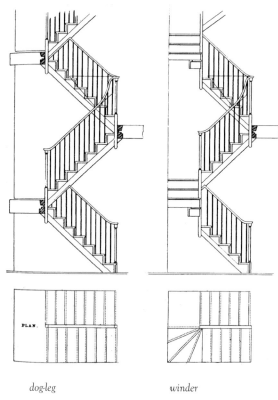

dog-leg   winder

Staircases

Staircases were placed in the hall when space was available, rather than in one of the main rooms. Because it was close to the front entrance the staircase created an early impression of the status of the house. Just before 1910, Halsey Ricardo explained that the staircase had originally connected the drawing room on the first floor with the downstairs sitting rooms. 'The staircase is thus the introduction to the principal room of the house' and should make a good impression but where the staircase led only to the bedrooms, it should be quite away from and at least out of sight of the front door.[1] Mrs Panton complained about this:

> That tiresome man, the builder, appears to consider, either that an entrance to a house is not necessary at all, or that the smaller it is, and the more the stairs are in evidence, the better and more appropriate it is to Angelina's lowly station in life.[2]

There were three basic designs – 'open newel' or well, the dog-leg and the winder. The well was found in medium and large houses. C. Jennings of Bristol's catalogue of 1914 recommended them as 'from a constructive and artistic point of view, the best form of stair there is'. The dog-leg was a cheaper alternative, making the maximum use of the space at the end of the hallway. It had no well-hole. It also created a mezzanine level. Jennings' catalogue stated that it would 'occupy less space than any other variety with the exception of the spiral, and for this reason are chiefly used in cottages and other small houses'. The winder consisted of two straight flights with angled steps around the 180 degree turn between them. It was used for small houses such as Geoffry Lucas' designs for Letchworth.

Wider plots and larger halls allowed the staircase to be made more than merely functional. Newel posts became more common. Screens and arches with fretwork decoration embellished the staircase as halls became reception rooms. Screens and arches could be assembled or taken down according to changing taste – In *Nooks and Corners* (1889) Mrs Panton had recommended arrangements such as a 'Moorish' scheme for a half-landing that would make a square room 'picturesque'. Jennings' catalogue claimed: 'The judicious use of our grilles will give the interior of your home a "modern" appearance ...' Fretwork screens were quite often found in the hall, at the foot of the stairs and on the first-floor landing. They served the real purpose of screening off the service parts from the private parts of the house.

Jewson's catalogue (1910–19) offered ten designs of newel post in a hierarchy of woods from deal to Austrian oak. The newel posts might be extended up to an arch over the staircase.

By 1914 C. Jennings was offering twenty-five different shapes of balusters, many of them round-turned. Square and fretwork balusters were top of the range. Woods such as oak, mahogany and teak raised the price still further.

Straight-flight wooden stairs were usually used only for access to cellars.

ABOVE: *'Moorish' scheme for a half-landing (1909)*

ABOVE: *balusters and newel post (1901)*

RIGHT: *foot of a Tudorbethan staircase, closed string staircase designed by Baillie-Scott (1921)*

ABOVE: *a double-height hall, with a balustraded landing (c.1920)*

ABOVE: *panelled staircase, designed by John Belcher (1920)*

DETAILS

The sides of the staircase were known as strings. Open string left the steps exposed. Closed string covered them, for example, the Tudorbethan staircase of The Tudors, Gerrards Cross. The handrail was supported by balusters. The norm was two per tread. They were usually turned. The handrails were normally of polished moulded hardwood; the most common moulding was known as 'toad's back'. There was a cheaper softwood alternative called 'frog's back'.

Metal balusters were the epitome of elegance but were mostly confined to grander houses.

After the middle of the nineteenth century, turned and carved balusters were fitted together with heavy, turned newel posts. The underside of the staircase was panelled, and cupboards were tucked underneath. The Queen Anne Revival saw the closed string in favour, sometimes with heavily moulded detail.

Extravagant revivalist staircases with Tudorbethan panelling could be bought 'off the shelf' from companies such as Gill & Reigate of Oxford Street.

ABOVE: *an 'off the shelf' Tudorbethan staircase from Gill & Reigate (1920)*

INTERWAR STAIRCASES

Naturally Tudorbethan revivalist staircases were still available after the war. M.H. Baillie-Scott continued the Tudorbethan approach at The Tudors, Gerrards Cross. John Belcher designed the hall staircase at Tatmore Place, Hitchin, Hertfordshire, with panelling up to the height of the first-floor landing and wooden screens around a cosy corner.

In 1920 Reginald Blomfield designed the entrance hall and staircase of 40 Upper Grosvenor Street. He gave it an open well, neo-Georgian staircase with a wrought iron balustrade. Lutyens also designed staircases for houses in the 'English Renaissance' style with wrought-iron balustrades as at Heathcote, Ilkley, Yorkshire (1920).

With the exception of some large houses, during the interwar period staircases became one of the prefabricated components which enabled speculative builders to build in great numbers. Medium-sized houses with double-height halls might enjoy flights of stairs lit by cathedral windows up to the first floor landing. Three-bedroom semi-detached houses were built with winders turning ninety degrees at the foot and at the head of a straight flight of stairs. Two bedroom non-parlour types were built with dog-leg stairs (see plans on page 132).

Modernists like Goldfinger even incorporated metal spiral staircases into their designs.

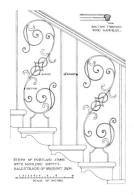

ABOVE: *design for neo-Georgian wrought iron balustrade (1920)*

LEFT: *40 Upper Grovesnor Street, designed by Blomfield (1920)*

ABOVE: *the foot of the spiral staircase at Goldfinger's house (1939)*

197

ABOVE AND RIGHT: *an Aesthetic interior (c.1890)*

ABOVE: *Bird and Anemone, an indigo discharge print designed by William Morris (1882)*

RIGHT: *Late Victorian colour combinations (1876)*

Terracotta/Cream/Rose

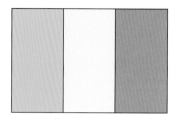

Yellow/Cream/Drab

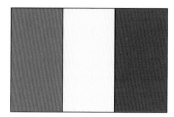

Plum/Cream/Red leather

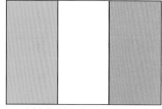

Old Gold/White/Pale Blue

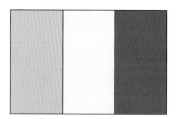

Lilac/Cream/Peacock Blue

ABOVE: *horizontal features picked out in white at Bedford Park (c.1880)*

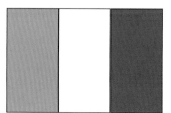

Drab/White/Chocolate

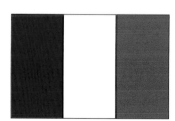

Prussian Blue/White/Crimson

Olive Green/Cream/Salmon

24

Colours

ABOVE: *a combined frieze, wall and dado wallpaper (c.1890)*

LATE VICTORIAN

ate Victorian colours were the result of reactions to the rich colours of the mid-Victorian period. Mrs Panton described these as 'sealing-wax reds, deep oranges, clear yellow and beautiful blues' (1869). They were synthetically produced from aniline dyes which were coal by-products.

Halsey Ricardo described how once a builder had finished the carcase of a house 'it passed for its completion into the hands of the furnisher' who followed the accepted form such as: 'Chintz was to be used for the bedrooms; the curtains to the drawing room were to be of silk', or damask; 'the paper on its walls was of French grey with sprigs of flowers in gold, or else of satinwood and the door and window cases were coloured and grained to match. Downstairs it was "oak" for the dining-room. The walls flatted in oil-colour or covered with a crimson flock paper, and the furniture upholstered in leather or in rep, with rep curtains to match. The library was treated in much the same way but the prevailing cast was rather more sombre, as befitting a "study".'[1]

Machine-made goods, including aniline dyes, superseded the furnisher's approach. The Arts & Crafts and Aesthetic movements developed in reaction to the flood of machine-made goods. Attempts to produce alternatives to products like aniline dyes led to experiments with vegetable dyes by William Morris among others. By the time he died, in 1896, Morris had endeavoured for over thirty years to produce cleaner colours by using techniques such as indigo discharge printing. There were a number of natural dyes which produced rather muddy colours which were used for cheap textiles. These colours were made by redyeing fabric already dyed woad blue in weld yellow. This produced colours such as puker green (a light khaki) and goose-turd green. The only bright colour produced by these means was Lincoln green.

Aesthetic colours were mocked by Gilbert & Sullivan as 'greenery-yallery'. The Grosvenor Gallery had opened in 1877 with a sage green and old gold interior. In *Patience* (1881) W.S. Gilbert included the lyric:

ABOVE: *sage green and old gold, the colour combination mocked as 'greenery-yallery' (c.1881)*

> A pallid and thin young man,
> A haggard and lank young man,
> A greenery-yallery, Grosvenor Gallery,
> Foot-in-the-grave young man

The late Victorian palette used combinations of colours such as terracotta, cream and rose; old gold, white and pale blue; olive green, cream and salmon. During the 1890s white, in a recognisable form, began to be used to pick out external woodwork and horizontal features.

RIGHT: *a colour scheme for a hall interior (c.1901)*

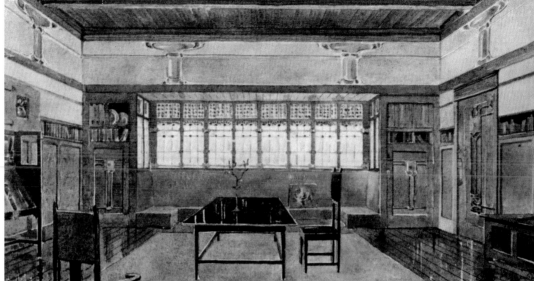

ABOVE: *distemper colour samples (1908)*

RIGHT: *Edwardian colours*

pale Blue

Old Gold

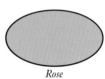

Rose

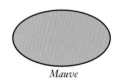

Mauve

ABOVE: *colour scheme for C.F.A. Voysey's own home at Chorleywood (1901)*

Maroon

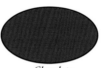

Chocolate

Neutral Brown

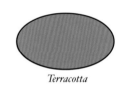

Terracotta

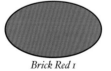

Brick Red 1

Brick Red 2

Stock Brick

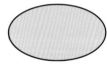

Pale Buff

ABOVE: *tobacco tin (c.1912)*

Pale Sage

Dark Sage

Pale Green

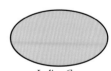

Indian Grey

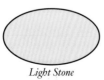

Light Stone

Blue Green

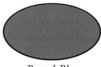

Peacock Blue

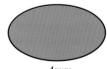

Azure

EDWARDIAN COLOURS

By the early 1900s internal colour schemes had become significantly lighter. Paler tints were not only more popular, they were more practical. New water-based paints offered a wide range, including numerous 'biscuit' colours and greys. These new paints were known as distempers. They were made from coloured limewashes, solutions in which the pigment was suspended rather than dissolved. Distemper relied upon the size in the solution to keep it fixed to the surface once the paint had dried. White distemper was most common but pastel colours were also available.

Edwardian oil paint was based on linseed oil. It was slow to dry and became progressively more yellow. It was used on unpapered wall surfaces, for example, the bathroom walls at Mr Straw's house, 7 Blyth Grove, Worksop. Such treatment required four coats. The first two coats were diluted. The final two were a much thicker mixture which caused it to dry so quickly that up to six workmen were needed to finish the job before the surface was completely dry or it would look uneven. The result was a matt finish. This was known as 'flatting'. A gloss finish could only be achieved by adding a clear varnish over the dry oil paint. Harland's Flat enamels had a pigment base with a varnish medium. They also claimed to be washable.

ABOVE: *an advertisement for a brand of distemper featuring a decorative scheme for a hall 1901)*

In 1905 *The Decorator* praised 'the enormous strides in public favour made by enamel paints during the last five years or so' because 'the enormous swing of the pendulum away from the so-called aesthetic style with its faded greens, bilious yellows, funereal drabs and general murkiness, was favourable to the introduction of a material which made for lightness, cleaness and simplicity' – white enamel paint.

Robert Tressell provided a contemporary description of painters at work:

> By Tuesday night all the inside work was finished with the exception of the kitchen and scullery. The painting of the kitchen had been delayed owing to the non-arrival of the new cooking range, and the scullery was still used as the paint shop. The outside work was also progressing rapidly, for, though, according to the specification, all the outside woodwork was supposed to have three coats, and the guttering, rain pipes and other ironwork two coats, Crass and Hunter had arranged to make two coats do for most of the windows and woodwork, and all the ironwork had one coat only. The windows were painted in two colours, the sashes dark green and the frames white. All the rest – gables, doors, railings, guttering, etc.– was dark green; and all the dark green paint was made with boiled linseed oil and varnish, no turpentine being allowed.[1]

ABOVE: *a copper fire screen with azure enamelled bosses*

In 1911 Halsey Ricardo advised: 'Put light colours where there is plenty of light, and rich colours where the light is not so dominant.' Rooms with north-facing windows should feature full colours like purple, brown or rich gold 'to preserve the steady dignity of the room'.[2]

Ricardo maintained that simplicity of colour was essential, especially in a light room, which involved limiting the number of tints in curtains and carpets. Either pictures or wall paper should provide the pattern. White should only be used if the ceiling is low. Too much white made a room look sterile. White walls should be complimented by a tinted ceiling.

White enamel was suitable for the panelling which was being installed in halls as part of the neo-Georgian revival. A typical dining-room scheme would have been red and gold with yellow and white ceilings and cream-coloured cornice. The drawing-room would have been more delicate in sparrow's egg blue, possibly embellished by stencilled or painted rush and grass designs. A change of pattern or colour completed the annual spring clean.

The architect John Cash agreed that walls on which pictures were to be hung should be plain or, if patterned, not too busy: 'If to be a foil for pictures, wall-hangings should be of plain tints or very nearly so. If the pictures are not important, then some indulgence in patterning cannot be objected to, but in every case the design must be quite in repose giving no impression of movement, and the colours neither many nor glaring.'[3]

ABOVE: *external woodwork such as window sashes was often painted a dark colour such as green (1913)*

Cash concluded that: 'the keynotes must be lightness and brightness ... in all a true alliance of beauty and purpose.'[4]

PART FIVE: DETAILS

RIGHT: *sample card showing different colours of Erinoid furniture handles*

FAR RIGHT: *bedroom with satin quilt, pink wallpaper and printed satin curtains (1934)*

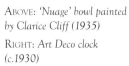

ABOVE: *'Nuage' bowl painted by Clarice Cliff (1935)*

RIGHT: *Art Deco clock (c.1930)*

RIGHT CENTRE: *Diakon acrylic samples*

FAR RIGHT: *modernist medicine cabinet (c.1939)*

BELOW RIGHT: *Clarice Cliff teaset (c.1933)*

ABOVE: *Art Deco colours*

RIGHT: *water jug with geometric design by Susie Cooper (1929)*

RIGHT CENTRE: *Shelley 'Vogue' cup and saucer*

FAR RIGHT: *Shelley 'Vogue' tea set (c.1935)*

INTERWAR COLOURS

The interwar period began by continuing the mood of lightness from before the war. This was possible because of the increasing availability of electric light. The choice of colours in newly built homes was usually restricted to whatever the developer offered. In vernacular or 'mock Tudor' homes dark woodwork might predominate but neo-Georgian style interiors could have a lighter touch. They could be achieved by making rooms such as the dining room neo-Georgian even in the dark interiors of a Tudorbethan semi-detached house which had 'Jacobean' oak-panelled walls with stained or parquet floors.

The mid-1920s brought the influence of Art Deco which found its way into homes through brightly coloured wallpaper patterns and ceramics from companies such as Shelley's or designs by either Clarice Cliff or Susie Cooper. Around 1931 these were being marketed as 'Jazz' and 'Vogue' ranges.

One of the most radical changes came in the form of new plastics. The first true plastic was phenol-formaldehyde which was given the trade name Bakelite. It was first marketed as 'fireproof celluloid'. It was a thermosetting plastic which had to be mixed with resins to prevent it from being too brittle. This limited it to dark colours such as black or brown. Telephones, clocks, radios and electric plugs had cases made from Bakelite. But formaldehyde could also be mixed with casein, a milk protein. Casein formaldehyde plastics could be brightly coloured. Products such as door handles or buttons were first sold under the Galalith and Erinoid trade names during the 1920s. Diakon was similar. It was an acrylic moulding powder used for bathroom fittings and cutlery handles. Bathroom fittings and accessories were also available in coloured earthenware. These might be styled in the 'Streamline Moderne' style with rounded corners. Most manufacturers were able to supply their fittings in green, blue, pink, ivory and black.

Dark brown was a popular colour for fitted carpets which were enlivened by rugs. Patterned linoleum squares were a cheap alternative to carpeting. Linoleum was available in 'Jazz-Modern' patterns.

Another radical change came through the influence of Modernism which brought in a fashion for plain painted walls. In all but the homes of outright Modernists like Erno Goldfinger, plain walls were offset by patterned curtain fabrics. Shiny fabrics such as satin might be combined with chromed furniture to create interiors influenced by the glamour of the cinema.

The characteristic colours of the 1930s were the 'autumn tints': shades of green, brown, orange and red.

ABOVE: *Modernists favoured plain walls (c.1938)*

ABOVE: *Autumn tints (1930s)*

ABOVE: *Art Deco tin*

LEFT: *Catesby's linoleum squares (1938)*

FAR LEFT: *buttons from a showcard that displayed the colours available in casein formaldehyde*

LEFT: *chart showing colours of Pyramid bathroom fittings (c.1935)*

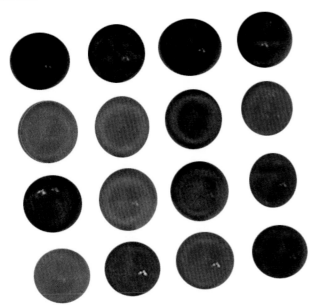

CATESBYS ONE-PIECE LINOLA SQUARES
FOR PRICES AND SIZES SEE FRONT OF BOOK

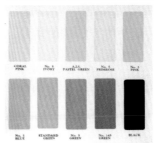

203

Part Five: Details

RIGHT: *graining – root of oak; note the simulated 'join' between two different pieces of wood*

FAR RIGHT: *graining – maple*

ABOVE: *good wood – oak, the right-hand side is varnished*

ABOVE: *good wood – maple, the right-hand side is varnished*

ABOVE: *beech, which was not regarded as good enough to be left unpainted*

RIGHT: *marbling – alabaster*

FAR RIGHT: *marbling – rouge roi*

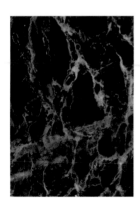

ABOVE: *marbling – tinos*

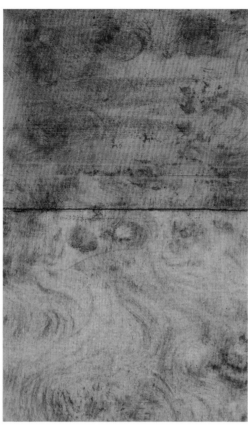

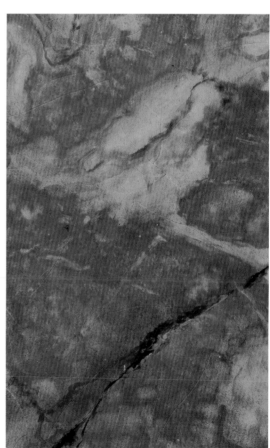

25

Paint Finishes

ABOVE: *Graining – 'flame', an example from 1923*

Paint effects were used throughout the Edwardian and interwar periods both on walls and woodwork. Only high quality woods such as oak, mahogany or walnut were left exposed, otherwise woodwork was painted to resemble hardwoods. The effect used to achieve this was called graining.

A painter gave the new wood three or four coats of plain paint. Then the grainer laid on his 'graining ground'. This varied according to the type of wood being imitated. The grainer would then draw various steel 'combs' across the surface while it was still wet. When it had dried it was sponged down with a mixture of beer and whitening before the final coat of varnish was applied. Graining could be applied to modest parts of the house such as internal doors and even the exterior of the cupboard under the stairs. For example, when Mr Straw's house was entirely refurbished in 1923, the cupboard under the stairs was grained with a 'flame' finish.[1] No furnisher's showroom was complete without sample panels of graining and, later, marbling on display. The examples shown here are taken from original sample panels.

Paint effects were subject to the dictates of fashion and the prejudices of the marketplace. As an effect was practised more widely it moved downmarket and the standard of execution tended to drop. Consequently it lost its appeal at the top end of the market. Each class avoided anything they thought their 'inferiors' were doing.

ABOVE: *even pianos were grained, if they were not walnut*

Marbling and graining had been fashionable throughout the eighteenth century. By the 1770s plastered walls were a recent development which awaited the attention of the paint brush. Ceilings were sometimes painted to resemble clouds. Painters were renowned for their 'three colours'; these were actually darker and lighter tints of the colour itself. Outside, stucco was given colour washes 'three times in oil' – at a cost of 8d a yard, 1s if sand was added.

During the Regency and early-Victorian periods new effects joined the repertoire: 'flame' was the most notable. During the 1820s ceilings began to be tinted rather than painted as clouds. During the mid-Victorian period anything that wasn't mahogany or oak was painted. The result was a plethora of 'fake' finishes, often poorly executed. Pianos were essential to a well-equipped house. They should have been walnut. If not, they were inevitably grained.

During the late nineteenth century graining became anathema to the up-to-date. Cast-iron baths and fireplaces were frequently 'japanned' – the application of marbling effects on metal.

ABOVE: *baths might be 'japanned' which was marbling on metal*

There had been a revival of stencilling since the 1880s led by Haywood & Sons. Such effects were favoured by the middle market, especially grass and reed designs. Friezes, either ready-made from frieze papers, or stencilled, were also popular. Painted effects provided a more exclusive alternative to wallpaper and plaster borders.

ABOVE: stencil decoration in
cream-white and warm brown
by Taylor Ingram

ABOVE RIGHT: a nursery with
a deep frieze (1906)

RIGHT: stencilled frieze for
a night nursery designed by
Florence Laverock (1901)

RIGHT: interior of a house
in Huddersfield with frieze
designed by Edgar Wood
(c.1901)

ABOVE: fireplace design to
be decorated with an enamel
panel from a sketch by Frank
Brangwyn (c.1901)

Painters' specialities also included staining and gilding. Robert Tressell described such a craftsman executing a 'Moorish' design:

> First of all, it would be necessary to take down the ugly plaster centre flower, with its crevices all filled up with old whitewash. The cornice was all right; it was, fortunately, a very simple one, with a deep cove and without many enrichments. Then, when the walls and the ceiling had been properly prepared, the ornamentation would be proceeded with: the walls divided into panels and arches containing painted designs and latticework, the panels of the door decorated in a similar manner; the mouldings of the door and window frames picked out with colours and gold, so as to be in character with the other work, the cove of the cornice, a dull yellow with a bold ornament in colour – gold was not advisable in the hollow because of the unequal distribution of the light, but some of the smaller mouldings of the cornice should be gold. On the ceiling there would be one large panel covered with an appropriate design in gold and colours, and surrounded by a wide margin or border. Great care would have to be used when it came to the gilding, because, while large masses of gilding were apt to look garish and in bad taste, a lot of the gold lines are ineffective, especially on a flat surface. Process by process he traced the work, and saw it advancing stage by stage until, finally, the large apartment was transformed and glorified.[2]

Walls were sub-divided into the dado, the part between it and the picture rail and the frieze between the picture rail and the cornice. The deep friezes of the Edwardian period invited decoration. *The Studio* featured stencilled decorations including a boudoir decorated with a frieze of the Water Babies designed by Winifred Horton (*see page 94*). Stencilled decorations and friezes were also highly desirable in nurseries. Individual frieze and stencil designs were regarded as 'handicraft, untouched by machinery', although a wide range of ready-made stencils were available to order in metal or paper. In 1901 Charles Holme expressed his approval:

> ... stencilling for walls, light hangings and subjects removed from immediate friction, is an instance of this; and here its transience is an element of charm, especially in the nursery where change is so welcome – for the children tire, more painfully than we realise, of durable surroundings. It need hardly be added that decoration of this kind should be carried out in materials proper to its spirit; the stencil in water colour, and on suitable paper rather than in a medium which assumes incongruous glaze. Canvas and silk, like the painted and panelled wall, demand a fuller decorative treatment ... making the best of slender opportunities, with limitations of structure, light and space.[3]

ABOVE: *ready-made stencil borders*

During the interwar period stencilling gave way to screenprinting, which made friezes and borders accessible to a wider market.

The lead compounds used in the enamel paints of the interwar period gave them very strong adhesion. But they took a long time to prepare. Despite this the exterior of a house could still be redecorated for as little as £5 in the 1930s.

ABOVE: *ready-made flowerpot stencil designs*

LEFT: *stencil design by Taylor Ingram*

Patterns

illiam Morris had died in 1896 but his work was to have a lasting influence on British interiors. He had established a classic tradition of pattern design based on floral motifs. In 1904 Muthesius stated:

> The father of the modern wallpaper is Morris. He devoted much of his energy to wallpaper and it was certainly through his wallpapers that he became known to the English people. Because he hated all modern manufacturing techniques, his wallpapers were not printed by machine but by hand ... he did not print them himself but had them done by the well-known firm of Jeffrey & Co Hand printed articles are, of course, fairly expensive. But the demand for really good quality is always so great in England that no one need shrink from producing expensive goods. Morris wallpapers became known far and wide.[1]

ABOVE: *advertisement for
Jeffrey & Co (1899)*

Morris had reverted to the traditional craft-based technique of block printing and evolved patterns suited to this. Morris's greatest achievements were in pattern design: wallpapers from 1864 followed by printed textiles from 1873. According to Muthesius two of his earliest designs, Daisy and Pomegranate, 'are as popular today (1904) as they were forty-five years ago when they first appeared.' After 1896 his company kept the tradition going through his successors such as John Henry Dearle, who took over as managing-director. But the archetypal pattern designer of both the Edwardian and interwar periods was C.F.A. Voysey. Voysey's designs were even simpler and flatter than those of Morris. Voysey had a number of aphorisms to make this point, including: 'Simplicity in decoration is one of the essential qualities without which no richness is possible.' Between 1893 and 1930 Voysey created hundreds of wallpaper designs for Essex & Co as well as textile designs for various manufacturers and retailers, including Liberty. In 1899 Essex & Co had joined Wall Paper Manufacturers (WPM). This was a joint stock company formed from an amalgamation of 31 factories. In 1923 Essex & Co became part of the Sanderson branch of WPM along with Jeffrey & Co. The wallpaper industry was becoming increasingly mechanised and specialised. By 1914, 140 different jobs were identifiable.

Shand Kydd was an independent company which was largely responsible for the fashion for frieze papers. By 1900 the firm employed five block-printers and twelve stencillers. There were other exponents of quality in Edwardian pattern design, such as the Silver Studio, who did not

ABOVE: *Bird and Rose,
designed by Voysey (1897)*

ABOVE: *Bird and Bramble,
designed by Voysey (1901)*

LEFT: *Edwardian frieze
papers (1911)*

PART FIVE: DETAILS

RIGHT: *a flat poppy design showing Voysey's influence from Alfred Chapman & Co wallpaper pattern book (1895)*

ABOVE: *Oak, a carpet design by Voysey*

RIGHT: *block-printed furnishing fabric designed by Lindsay Butterfield for G.P. & J. Baker (1903)*

FAR RIGHT: *roller printed furnishing fabric designed by Silver Studio for Liberty (c.1899)*

ABOVE: *cotton furnishing fabric designed by Silver Studio for Liberty (1900–05)*

reject commerce as adherents of the Arts & Crafts movement did. Arthur Silver had followed the example of Christopher Dresser by setting up the Silver Studio in 1880 at a time when most commercial pattern studios were French.

Voysey's influence was apparent in a 1903 block-printed furnishing fabric designed by Lindsay Butterfield for G.P. & J. Baker. Another example of Voysey's flat style came from an Alfred Chapman & Co wallpaper pattern book of 1895. In 1904 W. Shaw Sparrow proclaimed: 'the new wallpapers have been so cheap and plentiful. No spring cleaning is considered complete without a change of pattern and colour.'[2]

There were plenty of wallpapers at the lower end of the market. The cheapest papers were pulps in which the natural colour of the paper formed part of the final surface. The next cheapest were ground papers on which the whole paper was machine printed with the background colour before the final design was overprinted. Satin papers were polished or glazed before printing by rotary brushes; embossed or stamped papers might be grained in imitation of oak. Gilded, marbled or flocked papers were available in numerous combinations. Relief papers for dados, friezes and ceilings also saw much experimentation and development. In 1902, 'relief papers were legion in their variety.'[3] Anaglypta even employed Dresser to design patterns suitable for different surfaces.

By the end of the nineteenth century 'sanitary' coloured papers and fabrics were proudly advertised. 'Sanitary' papers were printed in oil-based inks and varnished so that the surface was washable. They were often used below the dado rail in halls and areas susceptible to hard wear but they were also available as wall and frieze papers. They were produced in lighter floral patterns for bedrooms. The non-toxic nature of the products was a prominent part of the sales pitch.

Special patterns for children and nurseries appeared which shared the lighter, brighter characteristics of the period. Ready-made products for walls and ceilings proliferated. A complete range existed, from fully moulded plaster to heavily embossed paper facsimiles.

LIBERTY ART FABRICS

About 1880 Liberty began to commission patterns from Dresser and from the Silver Studio. The textiles were sold as 'Liberty art fabrics', which became an advertising by-line asserting their superiority to rivals' products. By 1898 Liberty had their own shop in Paris as well as supplying L'Art Nouveau and other outlets. In Italy, Art Nouveau was known as 'Le Stile Liberty'.

By 1905 the British textile industry began to face competition from imported designs. This even alarmed English designers, like Harry Napper, who had previously been open to continental ideas. The resemblance of Art Nouveau to English designs made Frank Warner of Warner & Sons call it 'a continental nightmare of design and colour ... a vulgar parody on English Art'.

ABOVE: *Seagulls – silk and wool double cloth designed by Voysey for Alexander Morton & Co (1895–98)*

ABOVE: *a sanitary paper suitable for a bedroom (1891)*

ABOVE: *Hawkweed, a wallpaper designed by Lindsay Butterfield for Essex & Co (1902)*

LEFT: *Bo Peep (top) and Simple Simon (below) – nursery wallpapers designed by Will Owen (1910)*

Part Five: Details

RIGHT: *Art Deco abstract borders, printed in silver and gold with stencil infills by Hayward & Son (late 1920s – early 1930s)*

FAR RIGHT: *combination of patterned and plain papers within a border, in a hall (1938)*

RIGHT BELOW: *hearth rug design in a catalogue for Times Furnishing Company (1935)*

FAR RIGHT BELOW: *detail of a 'Crocus' corner (1934)*

ABOVE: *'Cactus' border (1937)*

RIGHT: *rug design by the Silver Studio (1934)*

INTERWAR PATTERNS

After 1925 Art Deco in the form of French patterns began to have a considerable impact on the English textile market; for example, Hayward & Son's abstract wallpaper borders. Great Britain was losing its position as the leading textile producer to foreign competition. The shrinking textile industry became cautious 'with a consequent decline in the whole level of floral design', according to textile designer Antony Hunt. The hearth became a focal point because its rug was the most striking element in the room. Rugs were often placed on plain brown carpets which meant that even designs in flat colours could catch the eye.

The wallpapers of the 1930s could be used in combinations of plain and patterned papers or with borders to enliven them. A patterned paper might be used to fill a panel as a contrast with the plainer paper used elsewhere. Narrow borders and matching 'corners' were popular. The patterns ranged from 'Jazz' abstract to floral. In 1934 John Line and Sons produced 'Crocus' which was both 'Jazz' and floral.

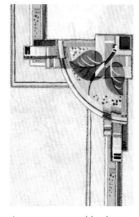

ABOVE: *corner and border (1934)*

ABOVE & LEFT: *rugs on a brown carpet in a recreation of a 1930s living room*

PART FIVE: DETAILS

RIGHT: *block-printed linen furnishing fabric designed by F. Gregory Brown for William Foxton & Co Ltd. This design won a gold medal at the Paris exposition in 1925*

FAR RIGHT: *screen printed linen furnishing fabric for Turnbull & Stockdale, designed by émigré German designer, Hans Aufseeser (1936)*

RIGHT: *roller printed cotton furnishing fabric designed by Minnie Mcleish for William Foxton & Co Ltd*

FAR RIGHT: *block printed on silk design by Charles Rennie Mackintosh for William Foxton & Co Ltd. (1918)*

RIGHT: *Crofton, rough weave cotton furnishing fabric, designed by Marianne Straub, for Helios (1938)*

FAR RIGHT: *Aircraft, screen printed rayon and linen furnishing fabric designed by Marion Dorn for Old Bleached Linen Co (1938)*

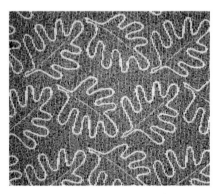

RIGHT: *Wychwood – screen printed cotton satin furnishing fabric designed by Noldi Soland for Helios (1939)*

FAR RIGHT: *colourways for textile designed by the Silver Studio (1934)*

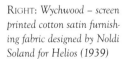

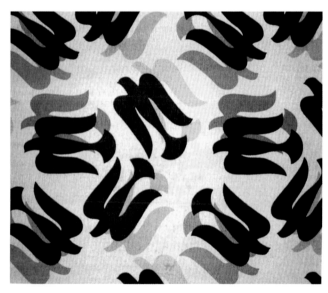
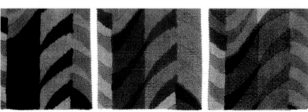

The only British firm to stand its ground against French and Austrian competition was William Foxton & Co. Ltd. One of their designs won a gold medal at the Paris exposition in 1925. Foxton, himself, was a founder member of the Design and Industries Association. Foxton was the only British company to produce designs by the Glasgow designer, Charles Rennie Mackintosh.

EMIGRE DESIGNERS

Modernism finally arrived with various émigrés such as the German designer Hans Aufseeser, who designed furnishing fabrics for Turnbull & Stockdale in 1936. Furnishing fabrics became increasingly important as the Modern movement influenced people to choose plain walls instead of patterned wallpapers. This was at the expense of the traditional floral patterns, but the Modern movement was more receptive to abstract and geometrical patterns. These factors contributed to the decline of companies such as Morris & Co. The combination of patterned fabrics and plain walls resulted in a common form of the compromise known as Moderne.

During the 1930s there was a revival of creativity in British textiles with companies such as Helios and Edinburgh Weavers. Helios was a progressive Bolton company established as an independent subsidiary of the Manchester firm of Barlow & Jones. The government introduced tariffs to protect the textile trade. The introduction of screen-printing coincided with a revival of block-printed textiles. Screen-printing was a development of stencilling. The new technique was cheaper than block-printing, with lower set-up costs; it was also suitable for short runs. During the interwar period screen-printing was manual.

Edinburgh Weavers developed textile patterns including Constructivist fabrics designed by Barbara Hepworth and Ben Nicholson. These used subtle colours and variations in tone. The use of a subdued palette and architectural patterns succeeded in creating a fashion for 'beigery' as exemplified by a Silver Studio design of 1935. Fabrics were available in various 'colourways'.

'Since 1928 the general tendency has been for paler and more uncommon colours,' Antony Hunt related, in 1937. 'The beige craze passed into one of still greater pallor and white and off-white became still more anaemic and flats like whited-sepulchres vaunted chalk-like chairs and pallid curtaining. Then, blood returning to the cheeks and money to the pockets, colour re-entered.'

Edward Bawden's approach to wallpaper was that of a graphic artist. He designed Woodpigeon for the Curwen Press in 1927. Curwen Press reproduced Bawden's designs by colour lithography on sheets rather than rolls of paper. Together with John Aldridge, Bawden produced the Bardfield Papers. This was a collection which included Moss, a 1939 design which combined Surrealism with a Regency-style pattern.

ABOVE: *Woodpigeon, designed by Edward Bawden for the Curwen Press (c.1927)*

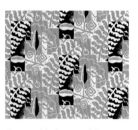

ABOVE: *block-printed linen furnishing fabric, designed by Bernard Adeney for Allan Walton textiles (c.1931–32)*

ABOVE: *Torro, a screen printed cotton furnishing fabric designed by Michael O'Connell for Edinburgh Weavers (c.1939)*

LEFT: *Moss, one of the Bardfield Papers, designed by John Aldridge (1939)*

FAR LEFT: *a textile design by Silver Studio which exemplified 'beigery' (1935)*

PART FIVE: DETAILS

RIGHT & MIDDLE RIGHT: *majolica porch tiles (c.1910)*

FAR RIGHT (TOP): *Doulton encaustic floor tiles (c.1900)*

FAR RIGHT (BELOW): *tiled fireplace cheeks and hearth (c.1910)*

BELOW RIGHT: *doorstep and front path (1910)*

ABOVE: *advertisement for Doulton ceramic products (1909)*

RIGHT: *mosaic tile floor from the Pilkington Company (c.1910)*

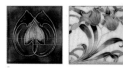

ABOVE: *Minton tiles (c.1905)*

27
Tiles

nglazed and glazed tiles were regular features of Edwardian and interwar houses, both indoors and outdoors. They were used in kitchens, conservatories, hallways and bathrooms. Tiled hearths and grates were also widespread.

A great expansion in the use of tiles had come in the 1850s, after the invention of the encaustic tile in 1840. Ceramic tiles greatly increased in use from 1871 onwards, especially in bathrooms because of their hygienic properties. By the late 1870s tiles were being used in halls up to the dado rail. The range of designs expanded to include Middle Eastern patterns and motifs. Later the undulating patterns of the 'New Art' also appeared as glazed ceramics, especially in porches and fireplaces as well as in hallways.

There was a vast increase in demand for tiles due to late Victorian and Edwardian house building. Builders bought in bulk from specialist producers such as Maw and Co. or builders merchants like Young and Marten.

Ceramic tiles were decorative, adaptable and hygienic. They provided cheap, up-to-date, colourful and easy to clean surfaces of any size. Ceramic wall and floor tiling was popular in kitchens, bathrooms, conservatories and hallways. Tiled hearths and grates enhanced reception rooms. Furnival reported an enormous demand for 'crimson-enamelled tiles, especially in the six by six inch briquette pattern'. They 'proved particularly suitable for dining-room and hall hearths'.[1]

Tiles had the advantage of being impervious to frost and were used outdoors for the forecourt and doorstep as well as porch walls where they might provide 'such permanent decoration which may "make or mar" the first glimpse of the home'.[2]

Tiled hearths were becoming popular. 'Hardly a mansion or even a dwelling-house, is now built without being fitted with glazed tile hearths of one kind or another.'[3] About 1900 complete sets of hearth tiles were available from companies such as Gibbons, Hinton and Co who were offering embossed and flat surface majolica.

Muthesius noted: 'there is now a steady demand for ceramic mosaic' for 'better class work such as vestibules, large conservatories, hotel-entrances, shop doorways and the like'. The installation of tiles and mosaics was elevated into a specialised trade. Furnival noted that ceramic came to be used for entire fire surrounds not just the cheeks and hearth. The surrounds were composed of specially curved or moulded briquettes 'available in a large variety of designs and glazes or enamelled in equally profuse variety'.[4]

Technical developments such as the invention of lead-free glazes brought about visual changes. These included hand painting and transfer-printing, relief moulded majolica glazing and tube lining which could be used to reproduce styles from the Aesthetic Movement to Art Nouveau, Adam or plain coloured tiles.

The top of the range in ceramic flooring was mosaic pavement which was available from firms like Doulton and Co of Lambeth. Mrs Humphry described it as 'a cheap yet novel and beautiful artistic flooring'. Demand for marble tesserae increased until 'some ten thousand tons of marble tesserae are annually imported into England ... it can now be laid down for but a few shillings per square yard'.[5]

ABOVE: *Georgian plain floor tiles (c.1750)*

ABOVE: *encaustic tiles*

ABOVE: *'New Art' tiles (1900–05)*

ABOVE: *transfer printed tiles (c.1885)*

RIGHT : *tesselated tiles by Gibbon, Hinton and Co (c.1910)*

ABOVE: *the Carter fireplace (1920)*

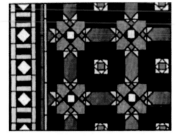

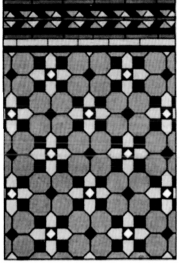

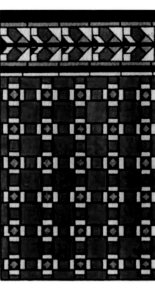

ABOVE: *tiled fireplace surrounds (1920s)*

The pattern of a mosaic pavement was drawn on paper, in reverse, at the tile works. The paper was cut into manageable sections for laying. The tesserae were placed face down onto the paper, glued ready to be taken to the site where they would be laid.

Medium-sized houses usually had tessellated flooring. This was composed of standard sized and shaped ceramic pieces which could be fitted together to form geometrical patterns to suit the space. Tessellated floors were composed of various types of dust pressed tile: either plain colours, vitreous or encaustic. Plain colours were made from the natural colours of the clay, usually red or buff. A metallic oxide such as manganese could be added to produce black, chocolate, greys or drab, salmon or fawn. Vitreous tiles were produced from feldspar, ball clay, china clay, Cornish china, stone and flint, which produced a white tile. Stains could be added to form blue or green. Pale pink and silver grey could also be made in this way but were more expensive and therefore rarer. Most hall floors used plain or vitreous tiles.

ABOVE: *fireplace with an entirely tiled surround, designed by Voysey (c.1910)*

The tiles were laid out on a prepared cement surface to check the fit, then guide strips were positioned in sections eighteen to thirty inches apart. Mortar was spread between them and levelled with a screed notched to allow for the tile thickness. When the mortar was stiff the tiles were laid and tamped down until they were level with the height of the guide strips. The guides were removed and work would begin on the next section. When the floor was complete the joints were grouted with pure cement and the excess rubbed off with sawdust.

ABOVE: *fireplace with tiled surround, at The Orchards, Chorleywood, designed by Voysey (1900)*

Wall tiling was done in a similar way, although the practice of 'buttering' the backs of individual tiles with mortar before setting them was also employed.

There were regional preferences for the colours of floor tiles. In Cardiff multicoloured designs were more popular than black and white. In London there was 'a distinct preference shown for black and white tiles; these being used most largely for outside forecourts, porches, and halls, also for scullery floors and underground conveniences.'[6]

Tiles had been set in the splayed sides of the fireplace surround since the late nineteenth century. Voysey and others led the way towards entirely tiled surrounds. He designed numerous fireplaces with entire glazed surrounds beneath high mantels, including those in his own home, The Orchards, Chorleywood.

ABOVE: *bathroom tiled up to the dado (1931)*

Around 1906 tiles were being integrated into ready-made fireplaces with tiled panels and hearths. W. Shaw Sparrow expressed his approval of such schemes as having 'a unity of materials welded into one intention by skilful manipulation, a charming combination of wood, metal, tiles or marble properly selected and fittingly used'. [7]

INTERWAR TILES

After the war, tile companies such as Carter & Co. Ltd of Poole, Dorset, were still offering fully integrated fireplace units. In 1920 the Carter Fireplace was advertised with surround, arch, hearth and back of tiled briquettes. It was claimed to be 'the last word in fuel efficiency'. Carter & Co. claimed that: 'Attractive and distinctive appearance, hygienic considerations and the ease with which cleanliness can be maintained are all powerful arguments for the wider use of tiles in domestic architecture for Floors and Walls.'

ABOVE: *bathroom tiled up to door height, with borders and coloured accent tiles (1936)*

The pre-war trend towards fully tiled surrounds became a feature of 1920s fireplaces, although the Art Deco influence made the surrounds less pictorial and more architectural. They also had to compete with other materials such as marble and slate.

By the 1930s fireplaces were becoming plainer and more functional. Fireplace surrounds might be made from marble and slate, with the inner fireplace of cast iron and fireclay.

In the bathroom tiling up to dado height was essential. In fact, the higher the tiles reached the better – although tiling up to door height was expensive. Best of all, and even more costly, was tiling the entire wall. Tiles became plainer. White was standard in local authority housing. Decorated or coloured tiles were used to provide accents of colour in geometric patterns or borders. Plain coloured tiles could match the colour of the bathroom suite.

ABOVE: *bathroom with coloured tiles (1930s)*

PART FIVE: DETAILS

FAR RIGHT: *cartoon of a design in stained glass for a hall window by Frank Brangwyn (c.1900)*

RIGHT: *'New Art' stained glass (c.1917)*

ABOVE: *'leaded glass' window in Worksop (c.1905)*

RIGHT: *front door with 'leaded glass' on side lights, fanlight and upper lights (1885)*

ABOVE: *'New Art' designs on fanlight and upper lights (c.1910)*

Stained & Coloured Glass

 tained glass 'is a decorative essential of the highest order', wrote the architect, John Cash, around 1910. He considered it to be both useful and beautiful in its own right, as valuable as wallpapers, good furniture, table glass and pictures:

Stained glass is a very comprehensive title to most people, if not to the glass stainer himself. It ranges from the flattest and most uninteresting of tinted squares to the largest and most elaborate of cathedral windows; all are mistakenly classed under the same heading. Unfortunately it is a subject difficult of illustration by any known process. Mere black and white is quite inadequate, and even with colour-printing both scale and transparency are lost, and transparency is perhaps its most essential quality. The play of light within the thick glass and the varied richness of the colour effects are in themselves delightful, but when 'framed in a suitable fretwork of thick lead lines, designed by one who understands his craft, stained glass is a decorative essential of the highest order – useful enough too, for it may shut out a distasteful view and its beauty be still an attraction.[1]

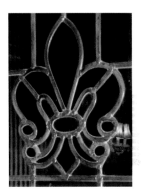

ABOVE: *'leaded glass' (c.1900)*

By 1900 stained glass had already filtered down from the expensive designs of the architects to more widely available commercial products such as 'cathedral windows' or bull's eye glass. *Cassell's Household Guide* (1912) noted 'many modern windows have an upper division either of decorative lead-lights or bull's eye glass, or sometimes merely plain glass in smaller panes.' In terms of domestic architecture 'cathedral windows' meant large windows lighting hall staircases. By 1915 these could be found in four-bedroom suburban houses. Stained glass was usually located around the front door and the hall of both large and medium-sized houses. Stained glass added to the impression of greater space in the vestibules and entrance halls of Edwardian houses. Stained glass windows might also form part of an inglenook or similar feature situated towards the front of the house. Edwardians referred to it as 'leaded glass' or leaded lights. It was the pattern of the glazing which was important. Coloured glass was an added attraction. An advertisement of 1910 claimed: 'a high class leaded art glass window adds to the beauty of the interior of a home ... the leaded art glass designs as viewed from the street also add much to the appearance of a house.'[2]

ABOVE: *front door with 'New Art' designs on upper lights and fanlight (c.1901)*

The ready availability of stained glass for speculatively built houses brought the usual scorn from architects. In 1895 Baillie-Scott warned that 'the average stock patterns of the manufacturer are more suggestive of the gin-palace than the private house, and should be carefully avoided'. He suggested that it was better 'to introduce in a pane of small squares or diamonds of clear glass a small heraldic or floral design in rich colouring, which in such a setting will have a brilliant jewel -like effect.'[3]

After 1900 designs altered from simple patterns of tulip, rose or heart motifs to the sinuous forms of the 'New Art'. Manufacturers came up with alternatives such as a glass screen from Powell and Cottier or Young and Marten Ltd's 'Lithoglas Transparencies in imitation of Stained Glass for Window decoration.'

ABOVE: *heraldic device in 'leaded glass' (c.1900)*

INTERWAR STAINED GLASS

Patterned glazing remained popular during the interwar period. This was usually achieved by installing leaded lights. Small pieces of glass called quarries were carried by 'H' section lead strips called cames. These could be as little as three sixteenths of an inch wide. Each quarry was inserted into the grooves in the cames, cemented in place with a mixture of plaster of Paris, linseed oil and lamp black, then the lead wings were folded back on to the surface of the glass.

Coloured glass was of two types: pot metal and flashed glass. Pot metal was uniformly coloured throughout. Flashed glass was clear glass with a coloured coating on one side. The central panel of a leaded light could be painted. Collages of flowers or animals were popular. This treatment was often reserved for the most prestigious application in the whole house. This was usually the upper panel, or panels, of the front door. The painted glass was made durable by firing after it had been painted.

The colours used for stained glass came from metallic oxides: reds from iron oxide, blues from cobalt, zaffre and copper, greens used iron oxide, peroxide of copper and chromium oxide. Tinted glass had trade names such as Opal glass, Cathedral glass and Opalescent glass.

The upper lights of interwar segmental bay windows might be embellished by decoration in coloured glass. This could be in addition to the fanlight, side lights and upper light of the front door. The archetypal interwar design for the upper light of the front door was the sunrise motif. By the 1930s embellishments to bay windows included Art Deco motifs such as chevrons. Simple diamonds of plain coloured glass could be added at the junction of the cames.

OPPOSITE: *Art Deco chevrons on the upper lights of the bay windows of a semi-detached pair in a Manchester suburb (c.1934)*

ABOVE: *plain glass diamonds at the junction of the cames of a bay window (c.1934)*

LEFT: *stained glass upper and side lights of a detached house (1933–36)*

ABOVE: *re-creation of the archetypal sunrise motif on the upper light of a front door*

ABOVE: *Art Deco motif on the upper lights of a bay window (c.1932)*

223

PART FIVE: DETAILS

RIGHT: *the sub-divisions of the wall were the equivalents of the parts of a classical column*

FAR RIGHT: *dado rail on the stairs of a house built c.1901*

ABOVE: *re-creation of an 1890s interior sub-divided into dado, wall and cornice*

cornice

frieze

wall

dado

RIGHT: *frieze and panelled wall of a dining room (1909)*

MIDDLE RIGHT: *stencilled frieze of a drawing room (1909)*

FAR RIGHT: *frieze and wall of a study (1909)*

ABOVE: *an interior with a plaster cornice, plain frieze and a plate rail (c.1906)*

29

Walls

ABOVE: *re-creation of the chair rail in an eighteenth-century interior*

nternal walls were divided horizontally into different sections for practical and decorative reasons. During the Edwardian period there were revivals of the earlier fashions for dado and picture rails. These rails sub-divided the wall between the skirting and the cornice. These traditional sub-divisions continued into the interwar period until a new fashion for plain walls left only the skirting which covered the junction of the wall and the floor.

The cornice covered the join between the wall and the ceiling. The architrave covered the junction of doors and walls.

The dado or chair rail had been introduced in the late eighteenth century to protect newly plastered walls from damage when chairs were placed up against them. A rail was fixed to the wall at the height of the back of a chair, about three feet above the floor. The part of the wall below the chair rail became known as the dado. Before the Regency period chairs and tables were moved into the centre of the room when required for dining. Once a room was permanently assigned to dining, chairs remained at the table and the chair rail became redundant.

ABOVE: *re-creation of a mid-Victorian interior with continuous wall from skirting to cornice and a brass picture rail*

The picture rail had been introduced in dining rooms and studies during the Regency and early Victorian periods. In medium-sized houses it was an iron or brass rod which ran round the room just below the cornice. By the mid-Victorian period, however, the wall was continuous from skirting to cornice.

Muthesius reported: 'In place of the Victorian papered wall that ran from floor to ceiling, they revived the dado. It became so important to the aestheticism of the 1880s as to be found almost indispensable to an artistic room. No less importance was attached to the frieze.'[1] The sub-divisions of the wall were equivalent to the parts of a classical column. These separations could be achieved by using wallpapers. Ready-made frieze papers became available. Speculative builders realised that the addition of a few carefully placed mouldings could make a house fashionable and saleable. 'No middle class house was considered perfect without it ... the lady whose rooms had dadoes looked down upon the lady who had none.'[2] Muthesius continued: 'The wall above the dado is usually painted, or it may be plastered, either colour washed or with a stencilled pattern ... larger rooms may have another, smaller frieze at the top, which then belongs rather to the ceiling and is separated from the main part of the wall by a picture-rail.'[3]

ABOVE: *plate rail in the dining room of a house in Barnt Green, Worcestershire (c.1901)*

The part between the cornice and the picture rail became the frieze. During the Edwardian period the depth of the frieze varied. Deep friezes invited further decorative treatment such as stencilling. Cheaper moulded wooden rails replaced the metal rods from which pictures were suspended. Muthesius remarked that picture rails with hooks were an English feature worth emulating. Cottage style encouraged a vernacular feature similar to the picture rail – the plate rail. Muthesius noted that panelling above head height terminated in a shelf 'on which decorative porcelain, pictures etc may be stood'.[4]

RIGHT: *an Edwardian hallway with a high rail at waist height*

ABOVE: *light coloured neo-Georgian panelling in the hall of Codicote Lodge, Hertfordshire (c.1920)*

ABOVE: *the dining room at Codicote Lodge (c.1920)*

RIGHT: *the drawing room at Kerfield House, Knutsford, Cheshire (c.1920)*

ABOVE: *neo-Georgian panelling in a Westminster drawing-room with fitted display cabinets (1920)*

The neo-Georgian revival included the re-introduction of panelling which was subdivided in the same way. It was painted in light colours, as in the hall at Codicote Lodge, Hertfordshire.

At The Orchards, Chorleywood, Voysey's design featured plain deep friezes with neither dado nor cornice. Only large houses could really support both dado and picture rail, so it was usually a choice between them. Picture rails were more common in reception rooms than dado rails.

The dado rail was considered necessary in the hall where impervious materials such as tiles or raised papers such as Anaglypta or Lincrusta might be fitted below it. By the Edwardian period the hall rail had been raised above waist height to protect the wall from being splashed by wet or muddy clothes. Fitted furniture conformed to the sub-division of the wall, for example, in the morning-room of Heathcote, Ilkley. Other architectural features could continue the line of the picture rail or the dado.

The bathroom required hygienic tiles at least up to dado height. The Edwardian bathroom had an even higher 'splash' rail and might also have tiles to the top of the wall. A scheme of 1909 suggested that the real sub-division was between the tiled part and the rest: 'dado of white tiles; pink and white paper above'.[5] Interwar bathrooms continued to try to be functional and hygienic. The sub-division between the tiled part and the rest became more marked as borders The use of occasional coloured tiles as an accent became fashionable. (see chapter 21 Bathrooms)

The neo-Georgian revival continued during the interwar period with lightly coloured panelled interiors such as the drawing room of Kerfield House, Knutsford, Cheshire, which was remodelled around 1920. At the same time several newly built houses in Westminster were given similar interiors. One had fitted display cabinets between the dado rail and the cornice.

The fashion for wallpaper borders sub-divided the wall into panel and background. The modern influence resulted in sitting-rooms of the 1930s with plain walls in pale colours without any cornice and simple skirting.

ABOVE: *hall of The Orchards, Chorleywood (c.1900)*

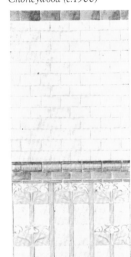

ABOVE: *bathroom tiles from the Pilkington company (c.1910)*

ABOVE: *fitted furniture in the morning-room of Heathcote, Ilkley, Yorkshire*

LEFT: *re-creation of a 1930s interior with plain wall and skirting*

PART FIVE: DETAILS

RIGHT: *basic shapes of mouldings*

FAR RIGHT: *re-creation of late seventeenth-century painted panelling*

ABOVE: *plaster cornice (c.1900)*

FAR RIGHT: *re-creation of mid-eighteenth-century painted panelling*

ABOVE: *panelling (c.1900)*

RIGHT: *re-creation of an Edwardian door surround and picture rail (Geffrye museum)*

Fillet (supporting element)

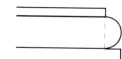

Corona – large fillet

Bead (right) cocked bead

Sunk bead

Torus same as bead but larger

Torus was always accompanied by a fillet

Ovolo convex of equal height and projection (left) unequal (right)

Cavetto (concave)

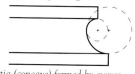

Scotia (concave) formed by curves with two different centres

Cyma recta of equal projection

Cyma recta of unequal projection

Cyma recta quirked with a fillet

Cyma recta quirked with a beaded fillet

30

Mouldings

The Edwardian neo-Georgian revival was based on late seventeenth-century and early Georgian forms. Naturally the mouldings used conformed to this. The original Georgian craftsmen had followed pattern books which were in circulation at the time. Edwardian producers of mouldings such as H. Gibbon and Sons, Cardiff, were able to reproduce the same forms much more economically using new machinery and imported timber.

Edwardian trade catalogues such as Jewson's displayed a vast selection of mouldings for a wide range of markets. These included over one hundred designs for architraves, thirty-three designs for skirtings and similar numbers for dado, picture rail and panel mouldings. They were produced in different sizes and sets. 'These mouldings which have been specially designed for use are arranged in series ... [which] enables you to have all mouldings alike throughout the house.' [1] As the use of machine-made mouldings spread so did criticism which condemned the 'meaningless assemblage of hollows and rounds that do duty for mouldings ... thanks mainly to the exigencies of machine production.' [2] By 1914 this kind of criticism resulted in a preference for simple mouldings, so that the catalogue prices of simple and complex mouldings were the same.

Panelling in wood such as oak or teak was fashionable around 1900. After 1905 panelling and plate rails filtered down into speculatively built houses in simplified forms. Before 1910 panelling retained its natural finish, but after 1910 neo-Georgian panelling was painted as the originals had been. Large houses had skirtings made of two pieces, but medium-sized houses had skirtings made from a single piece. Machines in use could cut any kind of profile but the forms used during the Edwardian period generally followed classical precedents.

The shape of mouldings was ultimately derived from the temple architecture of ancient Greece. where these features originally served a purpose as well as being decorative. The cornice covered the join between the roof and the wall and was designed to throw the rainwater off the wall; the fillets acted as drip-moulds. When transferred to Edwardian interiors, similar shapes continued to be used on architraves, covering the junction of doors and windows with wall and skirting. Architraves were also used on fireplace surrounds.

Mouldings appeared complex but were actually composed of several basic elements. These were variations on the flat-faced, right-angled fillet and the curved quadrant.

The quadrant was either concave or convex. The curve could be undercut to emphasise it by throwing a shadow. This was called quirking. Curves were used in combination with each other to build up distinctive forms, such as the cyma recta or convex curve. Shapes could also be concave rather than projecting. This was called cavetto.

The flat fillet served as punctuation to the curved mouldings. It varied in size in proportion to the quadrants, depending on whether it was a supporting or a main element.

Ceiling mouldings consisted of central decorations, borders, cornice, coving – even a wall frieze below the cornice. They were cast from plaster or alternatives such as fibrous plaster panels.

ABOVE: *a panelled interior by Morris & Co. (1901)*

ABOVE: *advertisement for Compoboard, a plaster alternative (1901)*

PART FIVE: DETAILS

RIGHT: *bolection moulding shapes*

FAR RIGHT: *bolection architrave*

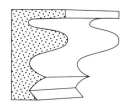 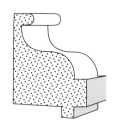 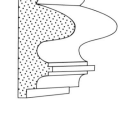 

RIGHT: *original Georgian moulding shapes*

FAR RIGHT: *reeded moulding*

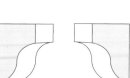 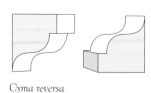 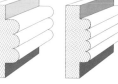

Cyma recta

Cyma reversa

Reeded mouldings

RIGHT: *neo-Georgian moulding shapes*

FAR RIGHT: *torus skirting*

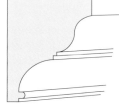   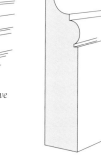 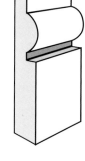

Cornice and coving

Dado

Architrave

Skirting

Torus skirting

ABOVE: *reeded mouldings on a closed stair string with cyma reversa mouldings on a cupboard below the stairs from a house built in 1910*

RIGHT: *fireplace surround (c.1900) with cyma reversa mouldings*

ABOVE: *cross section of 'frog' handrail moulding*

Wood accounted for the rest – architrave, panel decorations, window mouldings, picture rails, plate rails, chair rails and skirting. Around 1900 reeded mouldings, which had been popular during the Regency period, still appeared occasionally on stair strings or panelling.

The shapes were referred to by numerous names. Ovolo, which simply meant a convex quadrant, was also known as echinus. (In Latin, ovolo means egg, and echinus means the shell of a chestnut.) Cyma reversa was often called 'ogee'. So was cyma recta which was not appropriate because cyma recta does not follow an ogee curve. The cyma recta gave a lighter look than its predecessor, the bolection.

PERIOD CHARACTERISTICS

Late Georgian handbooks showed cyma recta mouldings for 'Architraves, Frize & Cornices for doors or windows'. The Edwardian neo-Georgian revival preferred the bolection because it was based on early Georgian forms rather than the discredited late Georgian.

Bolection had been the characteristic moulding of early Georgian wooden panelling. Bolection was a deeply quirked cyma reversa. Georgian handbooks had recommended that the width of an architrave was one sixth of that of the door opening itself. This proportion always decreased relative to the size of the house.

The mid-Victorian look was altogether darker and heavier. The most popular moulding was the cyma reversa. Doors had four panels which often accommodated mouldings. They were finished in dark paint. The torus design was widely used for skirting boards. The 'frog' handrail to the stairs was often the only bit of hardwood in the house and was proudly exposed.

Towards the end of the nineteenth century and throughout the Edwardian period the earlier Georgian preferences for bolection and cyma recta re-asserted themselves.

During the interwar period speculatively built houses continued to use traditional mouldings. Perhaps the only interwar innovation in terms of mouldings came in the form of plastic products such as Bakelite door handles which had stepped edges. Book cases were also stepped but they had plain edges, and skirting often only had a chamfered top.

ABOVE: *a design with teak panelling up to the plate rail (c.1901)*

ABOVE: *interwar mouldings – Bakelite door handles with stepped edges*

LEFT: *plaster swags on a fireplace surround designed by Baillie-Scott (1921)*

RIGHT: *Artefacts montage*

ABOVE: *Key to Artefacts
montage – see chapters
on Social & Economic
Background, Telephone &
Wireless, Lighting & Electrical
Appliances and Colours*
1 *Cadbury's Cocoa Essence
(c.1908)*
2 *Colmans 1905 poster*
3 *poster promoting suburbs
served by the new Underground
Railway (1909)*
4 *Radio Times (1938)*
5 *poster promoting Southern
electric trains (1935)*
6 *Sunlight Soap (1885
onwards)*
7 *BVC non-electric vacuum
cleaner (1908)*
8 *Philips 930A wireless
(1930)*
9 *Davis Estates (1938)*
10 *Oxo cubes tin (c.1930)*
11 *Pye wireless (1932)*
12 *poster advertising
electrification of Southern
railways (c.1932)*
13 *illustration from* Modern
Furnishing and Decoration
by Derek Patmore (1936)
14 *Metro-Land promotional
publication (c.1928)*
15 *Smoothwell electric iron
(c.1928)*
16 *Erinoid samples (c.1936)*
17 *Nestlé 'Honey Queen' milk
chocolate bar (c.1937)*
18 *illustration from a Twyfords
catalogue (c.1935)*
19 *Vac-Tric de luxe (c.1937)*
20 *Lifebuoy Carbolic soap
(1894 onwards)*

BIOGRAPHIES

BAILLIE-SCOTT, MACKAY HUGH (1865–1945) Born in Ramsgate, his early training was in Bath. In 1889 he moved to the Isle of Man, where he set up his own architectural practice. He knew and worked with the artist and designer Archibald Knox on some of his interior design features. He exhibited furniture, metalwork and wallpaper at the 1896 Arts & Crafts Exhibition. He returned to England in 1901, where he designed suburban homes, including the Tudors, Gerrards Cross (1921) until 1939. He favoured the use of structural timbers. Many of his designs were published in Builder's Journal, Building News and The Studio. *See* HALF-TIMBERED.

ABOVE: *electrolier designed by W.A.S. Benson*

BENSON, WILLIAM ARTHUR SMITH (1854–1924) Benson met William Morris while he was working as an architect in the office of Basil Champneys. In 1880 he set up a metalworking workshop. His business grew into a well-equipped factory. From 1887 he had a shop in Bond Street. Benson was a pioneer in the design of electric light fittings. Muthesius regarded him as 'the leading spirit in electric lighting-appliances'. He designed numerous electric light fittings for Morris & Co. – including commissions such as Standen, Sussex. He was an active founder member of the Art Workers' Guild, but as a metalworker he was more open to mechanisation than other Arts & Crafts designers, such as Walter Crane. After Morris' death, Benson took over as chairman of Morris & Co. In 1914 he became a founder member of the Design & Industries Association.

BLOMFIELD, REGINALD (1856–1942) Educated at Haileybury and at Exeter College Oxford, in 1881 he trained as an architect in the office of his uncle Sir Arthur Blomfield and at the Royal Academy. In 1883 he set up on his own as an architect He became one of the early members of the Art Workers Guild. His architectural practice mainly consisted of country houses. He was also a prolific writer on the history of architecture and gardening; his advocacy of the formal garden led him into conflict with William Robinson. In 1913 he was awarded the RIBA Gold Medal and was elected to the Royal Academy in 1914.

ABOVE: *twisted vase designed by Christopher Dresser (1892–95)*

CLIFF, CLARICE (1899–1970) interwar ceramic designer and artist. Her designs were so bright and colourful some considered them gaudy. She and Susie Cooper were the outstanding Art Deco ceramic designers. *See* COOPER, SUSIE.

COOPER, SUSIE (1902–1995) interwar ceramic designer who began as a paintress at A.E. Gray pottery. She became the resident designer. In 1929 she set up her own company which introduced new shapes and lithographed transfer patterns including the Kestrel shape (1932), and her most famous lithograph pattern, 'Dresden Spray.' (1935)

DRESSER, CHRISTOPHER (1834–1904) Trained at the Government Art Schools. He was one of the few designers who was not also an architect. Dresser managed a commercial art studio. He produced designs for over fifty companies. He was described by *The Studio* magazine in 1899 as 'the greatest of commercial designers'. Some of his designs were so avant garde that they were never reproduced. His influence on design was perpetuated by his publications *Principles of Decorative Design* (1873) and *Studies in Design* (1876). He produced the botanical drawings for Owen Jones' *Grammar of Ornament*. On his return from Japan, in 1882, he published a book, *Japan, its Architecture, Art & Art Manufacture*.

ABOVE: *yellow glass vase designed by Christopher Dresser (1892–96)*

FORSTER, E.M. (1879–1970) Edwardian and interwar novelist, a member of the Bloomsbury Group and a friend of Virginia Woolf, Leonard Woolf, Lytton Strachey, and Roger Fry. *Howard's End* (1910) was his first major success. His most famous novels were *A Room with a View* (1908) and *A Passage to India* (1924).

ABOVE: *Goddards,
Godalming, Surrey, garden
designed by Gertrude Jekyll,
house by Lutyens*

ABOVE: *Inigo Jones*

ABOVE: *Deanery Gardens,
designed by Lutyens, for
Edward Hudson, owner of*
Country Life *(1901)*

GALSWORTHY JOHN (1867–1933) author of a series of novels about a property owning family – the Forsytes. The Forsyte saga began with *The Man of Property* (1906) and continued through the interwar years until *Over the River* (1933).

HOLME, CHARLES (1848–1923) textile manufacturer, entrepreneur and author of numerous books on art. He formed a partnership with Christopher Dresser to deal in Japanese and oriental goods. Holme acquired several houses including the Manor House, Upton Grey, Hampshire. He was also the founder and owner of *The Studio* magazine. *See* STUDIO, THE

JEKYLL, GERTRUDE (1843–1932) Gertrude Jekyll trained at the South Kensington School of Art and embarked on a successful career as an artist and craftswoman. At first she worked in a variety of media including photography and embroidery. But her deteriorating eyesight forced her to concentrate on horticulture. She was influenced by Robinson and contributed to his publications as well as other magazines such as Country Life and The Garden. She added an artist's use of colour, texture and form to Robinson's ideas.

Jekyll first met the architect Edwin Lutyens in 1889 when she was 48 and he was 20. They worked together on numerous commissions as garden designer and architect. She introduced Lutyens to some of his first clients, and he designed her own house, Munstead Wood, in 1896. She designed some 300 gardens, including 100 with Lutyens. She became a household name through her gardens, books and articles. Wood and Garden (1899) was one of her most influential publications. Muthesius described her as 'Miss Jekyll, the celebrated writer on gardens.' He remarked on her 'strong preference for the woodland garden'

JONES, INIGO (1573–1652) the first English architect to apply the Palladian approach to classical proportions. Jones was the King's Surveyor. One of his innovations was the first up-market terraced housing in Covent Garden, London.

LUTYENS, EDWIN (1869–1944) Lutyens studied architecture at South Kensington School of Art, from 1885 to 1887. After college he joined the Ernest George and Harold Ainsworth Peto architectural practice. He began his own practice in 1888, his first commission being a private house at Crooksbury, Farnham, Surrey. During this work, he met the garden designer and horticulturalist Gertrude Jekyll. In 1896 he began work on a house for Jekyll at Munstead Wood, Godalming, Surrey.

Lutyens' fame grew largely through the popularity of the new lifestyle magazine *Country Life* created by Edward Hudson, which featured many of his house designs. Hudson commissioned Lutyens for a number of projects, including Deanery Garden, Sonning, Berkshire, in 1901.

Initially, his designs utilised the vernacular forms, but about 1906 his work became more classical in style. His commissions varied from private houses, initially, followed by two churches for Hampstead Garden Suburb, London, to Castle Drogo, Drewsteignton, Devon, and on to his contributions to India's new imperial capital New Delhi. After the First World War, he was involved with the creation of monuments to commemorate the fallen, including the Cenotaph, Westminster. He was knighted in 1918, and elected to the Royal Academy in 1921.

MORRIS, WILLIAM (1834–1896) Born into a wealthy family in Walthamstow and educated at Marlborough School, Morris went up to Exeter College, Oxford, to study theology. There he met fellow student, Edward Burne-Jones. They both read Ruskin, in particular The Stones of Venice (1853), in which Ruskin argued that 'art was an expression of man's pleasure in labour'. Both young men were convinced by Ruskin's opinion that artists should learn craft skills and master techniques of production as well as paint pictures and produce designs.

They left university to pursue careers in art. Morris went to work at the offices of the architect G.E. Street, and Burne-Jones began to paint. Philip Webb was already chief clerk for Street.

Morris soon met Dante Gabriel Rossetti, who persuaded him to paint. In 1857 Morris, Rossetti and Burne-Jones were involved in redecorating the Oxford Union debating hall. Here he met his future wife Jane Burden.

In the summer of 1860 Morris and his wife moved into the Red House, Bexleyheath, Kent. The house was designed for Morris by Philip Webb. Morris recalled: 'I got a friend to build me a house in a very medieval spirit in which I lived for five years, and set myself to decorating it. We found, I and my friend ... that all the minor arts were in a state of complete degradation ... and accordingly in 1861 with the conceited courage of a young man set myself to reforming all that, and started a firm for producing decorative articles.'

ABOVE: *Strawberry Thief, a wallpaper designed by William Morris in 1883*

In 1883 the *Spectator* pronounced 'Morris has become a household word for all who wish their material surroundings to be beautiful yet appropriate for homely use.' It continued 'all the better kinds of designs in the shops, as far as they are good, are cribs from Morris, just sufficiently altered to prevent unpleasantness'.

Through his leadership and his example, Morris became one of the authorities of the Arts & Crafts movement. Other members of the movement quoted him to justify their opinions, even Walter Crane, the President of the Arts & Crafts Exhibition Society. *See* MORRIS & Co

ABOVE: *Windrush was designed by Morris in 1883*

MUTHESIUS, HERMANN (1861–1927) Muthesius was a German architect attached to the German embassy as a cultural attaché. He lived in London from 1896 to 1903. He admired English domestic architecture and interiors. Muthesius wrote about the English house in the hope that his own countrymen could learn from it, for example about sanitation. In 1904, his investigations were published in Berlin, in three volumes, as *Das Englische Haus* (*The English House*). It is a record of English domestic architecture and applied art of the period 1860-1900. While in London he became friends with Walter Crane, Charles and Margaret Mackintosh.

The English House was not published in England until 1979, in an abridged version with English translation by Janet Seligman and introduction by Dennis Sharp. It is this translation which is quoted in this book. The full three-volume edition was published in England in 2007.

ABOVE: *a cottage garden as championed by William Robinson*

NESFIELD, WILLIAM EDEN (1835–1888) He was an architect and friend of R. Norman Shaw, with whom he shared offices. They never collaborated but they both studied English vernacular architecture and developed the vernacular revival.

ROBINSON, WILLIAM (1838–1935) Robinson was influential through his publications and for advocating the wild rather than the formal garden. He founded *The Garden* magazine (1871-1927) and *Gardening Illustrated* for the wealthier middle classes. His most famous book was *The English Flower Garden* (1883).

In 1867, on a visit to France, Robinson noticed that Parisians had introduced tropical foliage plants into their gardens to provide cover against harsh weather. On his return he began to advocate a similar approach. This involved planting in natural looking groups but with hardy specimens among the tender plants. The formal Victorian garden had featured topiary, hedges, geometric designs and mass carpets of colourful bedding. Robinson led a reaction against this. Robinson called his alternative approach the 'wild garden'. In *The English Flower Garden* he argued: 'To make a flower-bed to imitate a bad carpet, and by throwing aside all grace of form and loveliness of bloom, was indeed a dismal mistake' and criticised 'Useless planting out in midsummer when half the flower charms of the year are past; misuse of the glass-houses which might grow welcome food in spring ...'

ABOVE: *terraced houses in Bedford Park designed by Norman Shaw (c.1877)*

SHAW, R. NORMAN (1831–1912) The best known architect of the Queen Anne Revival. His designs for the suburb of Bedford Park in west London, published in *The Builder*, featured both the red-brick Queen Anne form and the half-timbered Old English form.

ABOVE: *the tower at Sissinghurst Castle Gardens, Kent, which Vita Sackville-West used as a study*

ABOVE: *Moorcrag, Gillhead, Cumbria, designed by Voysey (1898–99)*

FIRST FLOOR PLAN

GROUND FLOOR PLAN

ABOVE: *plans by Unwin for the Tudor Walters Report (1918)*

RUSKIN, JOHN (1819–1900) Ruskin was the son of a prosperous wine merchant. He studied at Oxford, where he won the Newdigate prize for poetry. Soon after graduating he met J.M.W. Turner and decided that he would try to rescue him from obscurity. His campaign included the first volume of his series on *Modern Painters* (1843), in which he highly praised Turner's work. In *Modern Painters II* (1846) he championed the pre-Raphaelites. In *The Stones of Venice* (3 volumes, 1851–3) he denounced 'soulless, repetitive industrialism'. He advocated direct observation of nature as the basis of art and design which he practised himself. In *Elements of Drawing* he advocated 'true perception of nature' because 'what we really see is areas of flat colour and shades which we perceive as form'.

He was a direct influence on William Morris and the architect and planner Raymond Unwin. In 1930 Unwin related that 'When young we all sat at [the] feet of Ruskin [and] hung upon his musical words'. By 1900 quotations from Ruskin were considered to be authoritative in British art and design.

SACKVILLE-WEST, VITA (1892–1962) Writer and influential gardener, who with her husband, Harold Nicholson, created the gardens at Sissinghurst Castle, Kent, after her own garden, at Long Barn near Knole, was threatened by development. She wrote a weekly gardening column for The *Observer* for sixteen years. She gardened all day and wrote into the night. She preferred old-fashioned roses that flower only briefly. She introduced other flowers into the rose garden to extend its season. In 1948 she became a founder member of the National Trust's garden committee.

SOISSONS, LOUIS DE (1890–1962) An architect and town planner who followed in the tradition of Parker and Unwin. De Soissons was appointed as architect/planner of Welwyn Garden City in 1920. He planned the town centre including the Parkway. He also designed the Shredded Wheat factory (1925).

UNWIN, RAYMOND (1863–1940) Architect and pioneer town planner. He began his career as a provincial architect in partnership with Barry Parker. They won the competition to design the first Garden City at Letchworth, Hertfordshire, in 1903. In 1907 they moved on to work on Hampstead Garden Suburb. In 1909 Unwin's book *Town Planning in Practice* was published. He reviewed historic patterns of residential development and put forward his arguments on housing density and layout. In 1910 he organised an International Town Planning Exhibition and Conference promoted by RIBA. he became the first Lecturer in Town Planning at Birmingham University (1911–1914) as a result of a grant from the Cadbury family.

In 1914 his partnership with Parker was dissolved. Unwin accepted an invitation to become Chief Town Planning Inspector to the Local Government Board. In 1918 he served on the Tudor Walters Committee, writing much of its report pressing for a state-subsidised housing programme, with standards and densities of housing based on those of the garden city. The 1919 Housing Act enacted the Tudor Walters Report and established the Ministry of Health as the department responsible for housing and public health. Unwin was appointed Chief Housing Architect at the Ministry of Health, a post from which he retired in 1928. He was President of RIBA from 1931 to 1933.

VOYSEY, CHARLES FREDERICK ANNESLEY (1857–1941) An architect and designer, influenced by Richard Norman Shaw, Voysey was responsible for the popularity of rough-cast finishes, deep gables and numerous other vernacular features copied by speculative builders in Edwardian suburbs. He designed hundreds of wallpapers, most of them for Essex & Co. with whom he was contracted. His work embodied the motto, 'Fitness is the basis for beauty'.

WEBB, PHILIP (1831–1915) Philip Webb was already chief clerk (assistant) for G.E. Street when he met William Morris. They became both friends and colleagues. In 1859, Webb designed the Red House, Bexleyheath, Kent for Morris. He also drew many of the birds and animals in Morris' fabric, tapestry and wallpaper designs. Webb often used Morris & Co. to furbish the interiors of houses he designed, such as Standen (1896) and Clouds, near East Knoyle, Wiltshire (1887 and redesigned in 1889, after it had been damaged by fire). Webb was a founding member, with Morris, of the Society for the Protection of Ancient Buildings (SPAB), a forerunner of the National Trust.

ABOVE: *Aesthetic Gothic room (c.1876)*

GLOSSARY OF TERMS

AESTHETIC MOVEMENT a reaction against the first generation of mass-produced (machine-made) goods. Aesthetics believed that art could improve and elevate. In 1878 in *Hints on Household Taste*, Charles Eastlake suggested the use of lighter, more 'aesthetic' styles, with simplicity being the desired effect. *The Burlington* magazine supported the Aesthetic Movement. The critic Walter Hamilton published *The Aesthetic Movement in England* in 1882. The motto 'Art for Art's sake' was popularised by Walter Pater (1839–94), who translated it from the French critic Theophile Gautier's expression 'L'art pour l'art'. Pater's most famous disciple was the young Oscar Wilde.
The sunflower was the best-known symbol of aestheticism. The Aesthetes also revived interest in Chinese blue-and-white porcelain. The architect E.W. Godwin was the outstanding Aesthetic exponent of the applied arts. Liberty's was the most famous retail outlet for Aesthetic wares such as Japanese fans and blue-and-white china. Aubrey Beardsley's illustrations were regarded as Aesthetic, but Kate Greenaway's illustrations were the most accessible of all the artwork associated with the Aesthetic movement.

Straight Arch Window Head.

Lintel or Relieving Arch
Wood Lintel
Exterior gauged brick

ABOVE: *straight arch and relieving arch*

ANAGLYPTA a raised and embossed wallpaper produced by the Anaglypta Company. Lincrusta was a rival type.

ARCH structural part of wall over an opening such as a door or window.

ARCHITRAVE lowest structural part of entablature, forming a lintel and uprights surrounding an opening. Architrave also referred to a moulding which covered the junction of doors and walls. *See* ENTABLATURE.

ABOVE: *Art Nouveau chair designed by A. H. Mackmurdo (1882)*

ART DECO Art Nouveau fell out of fashion in the years immediately preceding the First World War. During the 1920s a wide range of new forms developed. These were based on sources as diverse as ancient Egypt (Tutankhamun's tomb had been discovered in 1922), Central America, the Ballets Russes, and the urban imagery of the machine age. Art Deco motifs included the chevron, the zigzag pattern and the sunrise.
Many international exhibitions helped promote Art Deco, but none was more important than the Paris Exhibition of 1925. Officially entitled the Exposition Internationale des Arts Décoratifs et Industriels Modernes, it was dedicated to the display of modern decorative arts. The exhibition brought together thousands of designs from all over Europe and beyond. It had over 16 million visitors.

ABOVE: *Art Deco – detail of the former Carreras cigarette factory, Hampstead Road, London (1928)*

ART NOUVEAU during the Edwardian period Art Nouveau was referred to as the 'New Art' or the 'New Style'. The name Art Nouveau came from a shop in Paris: Le Maison de l'Art Nouveau. Curvilinear forms were characteristic of Art Nouveau. Its linear geometric variations, as exemplified by Aubrey Beardsley and Charles Rennie Mackintosh, provided the 'modern forms and decorative motifs' sought by a new generation of designers. In 1899 the illustrator and

ABOVE: *curvilinear design by Walter Crane*

ABOVE: *wood block-printing*

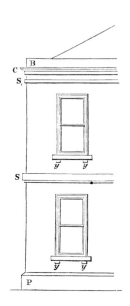

ABOVE: *Blocking course– key is in text (right)*

designer Walter Crane said: ' Line is all important. Let the designer, therefore, in his adaptation of his art, lean upon the staff of his line – line determinative, line emphatic, line delicate, line expressive, line controlling and uniting'.

In terms of interior design Art Nouveau meant creating a room or even a house in a single style. English architect-designers were influenced by Japanese art but the architect W.H. Bidlake insisted that 'we do not need a "new art".' He wrote in 1901 that, fortunately, the 'New Art craze' 'has not taken any real hold on British domestic architecture, which has quietly and steadily progressed, unaffected by New Art eccentricities.'

ARTS & CRAFTS MOVEMENT one of the reactions against the first generation of mass-produced (machine-made) goods as showcased at the Great Exhibition of 1851. The Arts & Crafts movement was an attempt to raise the standard of the arts as applied to interiors. Its equivalents in terms of exteriors were the vernacular and Queen Anne revivals. Although many Arts & Crafts designers trained or practised as architects, the Arts & Crafts movement mainly affected interiors particularly wallpapers, furniture and fabrics. Its exponents advocated the principles of hand skills and quality of materials. Consequently, most of its products were expensive and its co-operative ventures short lived. It suceeded in improving the quality of the applied arts by reducing the distinction between fine and applied arts, and the standard of products such as wallpapers through the designs of exponents such as William Morris.

ART WORKERS GUILD founded in 1884 by exponents of the Arts & Crafts movement to break down the distinctions between the fine and applied arts by creating contact between members of different artistic professions. Members included William Morris, W. A. S. Benson, Reginald Blomfield, L. F. Day and Walter Crane.

ASHLAR stone finished so that it could be laid square with finely fitting joints.

ASPECT was an original Georgian concept that a house should look pleasant, thus having a good aspect.

ATTIC room in the roof or upper storey of a building, often half-hidden behind the parapet.

BALCONY external walkway accessible from inside the house.

BALUSTER supporting post of handrail, usually decorated.

BALUSTRADE series of balusters supporting a rail or coping; identifiable as an Italianate feature, common from 1840s onwards.

BARGE BOARD vertically hung boards to protect the ends of the roof timbers (eaves) from the weather; vernacular feature, in keeping with Gothic style.

BAY WINDOW window projecting out from the face of the building, on one or more storeys, from the lowest level upwards.

BLOCKING COURSE continuation of the wall past the the junction of wall and roof to conceal the eaves, also known as a parapet In the diagram (*left*) B is the blocking course, C = Cornice, S = String course(s). P = Plinth and y = bracket(s). *See* BRACKET, CORNICE, PART-PARAPET.

BLOCK-PRINTING the traditional craft-based technique of printing wallpapers and furnishing fabrics; each colour was applied by hand using wooden blocks. William Morris sub-contracted his printing to Jeffrey & Co.

BOUDOIR a lady's private room.

BRACKET projection designed as a support. See diagram (*left*).

BUILDING ACTS acts regulating new building, usually with only local jurisdiction. To force local authorities to take action the national government had to issue Model By-Laws, which local authorities had to enact, albeit in a modified form. *See* BY-LAWS.

BUILDING SOCIETIES these organisations began as housing co-operatives which only lasted as long as it took to house their original members ('terminating societies'). Later, as permanent organisations, they lent their investors' money to builders for interest. The great change came after the First World War, when they began to lend money to builders who were building houses for sale rather than for rent. This caused their total lending to grow from £14 million in 1914 to £700 million in 1938.

BULL'S EYE a round opening or detail.

BULL'S EYE GLASS a thick knob or protuberance left on glass by the end of the pipe through which it was blown.

BUNGALOW derived from Hindustani 'bangla' (from Bengal): a single storey house with a pitched roof; a popular interwar type in seaside resorts and suburbs.

BY-LAWS acts with only local jurisdiction. The 1877 Model By-laws Act forced local authorities to enforce the 1875 Public Health Act. *See* PUBLIC HEALTH ACTS.

CAMES strips of lead or soft copper holding glass quarries in leaded window lights.

CAPITAL decorative top of a column immediately below architrave. *See* ENTABLATURE.

CASEMENT window (or door) hinged on vertical side.

CHALET a house built in the style of a Swiss cottage, a popular interwar type.

CHIMNEY BREAST structural part of a chimney, containing fireplace and flues carrying smoke up from other fireplaces directly below.

CLASSICAL STYLE style of decoration originating in ancient Greece and Rome, depending on symmetry, proportion and an ordered vocabulary of ornament. *See* PALLADIAN PROPORTIONS, ENTABLATURE.

COCK-LOFT, a form of dormer window with a pitched roof *See* DORMER.

CONSERVATORY structure built from glass panels set in a framework often of cast iron, originally to house tropical plants.

ABOVE: *bargeboards*

ABOVE: *bull's eye glass*

ABOVE: *cames, leaded window lights (1936)*

ABOVE: *teapot designed by Clarice Cliff*

ABOVE: *new shapes and patterns by Susie Cooper (c.1932)*

ABOVE: *'Dresden Spray' lithograph transfer printed pattern by Susie Cooper (1935)*

ABOVE: *moulding in an Interwar interior (1923)*

ABOVE: *dentils under the eaves of an original Queen Anne house (1703)*

ABOVE: *Bedford Park, in west London, brought the domestic, vernacular or Queen Anne revival to medium sized houses for the middle-classes*

CORNICE upper projecting part of classical entablature; designed to stop rain running down the face of the building *See* ENTABLATURE.

COURSE continuous layer of brick or stone of equal height in a wall. The course surmounting the wall is the Blocking Course. The wall may be sub-divided by a String Course. The plinth completes the wall at the base. *See* BLOCKING COURSE, STRING COURSE.

COVE curved moulding, usually joining wall to ceiling. *See* MOULDING.

DADO means a base, from the Italian word 'die'. Originally it referred to the base of a column. After the introduction of the chair or dado rail, it was also applied to the part of an internal wall between the chair rail and skirting.

DADO RAIL a rail fixed to plaster walls at chair height. Originally it was intended to protect the plaster from damage when chairs were placed against the wall.

DENTIL a projecting rectangular block, or brick, under the cornice in a classical order or under the eaves of a building.

DESIGN REFORM MOVEMENT one of the reactions against the first generation of mass-produced (machine-made) goods as showcased at the Great Exhibition of 1851. It suceeded in improving the quality of design education through the creation of the National Art Schools; the one at South Kensington became the Royal College of Art.

DISTEMPER matt-finish, water-based paint with whiting as the pigment and glue size as the binding.

DOMESTIC ARCHITECTURE, private, as opposed to public, buildings such as houses.

DOMESTIC REVIVAL a style developed by a number of architects, including R. Norman Shaw, W. E. Nesfield and George Devey. It was based on traditional features such as gables, low eaves, roughcast finishes and half-timbering. It became popular from the 1870s. *See* QUEEN ANNE REVIVAL, VERNACULAR ARCHITECTURE.

DORMER window projecting from the slope of a roof and possessing a roof of its own.

EAVES structural part of the roof where it meets the wall. The ends were always protected from the weather, either by a parapet or, if they were allowed to project, by bargeboards, plaster or brackets.

EDWARDIAN King Edward VII succeeded Queen Victoria as monarch in 1901. He himself died in 1910 and was succeeded by his son, King George V. The Edwardian period of domestic architecture may be regarded as extending from 1900 until the end of the First World War in 1918. This period saw a number of architectural forms which drew from both classical and vernacular traditions. Architects were, once again, influential, most notably Lutyens for his re-interpretation of early Georgian forms. The Neo-Georgian designs of Lutyens and others were increasingly taken up by the speculative builders in the years immediately preceding 1914.

ELEVATION a view of all the parts of a building facing in one direction – front, rear or side.

ENAMEL an oil-based paint. Edwardian enamel paint came from linseed oil, which was made from crushed flax seed. It was matt unless it received an additional coat of varnish, which gave it a gloss finish.

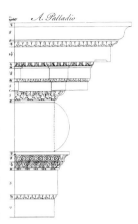

ENCAUSTIC a process for creating coloured tiles. Encaustic tiles were produced by inlaying different coloured clays which were fused together when fired. (Encaustic means 'burnt in'.) This allowed elaborate designs to be built up using relatively inexpensive tiles. The process began when earthenware clay was pressed into a moulded wooden frame. The frame was removed. Then a watery clay of a different colour (known as 'slip') was poured into the hollow gaps made by the mould. Any excess was scraped off. After the applications of slip had been completed, the completed tile was fired. Geometrical patterns were produced using the natural colours of the clay – white, cream, black and red. This suited the contemporary emphasis for detail and surface decoration. Blue, green and lilac became available after chemical dyes were introduced in 1856.

ABOVE: *entablature*

ENGLISH RENAISSANCE Edwardian commentators regarded the late seventeenth and early eighteenth centuries as the English Renaissance of domestic architecture.

ENTABLATURE classical lintel comprising architrave (main structural component), decorative frieze and cornice. *See* ARCHITRAVE, CORNICE, FRIEZE, LINTEL

ERINOID trade name for casein formaldehyde. *See* GALALITH.

EXCEPTIONAL as opposed to typical, large, houses; exceptional houses were designed by architects for the very rich such as Sir Ernest Debenham (the Debenham House).

FACADE the face of a building, usually the principal one.

FAIENCE glazed earthenware or porcelain.

ABOVE: *a decorative frieze in a bedroom design (c.1906)*

FANLIGHT window above the front door , intended to light the hallway, originally semi-circular and often decorated with radiating bars in the shape of a fan.

FINIAL ornament crowning a gable, or roof ridge.

FITMENT the Edwardian term for built-in furniture such as dressers or cupboards.

FLUE opening which carried smoke from a fireplace up to the chimney, where it escaped.

FRENCH WINDOW Casement door, fully glazed.

FRIEZE part of a wall between the cornice and the picture rail *See* ENTABLATURE.

GABLE upper part of a wall rising into the roof.

ABOVE: *fitment – a 1930s wooden dresser*

GALALITH trade name for casein formaldehyde. Casein is a milk protein which formed a plastic when mixed with formaldehyde. Unlike phenol-formaldeyhyde, casein formaldehyde could be brightly coloured. Erinoid was another trade name for Casein formaldehyde.

ABOVE: *Letchworth, Hertfordshire – the first Garden City (begun in 1903), terraced houses with front gardens*

ABOVE: *early Georgian terrace (c.1728)*

GAMBREL a curved section of roof, in the shape of a horse's hind leg.

GARDEN CITY MOVEMENT a movement for urban reform begun by the ideas of Ebenezer Howard. It aimed at the relocation of both the urban population and industry to rural satellite locations. The first Garden City was begun at Letchworth, Hertfordshire, in 1903. The second was at Welwyn, Hertfordshire, in 1920.

GARDEN SUBURB a suburban housing development which tried to retain rural features such as trees, greens and road layouts. The original Garden Suburb was begun at Golders Green in 1907. It was called Hampstead Garden Suburb because it was built on land adjoining Hampstead Heath – Other Garden Suburbs followed, for example, Valentine's Park, Ilford and Gidea Park, Chelmsford.

GEORGIAN STYLE early, mid and late Georgian were successive styles of domestic architecture during the years 1714–1810. Early Georgian was a development of the Queen Anne style. Late Georgian was the most severe phase of a whole period of development. It was accused of being formulaic. Most Georgian domestic architecture was based upon classical, Palladian principles which began in the seventeenth century. *See* CLASSICAL, PALLADIAN.

G.E.R. Great Eastern Railway

GLAZING BAR support for panes of glass set within the window-frame.

GRAINING a paint effect used to simulate the grain of a hard wood such as maple.

HALF-TIMBERED timber framed method of construction in which the structural timbers were formed from halved logs. Very few Edwardian or interwar houses had structural timbers. Most houses of these periods merely had wooden planks nailed to brickwork with a plaster infill. Some houses designed by M.H. Baillie-Scott were exceptions.

HANGING TILES tiles fixed vertically to an external wall to weatherproof it.

HEADER a brick laid so its end is visible.

HIP or **HIPPED** part of a pitched roof set at an angle to the main pitch.

INGLE, INGLENOOK space under a firehood or beside a fireplace.

JAPANNING marbling on metal such as cast-iron. *See* MARBLING.

JERRY BUILDING term used to describe shoddy, inadequate or downright bad work; from the nautical expression 'jury-rig', meaning temporary repairs to masts and rigging. In practise jerry-building usually meant skimping on materials or labour. For example, using up any half-bricks in place of headers resulting in the inner and outer layers of a brick wall remaining 'unbonded' and therefore structurally weak.

JAQUARD LOOM a weaving technology developed in 1801 by Joseph-Marie Jacquard. The Jacquard loom could automatically weave patterns into cloth at much the same rate as plain lengths of fabric could be generated. Jacquard's loom was able to control the action of the weaving process by interfacing the behaviour of the loom to an encoding of the pattern to be reproduced.

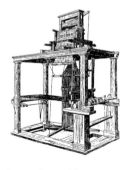

ABOVE: *Jaquard loom*

The pattern was encoded as a groups of holes 'punched' into a sequence of pasteboard cards. Each card contained the same number of rows and columns, the presence or absence of a hole mechanically determined the actions of the loom. By combining a 'tape' of cards together the Jacquard loom was able to weave (and reproduce) patterns of great complexity. It was widely adopted during the first generation of mechanised production.

KITCHENETTE a feature of interwar houses which was little more than a passage from the entrance hall through to the back door, fitted with a cooker, worktop and sink. It could be as small as nine feet by six feet.

LANDING space at the top of a staircase.

LARGE large urban or suburban houses were lived in by the wealthy. Some were designed by architects but this was unnecessary because builders were capable of building to the latest criteria without their involvement.

LAVATORY during the Edwardian period the term was used for a wash hand basin rather than a WC.

LATTICE WINDOW window with diamond or square shaped, leading and panes.

L.C.C. The London County Council (LCC) was created in 1889, as part of the Local Government Act (1888). Its main responsibility was to provide infrastructure to cope with London's rapid growth. It replaced the Metropolitan Board of Works which had been an appointed rather than elected body.

ABOVE: *Liberty's 1927 'Tudor' building, Great Marlborough Street, London*

LEAN-TO outbuilding or extension partly supported by the main building.

LIBERTY company begun by Arthur Lasenby Liberty to import Oriental wares. He opened his own shop in 1875. A Liberty catalogue of Eastern Art Manufactures, dating from 1880, included antique Chinese and Japanese bronzes, enamels, jade and ceramics, and embroideries and rugs from the Near and Far East. Liberty commissioned fabrics, furniture, silver and pewter from designers such as Archibald Knox, Christopher Dresser and Silver Studio. Liberty's fabric designs earned them the compliment that in some parts of Europe the expression for Art Nouveau was Stile Liberty. After Liberty himself died in 1917 the company ceased to commission entirely new designs. In 1927 Liberty opened its new Tudor building in Great Marlborough Street, London. This brought a change in its furniture to styles such as Stuart, Jacobean and early Georgian.

LIGHTWELL a window or skylight which allowed natural light into dark parts of a house, usually staircases.

LINOLEUM a patent floor covering of canvas coated with oxidised linseed oil. It could be printed with wood effects or bright patterns.

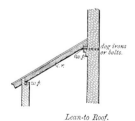

Lean-to Roof.

ABOVE: *'Lean to' construction*

LINTEL flat structural top of an opening. *See* ARCH.

LITHOGRAPHY printing technique which utilises the fact that oil and water do not mix.

LOFT low upper room, immediately beneath the roof, with no ceiling.

ABOVE: *Moderne – a compromise with a hipped roof over smoothly rendered walls and steel 'sun-trap' windows*

LOGGIA an open-sided extension of a house.

LOUVRE ventilation opening covered with slats to reduce entry of both rain and light.

MAJOLICA ceramic coated with an opaque white enamel, decorated or ornamented with colours.

MARBLING a paint effect used to simulate stone. *See* JAPANNING.

MEDIUM medium-sized houses could be identified by corridor access to all main rooms until 1900. Up to 1900 medium-sized houses were usually speculatively built to be rented out but increasingly, after 1900, for sale. After the First World War they were invariably built for sale.

MEWS originally where hawks were kept but after the seventeenth century mews meant a row of stables. Ideally the mews were built at the back of townhouses with accomodation for servants on the first floor, stables and storage for vehicles were on the ground floor.

MEZZANINE a level between two others, usually the ground and first floors.

MINTON & CO (1796–1968) innovative tile producers. They were already producing majolica and encaustic tiles by the time of the Great Exhibition (1851). Around 1900 they began producing Art Nouveau tiles.

MOCK TUDOR mock Tudor was an interwar style which emulated the timber construction of houses of the sixteenth century. *See* HALF-TIMBERED, TUDORBETHAN, OLD ENGLISH.

MODERNE was a compromise between Modernism and traditional design such as putting a hipped roof over a house with flush rendered walls and steel windows. A moderne interior might have plain walls and patterned fabrics.

ABOVE: *De La Warr Pavilion, Bexhill on Sea, designed by Serge Chermayeff (1935)*

ABOVE: *High Point One, the first high rise block of flats built in the UK (1935)*

MODERNISM was a movement in architecture which did not affect building in Great Britain until the 1930s. The ideas of modernism had been propagated in Europe since 1919. At the Bauhaus School in Weimar, Germany, Walter Gropius, in his text *Idee und Aufbau* (1923), included the idea that workers in all the crafts should design for a better world using the idea of machine production as a stimulus. The same year Le Corbusier stated that 'A house is a machine for living in.' in his manifesto *Vers Une Architecture* ('Towards a New Architecture'). Further new thinking on minimalist design and creating space was pioneered by the German Ludwig Mies van der Rohe, who declared 'less is more', and demonstrated this in his Barcelona Pavilion (1929).

Modernism arrived in Great Britain during the 1930s. It was introduced by immigrants including the New Zealander Amyas Connell, the Russian-born Serge Chermayeff, the German, Berthold Lubetkin, and the Canadian, Wells Coates. Amyas Connell designed High and Over, a luxurious private house in Amersham, Buckinghamshire (1931). Serge Chermayeff designed the De La Warr Pavilion in Bexhill on Sea, East Sussex (1935). Lubetkin designed the first high rise block of flats, Highpoint One, Highgate, London (1935). In 1933 Coates wrote; 'As young men, we are concerned with a Future which must be planned rather than a Past which must be patched up, at all costs ... As architects of the ultimate human and material scenes of the new order, we are not so much concerned with the formal problems of style as with an architectural solution of the social and economic problems of today.'

MODERNISTIC compromise between Modernism and traditional style, like Moderne see MODERNE.

MODERNISTS were proponents of modernism.

MODILLION projecting bracket, usually supporting a cornice. *See* BRACKET.

MORNING CALLS 'morning calls' were carriage visits from one local hostess to another for a quarter of an hour's polite conversation. They took place during the afternoon.

MORNING ROOMS morning rooms had first appeared in the early nineteenth century when they served as sitting rooms for the ladies. , sometimes also called 'saloons'..

MORRIS & CO company which began, in 1861, as Morris, Marshall, Faulkner & Co. The original partners were William Morris, Dante Gabriel Rossetti, Ford Maddox Brown, Edward Burne-Jones, Philip Webb, the surveyor Peter Paul Marshall and a mathematician and Oxford don, Charles Faulkner. They regarded themselves as 'Fine Art Workmen'. Each partner contributed share capital of £1, and the firm began trading with a loan of £100 borrowed from Morris' mother.

Activities at the Red House gave them a bias towards handmade goods. They introduced the practice into the company. The firm began as a co-operative. They collaborated on mural decoration, carving, stained glass, metalwork, jewellery, tiles, furniture and embroidery. They took turns in painting the designs before they were fired in a kiln installed in the basement.

Much of their early work was in stained glass commissions for churches through architect contacts such as G.F. Bodley. Early attempts at painted furniture were not universally admired. *Building News* regarded their medieval designs as 'useless' and only suitable for a family which had awakened from 'a sleep of four centuries and which was content to pay enormous prices ... to furnish a barn'. They abandoned medievalism for a simpler and more economical style. This included the turned wood and rush-seated 'Sussex' chairs which were light and could be lifted with one hand. The 'Sussex' chairs were praised for being 'comfortable for use, pleasant to look at and cheap in price'. They were sold for prices from ten to thirty shillings each and remained in almost constant production until 1940.

The small craft phase of the company lasted until 1865. The next decade saw its expansion into a large professional business with workshops at Queen's Square, Ormond Yard, and retail showrooms in Oxford Street. By 1872 much of the production of items like tiles was 'outsourced' to William de Morgan's Chelsea workshops. In 1874, the firm was reorganised as Morris & Co. Morris became the sole director. The first Morris designs for carpets appeared in 1875. These were machine woven by companies such as the Royal Wilton Carpet Works. Machine woven carpets were within the price range of the middle classes. Morris' carpets were manufactured in large rectangles with wide boarders. They cost about five shillings a square yard and were different in two ways. First of all, they were designed to be 'loose fitting' rather than fitted up to the skirting/walls. Secondly, the patterns were strictly two-dimensional. Their repeats were regular and emphatic.

Morris & Co had its most substantial effect on Victorian and Edwardian style through floor coverings, textiles and wall papers. The wallpapers reached the largest market. They cost between six and sixteen shillings a roll. They even appealed to those with 'progressive' tastes and appeared in the artistic colony at Bedford Park, in west London. After Morris died in 1896, Morris & Co. continued until 1905, when it was renamed Morris & Co Decorators Ltd. Morris's protégé, John Henry Dearle (1860-1932), took over as artistic director. W.A.S. Benson took over as chairman.

ABOVE: *High and Over, a modern house in Amersham, Buckinghamshire, designed by Amyas Connell (1931)*

ABOVE: *Blackthorn was designed by Morris' assistant, John Henry Dearle in 1892.*

ABOVE: *'Sussex' chair made by Morris & Co.*

245

By the interwar period Morris & Co products were becoming staid as tastes changed. Business declined during the Depression, and the company was finally liquidated in 1940. Arthur Sanderson & Sons Limited acquired the original wallpaper printing blocks from Jeffrey & Co *See* MORRIS, WILLIAM.

MORTAR mixture of sand, lime and sometimes clay used to bind bricks and stones together.

MOTOR HOME an Edwardian and interwar term for a garage.

MOULDING linear feature of wood or plaster with a decorative profile. There were numerous forms, such as Cyma Recta and Bolection. *See* ENTABLATURE.

MULLION part of the frame of an opening, such as a window.

MUNTING inner vertical timber, of a wall or door.

NEWEL post at the end of a flight of stairs supporting the outer string and handrail.

ABOVE: *proportions as applied to a large, mid Georgian house (c.1750)*

OLD ENGLISH originally the rural form of the Queen Anne Revival, Old English was characterised by its romantic adoption of vernacular features such as half timbering. It really came into its own as part of the speculative builders repertoire in the Edwardian period. *See* MOCK TUDOR, TUDORBETHAN.

OGEE an 'S' shaped curve.

ORIEL projecting window bracketed out from a wall.

PALLADIAN PROPORTIONS speculative builders simplified classical, Palladian proportions down to a modular approach, based on the circle and the square. (The diameter of the circle was equal to the width of the square.) The width of the window formed the basic module, which was one square/circle wide. The most prestigious parts of the house (the first-floor windows) received the most expansive treatment, usually two modules deep for a large house. Although the height was an exact number of modules, the width of an individual house often was not because the overall proportions of a terrace took priority over individual dwellings.

Another device used in the classical scheme was the 'Golden Rectangle'. The proportions were 7:5. This was applied to the facade of a large house (*illustrated left*). The depth of windows on the less important floors was one square. This was also the width of the 'pier' between the windows of the house.

ABOVE: *the golden rectangle as applied to a large, late Georgian house*

PALLADIO, ANDREA (1508 -1580) sixteenth century Italian who studied and checked the proprtions listed by the ancient Roman architect Vitruvius. He published his conclusions which were in turn checked by Inigo Jones while he was himself in Italy. The Palladian approach to classical proportions became predominant during the course of the eighteenth century.

PANTILES brick roofing tiles, usually red, curved in section.

PANTRY storeroom for food, originally flour and bread – later associated with the butler, the senior household servant.

PARAPET top of wall, sometimes projecting above the roof. *See* BLOCKING COURSE.

PARGETING plasterwork, usually decorated with inscribed or raised patterns.

PARLOUR private room, accessible by an internal door – a major aspiration for those who lived in small houses. A room of this kind could be set aside for receiving guests and special occasions. During the nineteenth century the designation 'parlour' was favoured by the working-class and consequently avoided by the middle-class. Originally the parlour was a room in a monastery where guests were received, from the French word 'parler' to speak.

PARTERRE a level space in a garden occupied by flower-beds or paths, ornamentally arranged

PART-PARAPET half-parapet which protects the underside of the eaves. The gutter itself conceals the edge of the slates or tiles.

PATERA flat round ornament in classical style, like a rosette.

PEDIMENT formalised classical gable, used to emphasise a part of the building.

PIANO NOBILE Italian term, meaning 'noble storey', that is to say the most important floor. The piano nobile was situated on the first floor and accommodated the most prestigious room in the house, the drawing room, where honoured guests were 'received'. The piano nobile gradually fell from fashion during the second half of the nineteenth century as the move out to the suburbs allowed a more expansive groundplan. This was able to accomodate all the reception rooms on the ground floor, with direct access to the garden.

PICTURE RAIL a moulding or projection from a wall, situated below the frieze originally for the hanging of pictures in the hall or library. If it projected far enough to carry an object it became a PLATE RAIL.

PITCH angle at which the roof slopes upwards from the horizontal.

PLATE RAIL a projection from a wall, large enough to accommodate an object such as a plate, situated below the frieze. *See* PICTURE RAIL.

PLINTH the supporting element of the base of a column or pedestal.

POLYCHROMY practice of combining materials of different colours to create decorative patterns on the exterior of a building.

PORCH covered entrance to a building.

POST vertical timber of a structure such as a bay.

PROSPECT an original Georgian concept, a house should have a good prospect or view.

PUBLIC HEALTH ACTS national legislation to improve hygiene. The first Public Health Act was in 1848. The second, in 1875, was highly effective. Builders had to show how sewage and ash would be disposed of before they could begin any new building.

QUARRY small pane of glass in a leaded light.

QUEEN ANNE REVIVAL also known as the domestic or vernacular revival, a style developed by a number of architects, which became popular in the 1870s. Loosely based on a mixture of traditional

ABOVE: *an example of pargetting from an Edwardian house in Victoria Park, Manchester*

ABOVE: *picture rail as a moulding in a recreation of an Edwardian drawing-room (Geffrye museum)*

ABOVE: *some Edwardian houses in Chelsea Park Gardens, London, still had drawing-rooms on the first floor, the piano nobile*

ABOVE: *Queen Anne revival, detached house in Bedford Park (1878)*

and classical motifs from the reign of Queen Anne (1704–14), its most famous exponent was R. Norman Shaw. The urban form was characterised by red-brick and white horizontal banding. It was quickly absorbed into the speculative builders' repertoire but disappeared around 1900. It was replaced by Old English, which had been introduced as the rural form of the Queen Anne Revival. *See* VICTORIAN, OLD ENGLISH.

QUOIN dressed or rusticated stone or brickwork which emphasises the corners of a building. *See* ASHLAR.

RAFTER timber onto which roof covering is fixed. *See* PANTILES.

RAIL horizontal structural part of a door or panelling.

REGENCY the Regency period (1811–37) proper began when George, Prince of Wales, became Prince Regent. He finally succeeded his father to the throne as King George IV in 1820. In 1827 he was himself succeeded by his brother who became King William IV. In terms of domestic architecture and interiors, the Regency period may be merged with the early Victorian years up to 1850, because medium and small houses did not benefit from the next generation of improvements and stylistic changes until after the middle of the nineteenth century (although Queen Victoria actually came to the throne in 1837). The style was predominantly classical. The period saw the beginnings of villa suburbs but also much unregulated building which resulted in unhealthy, overcrowded working-class areas of housing.

ABOVE: *roughcast rendering (c.1909)*

RENDERING general term for a weatherproof coat on the outside walls of a building.

REVEAL rebate or jamb between the frame of door or of a window and the outer face of a wall

RIBA Royal Institute of British Architects.

RILL an artificial water-course or rivulet in a garden

ROCOCO a light, curvaceous form of decoration current during the eighteenth century.

ROUGH-CAST external rendering made from sand and cement with crushed stone, gravel or pebbles, also known as pebbledash.

SASH WINDOW window where the moveable elements are hung from the top rather than hinged at the side.

SCREEN-PRINTING a development of stencilling, beginning in 1932, in which printing ink is forced through a mesh. Patterns could be reproduced photographically.

ABOVE: *Regency – Carlton House Terrace, London (c.1830)*

SCULLERY small service room, first appeared in the Regency period as plumbing and water supply improved. Washing then began to be separated from cooking both by its location in the scullery and by its inferior status in the hierarchy of chores.

SEMI-DETACHED PLAN pair of houses joined together, usually so that one is the mirror image of the other. Began to appear in great numbers after 1851 as the suburban railway network expanded to cater for increasing numbers of middle-class commuters able to take advantage of cheaper land values further out from the town or city centre. Semi-detached houses no longer needed to locate the services in the basement.

SHELLEY Shelley china began in 1860. From 1920 to 1940 the company produced art deco ceramics under the artistic direction of Fredrick Rhead and Eric Slater.

SERVICE ROOM room used for household tasks such as food preparation, washing or storing goods, such as cleaning materials.

SHUTTERS movable panels or screens usually fitted to windows.

SIDETONE a side effect of using a telephone up to around 1930. The speaker could hear his own voice like an echo.

SILL (or cill) base of wall or window.

SKIRTING panelling at the foot of the wall covering the join with the floor.

SLATE specific type of impermeable stone which can be split into thin layers usually for covering roofs or making a damp-proof course.

SMALL small houses were for the working classes. During the Edwardian period the first publicly subsidised houses were built for the working classes to rent. During the interwar period publicly subsidised houses were built on a national scale, but it was the speculative builders who built the majority of small houses, for sale rather than rent. Only those in regular employment could afford them.

SMOKE DOCTOR a cowl fitted over the opening of a chimney stack to prevent downdraughts from forcing smoke back down the chimney.

STENCILLING a paint effect using pre-cut masks to achieve decorative effects.

STOREY floor, particularly the space between the two floors.

STRETCHER a brick laid with its longest face parallel to the length of a wall.

STRING timber support for stair.

STRING COURSE single layer of bricks projecting from wall, often at first-floor level, in Georgian architecture. *See* BLOCKING COURSE, COURSE.

STUCCO form of hard, smooth render, in imitation of stone.

STUDIO, THE an art magazine founded and owned by Charles Holme (1848–1923) in 1893. It favoured the Arts & Crafts movement, giving equal weight to both the fine and applied arts. Holme was a businessman from Bradford. Its first editor was Gleeson White, but he resigned in 1895, and Holme subsequently edited the magazine himself. It was the first art magazine to use exclusively photo-mechanical means of reproduction for its images. Other publications were still using a mixture of wood and photo engravings. Before the First World War it had an international circulation but it never subsequently regained its pre-war level of success.

ABOVE: *Shelley blocks pattern and Eve shape (c.1932-3)*

ABOVE: *interwar models of telephone such as the 332 no longer had the problem of 'sidetone' (c.1930)*

ABOVE: *the ground floor of this mid-Georgian house has been rendered with stucco (c.1750)*

STYLE outer vertical timber, of a wall or door.

SUBURB outlying urban area.

SUN-TRAP features designed to maximise the effect of sunshine such as Crittall's curved metal-framed windows, part of a 1930s fashion known as the 'sun-cult'.

SWAG also known as festoon, decorative device in a light classical vein.

TERRACE row of joined houses, often similar and designed as a whole but sometimes the work of numerous different builders. Whether or not this showed was due to the degree of control, or lack of it, exercised by the landlord or developer.

ABOVE: *interwar suburban terrace*

TERRACOTTA moulded brickwork, readily available from around 1875 onwards.

TILE flat baked clay or split stone slab used for floor, roof or wall covering.

TRANSOM horizontal bar set across an opening, such as a window.

TRUSS transverse structural timber designed to support a roof.

TUDORBETHAN another term for the style which emulated the timber construction of houses of the reigns of the Tudor monarchs including Queen Elizabeth I (1558–1603). *See* MOCK TUDOR, OLD ENGLISH.

VERNACULAR ARCHITECTURE forms of domestic building indigenous to England and Wales, either developed or traditionally used here: for example timber framed, jetty construction. The re-adoption of traditional features during the late nineteenth-century was known as the domestic or vernacular revival.

ABOVE: *vernacular architecture – an early seventeenth century farmhouse* (Weald & Downland Museum)

VICTORIAN Queen Victoria came to the throne in 1837 and reigned until 1901, a period spanning three generations. It was not until mid-century that changes which represented a comprehensive Victorian style affected all three classes: upper, middle and the recently named 'working' class. The middle generation, approximately 1850–75, may be regarded as the mid-Victorian period. The mid-Victorian style was the first heterogeneous style – having numerous different forms which shared common elements which made it an identifiable style. The most notable example was the straight sided, or cant, bay-window. Further development of Victorian style occurred 1876–1900. These developments included the Queen Anne and vernacular revivals.

VILLA detached suburban house.

WAINSCOTING internal panelling made of oak or painted softwood.

WASH HOUSE, a service room in small houses used for washing up, laundry and bathing.

WC water-closet, as opposed to EC, earth-closet.

LEFT: *recreation of laundry in a wash-house or scullery* (Church Farmhouse Museum)

NOTES

Chapter 1 Social & Economic Background to the Edwardian & Interwar Eras
1 quoted in Laver J. *Edwardian Promenade* (1958)
2 Peel C.S. *Life's Enchanted Cup* (1933)
3 Hattersley R. *The Edwardians* (2004)
4 Weaver L. *Small country houses of today* (1910)
5 Crane W. *The Claims of Decorative Art* (1892)
6 Newton E. on 'Domestic Architecture of today' in *The House and its equipment* ed. Weaver L. (1911)

7 *ibid*

8 Tressall R. *The Ragged Trousered Philanthropists* 1927 edition

9 *The Dudley Report on the Design of Dwellings* (1944)

10 Forster E.M. *Howards End* (1910)

Chapter 2 Introduction to Edwardian Domestic Architecture

1 Holme C. (ed.) Prefatory note *Modern Domestic British Architecture & Decoration* (1901)

2 Morris W. in *Essays by members of Arts & Crafts Exhibition Society*, 1893

3 Bidlake W.H. in 'The home from Outside' in *The Modern Home* ed. Sparrow W.S. (1906)

4 *ibid*

5 *ibid*

6 Muthesius H. *Das Englische Haus* (1904) English translation (*the English House*) by Stamp D. (1979)

7 *ibid*

8 *ibid*

9 *ibid*

10 *ibid*

11 Prior E.S. from 'Upon House-building in the Twentieth Century in *Modern Domestic British Architecture & Decoration* ed. Holme C. (1901)

12 in preface to *Recent English domestic architecture* Macartney M.E. ed. (1920)

13 Muthesius H. op cit

14 in the foreword to *The Modern Home* Sparrow W.S. ed. (1906)

15 Sackville-West V. *English country houses* (1945)

16 Forster E. M. *Howards End* (1910)

17 *ibid*

18 Priestley J.B. *English Journey* (1934)

19 quoted from a leaflet about Bourneville in Priestley J.B. *English Journey* (1934)

20 Gissing G. *The Nether World* (1889)

21 quoted from a leaflet about Bourneville in Priestley J.B. *English Journey* (1934)

22 Howard E. *Garden Cities of To-morrow* (1902 edition)

23 *ibid*

24 Barnett H. quoted in Miller M. & Gray A.S. *Hampstead Garden Suburb*

25 Unwin R. *Town Planning in Practice* (1909)

26 LCC–Boundary St, Tower Hamlets (1900), Chelsea–Beaufort Street (1902-4), Southwark–Borough Road (1902), Westminster–Millbank (1903)

27 quoted in Johnson A. *Understanding the Edwardian and Interwar House*

Chapter 3 Introduction to Edwardian Interiors

1 Ruskin J. *The Stones of Venice* (3 vols, 1851–53)

2 Ruskin J. *Elements of Drawing* from Letter I 'On first practise'

3 Eastlake C. *Hints on Household taste* (1878)

4 Ricardo H. in *The Modern Home* ed. Walter Shaw Sparrow. Hodder & Stoughton (1906)

5 Eddis R. *Decoration & Furniture of town houses*, 1881

6 Morris W. in *Essays by members of Arts & Crafts Exhibition Society* (1893)

7 Crane W. in *Essays by members of Arts & Crafts Exhibition Society* (1893)

8 *ibid*

9 Morris W. *News from Nowhere* (1890)

10 Muthesius H. op cit

11 quoted in *Modern Architecture and Design* (1901)

12 S.J. Waring of Lancaster merged with the Lancashire firm of Gillows in 1903 to form Waring and Gillow

13 W.H.Bidlake in *The Modern Home* ed. W.S. Sparrow (1906)

Chapter 4 Large Edwardian Town Houses
1 *Modern buildings their planning construction & equipment* ed. G.A.T. Middleton vol 2 (c.1910)
2 Peel C.S. *Life's Enchanted cup* (1933)
3 Ricardo H. on The Interior and its Furniture in *The Modern Home* Sparrow W. S. (ed.) 1906
4 *ibid*
5 Inigo-Triggs H. on Outdoor dining rooms in *The House and its Equipment* ed. Weaver L. (1911)

Chapter 5 Medium Edwardian Town Houses
1 Charles Booth *Life & Labour* 2nd series (1903)
2 *Hendon & Finchley Times*, 23 August 1907
3 S.J.Waring's and Gillows were separate firms until 1903 when they merged to form Waring & Gillow but they continued to publish their own catalogues.
4 Bidlake W.H. in 'The home from Outside' in *The Modern Home* ed. Sparrow W.S. (c.1910)

Chapter 6 Small Edwardian Town Houses
1 To the Joint Select Committee of Lords and Commons on London underground railways, 1901
2 Curtis A.C. *The Small Garden Beautiful* (1906)

Chapter 7 Edwardian Country Houses
1 Newton E. on 'Domestic Architecture of today' in *The House and its Equipment* ed. Weaver L. (1911)
2 *ibid*
3 Quoted in Waller P.J. *Town, City & Nation: England 1850–1914* (1983)
4 Newton E. *op.cit.*
5 Sackville-West V. *English Country houses* (1945)
6 Lutyens E. *A Goldfish Bowl* (1972)
7 Kerr R. *The Gentleman's House* (1830)
8 Sackville-West V. *The Edwardians* (1945)
5 'A Foreign Resident' on 'Society in the new reign', in *Edwardian Promenade* ed. Lavery J.(1958)
6 *The Modern Home* ed. Walter Shaw Sparrow (1906)
8 Sackville-West V. *English Country houses* (1945)
9 Asquith C. in *The Day Before Yesterday* (1956)
10 *ibid*
11 Muthesius H. op cit
12 *ibid*
13 Weaver L. in the introduction to *The House and its Equipment* ed. Weaver L. (1911)
14 Bidlake W.H. in 'The home from Outside' in *The Modern Home* ed. Sparrow W.S. (c.1910)

Chapter 8 Country House Gardens
1 Bidlake W.H. on 'The home from outside' in *The Modern Home* ed. W.S. Sparrow (1906)
2 Jekyll G. 'On Garden Design Generally' in *The House and its Equipment* ed. Weaver L. (1911)
3 W. MacQueen-Pope in *The Age of Extravagance* (1956)
4 *English Country houses* (1945)

Chapter 9 Interwar Front
1 Daughton M. on Housing in *The Cambridge Social History of Britain 1750-1950*, vol 2 ed. F.Thompson (1990)
2 from preface to *Recent English Domestic Architecture* ed. McCartney M.E. (c.1920)
3 *ibid*
4 Manchester Corporation *City of Manchester plan* (1945)
5 *ibid*

Chapter 10 Interwar Plan
1 Mass Observation, *The Sort of Home the Englishman Wants*, 1943, *Design of Dwellings*, The Dudley Report (1944)
2 Manchester Corporation *City of Manchester plan* (1945)

Chapter 12 Roofs
1 W.H.Bidlake in 'The home from Outside' in *The Modern Home* ed. Sparrow W.S. (1906)

Chapter 13 Brick & Stone
1 W.H.Bidlake in 'The home from Outside' in *The Modern Home* ed. Sparrow W.S. (1906)
2 *ibid*
3 *ibid*

Chapter 14 Windows
1 Muthesius H. *op.cit.*
2 *ibid*

Chapter 17 Fireplaces
1 Muthesius H. *op.cit.*
2 Muthesius H. op.cit.

Chapter 18 Kitchens & Cooking
1 London J. *The Children of the Abyss* (1903)

Chapter 20 WCs
1 Cash J. in *The Modern Home* ed. W.S. Sparrow (1906)

Chapter 21 Lighting & Electrical Appliances
1 Maurice Hird on Electric light in country houses in *The House and its equipment* ed. Weaver L. (1911)
2 *ibid*
3 W.H.Bidlake in 'The home from Outside' in *The Modern Home* ed. Sparrow W.S. (1906)
4 Muthesius *op.cit.*

Chapter 22 Telephone & Wireless
1 Peel C.S. *Life's Enchanted cup* (1933)
2 Maurice Hird on Telephone Installations in *The House and its Equipment* ed. Weaver L. (1911)
3 Priestley J.B. *English Journey* (1934)
4 *ibid*
5 *Hope and Glory*, Columbia Pictures (1987)

Chapter 23 Staircases
1 Ricardo H. on 'The interior and its furniture' in *The Modern Home* ed. Sparrow W. S. (1906)
2 Panton J. E. *From Kitchen to Garrett* 1887

Chapter 24 Colours
1 Ricardo H. in *Modern Domestic British Architecture & Decoration* (1901)
2 Tressall R. *The Ragged Trousered Philanthropists* 1927 edition
3 Ricardo H. on 'colour in the House' *The House and its equipment* ed. Weaver L. (1911)
4 Cash J. on Some decorative essentials in *The Modern Home* ed. Sparrow W. S. (1906)
5 *ibid*

Chapter 25 Paint Finishes
1 7 Blyth Grove, Worksop, Notts. was built in 1905. In 1920, a local grocer, William Straw bought the house. He had the house redecorated when he moved in with his family during 1923. The house has been unchanged since 1932. *see PLACES TO VISIT*

NOTES &
FURTHER INFORMATION

2 Tressall R. *The Ragged Trousered philanthropists* 1927 edition
3 Holme C. on Decoration and Embroidery in *Modern Domestic British Architecture & Decoration*
ed. Holme C. The Studio (1901)

Chapter 26 Patterns
1 Muthesius H. *op.cit.*
2 Sparrow W. S in *The British Home of Today* (1904)
3 Pearce W. *Painting & Decorating* 1902

Chapter 27 Tiles
1 Furnival W. J *Leadless Decorative Tiles, Faience and Mosaic* 1904
2 *ibid.*
3 *ibid.*
4 *ibid.*
5 *ibid.*
6 *ibid.*
7 Sparrow W. S. *The British Home of Today* (1904)

Chapter 28 Stained & Coloured Glass
1 Cash J. on Some decorative essentials in *The Modern Home* ed. Sparrow W. S. (1906)
2 Sears Roebuck and Co *Home builders' Catalogue* 1910
3 Baillie-Scott M. H. on 'The Decoration of the Suburban House' in *The Studio*, V

Chapter 29 Walls
1 Muthesius H. *op.cit.*
2 Jennings H. H. *Our homes and how to beautify them* 1902
3 Muthesius H. *op.cit.*
4 *ibid*
5 Allen J. G. *The Cheap Cottage and the small house* 1913

Chapter 30 Mouldings
1 H. Gibbon and Sons *Catalogue of Mouldings* 1909
2 Ellis G. *Practical Modern Joinery* 1921

ABOVE: *Arbutus, a late Morris & Co print, available from Sanderson, designed by Kathleen Kersey (c.1914).*

FURTHER INFORMATION: DECOR

DULUX: heritage collection of authentic paint colours, containing Georgian, Victorian, Edwardian & Art Deco ranges
ICI Paints, Wexham Road, Slough, Berkshire, SL2 5DS
Telephone: 01753 550555
Website: www.heritagepaints.co.uk/edwardian_colours.html

HAMILTON WESTON WALLPAPERS: modern reproductions of historic wallpapers, archive, reference library
18 St Mary's Grove, Richmond, Surrey TW9 1UY
Telephone: 020 8940 4850
Website: www.hamiltonweston.com
Email: info@hamiltonweston.com

SANDERSON: fabrics and wallpapers including Morris & Co. designs
UK Head Office: Chalfont House, Oxford Road, Denham, Middlesex, UB9 4DX

Telephone: 01895 830044
Email: enquiries@a-sanderson.co.uk
UK Showroom: Chelsea Harbour Design Centre, Unit G9, Lots Road, London, SW10 OXE
Telephone: 08708 300066
Website: www.sanderson-online.co.uk

AIDS TO RESEARCH

LOCAL STUDIES: for information about specific houses in any area contact the relevant local studies/history library. Staff will help you to find the information through large scale Ordnance Survey maps, records and archives.

REPRODUCTIONS OF ORDNANCE SURVEY MAPS: available from Alan Godfrey Maps, The Off Quay Building, Foundry lane, Newcastle-upon-Tyne, NE6 1LH
Website: www.alangodfreymaps.co.uk

NATIONAL ORGANISATIONS

NATIONAL TRUST (NT)
Heelis, Kemble Drive, Swindon, SN2 2NA
Telephone: 0870 458 4000
Website: www.nationaltrust.org.uk
Email: enquiries@thenationaltrust.org.uk

ENGLISH HERITAGE: conservation and restoration advice
PO Box 569, Swindon, SN2 2YP
Telephone: 870 333 1181
Website: www.english-heritage.org.uk

ABOVE: *the Geffrye Museum, which is set in almshouses built c.1705*

MUSEUMS & COLLECTIONS

BLACK COUNTRY LIVING MUSEUM: an open air museum with over 40 relocated buildings, including early twentieth century workers' houses, shops, re-enactors, working trams and trolleybuses
Black Country Living Museum, Tipton Road, Dudley, DY1 4SQ
Telephone (shop): 0121 521 5601
Website: www.bclm.co.uk

GEFFRYE MUSEUM: period room sets and garden displays
Kingsland Road, London, E2 8EA
Telephone: 020 7739 98
Website: www.geffrye-museum.org.uk

MoDA (MUSEUM OF DOMESTIC DESIGN & ARCHITECTURE): permanent exhibitions include displays of early twentieth-century interiors 1900–60. Study Room to examine collection. Admission is free to everyone
MoDA is situated at Middlesex University's Cat Hill Campus. Admission is free to everyone.
Middlesex University, Cat Hill, Barnet, Hertfordshire EN4 8HT

ABOVE: *early twentieth century household artefacts in the Science Museum, including a Hoover vacuum cleaner and a Smoothwell electric iron*

255

Telephone: 020 8411 5244
Website: www.moda.mdx.ac.uk

SCIENCE MUSEUM: collection includes twentieth century artefacts such as early plastics and electrical appliances
Open 10am to 6pm every day except 24 to 26 December.
Exhibition Road, South Kensington, London SW7 2DD
Lambeth Palace Road, London SE1 7LB
Telephone: 020 870 4868
Website: www.sciencemuseum.org.uk

V & A (VICTORIA & ALBERT MUSEUM): collection includes early light fittings and wireless sets as well as original Arts & Crafts artefacts
V&A South Kensington
Cromwell Road, London SW7 2RL
Telephone: 020 7942 2000
Website: www.vam.ac.uk/your_visit/index.html

ABOVE: *Broad Leys, designed by C.F.A. Voysey, now the home of WMBRC who offer B&B during the week*

WHITWORTH ART GALLERY: collection includes textiles and wallpapers
The University of Manchester, Oxford Road, Manchester M15 6ER
Telephone: (161) 275 7450
Website: www.whitworth.manchester.ac.uk

PLACES TO VISIT: (NT) denotes a National Trust property

BEDFORD PARK from Turnham Green Underground station turn right onto the Bath Road. The original parts of Bedford Park lie between Gainsborough and Arbinger Roads on the east side and Marlborough Crescent on the northwest. From South Parade, Bath Road and Flanders Avenue, they extend northwards as far as Blenheim Road.
The Bedford Park Society, 31 Priory Avenue, Bedford Park, London W4 1TZ
Website: www.bedfordpark.org/

ABOVE: *Hidcote, Edwardian and interwar gardens*

BOURNVILLE George Cadbury's 1895 development to house his own employees and others in a pleasant environment near his new factory outside Birmingham.
Bournville, Birmingham B30 2LU
Website: www.cadbury.co.uk/EN/CTB2003/about_chocolate/history_cadbury/social_pioneers/bournville_village.htm

BROAD LEYS: the largest country house designed by C.F.A.Voysey. It is now the home of Windermere Motor Boat Racing Club (WMBRC), who offer Bed and Breakfast (B&B) accommodation (Monday to Thursday only)
Broad Leys, Ghyll Head, Windermere, Cumbria, LA23 3LJ
Telephone: 015394 43284
Website: www.wmbrc.co.uk/Default.htm

COLETON FISHACRE (NT) 1920s house and garden built as a holiday home for Rupert D'Oyly Carte and his family
Brownstone Road, Kingswear, Devon TQ6 0EQ
Telephone: 01803 752466
Website: www.nationaltrust.org.uk/main/w-vh/w-visits/w-findaplace/w-coletonfishacrehouseandgarden

HAMPSTEAD GARDEN SUBURB: from Golders Green Underground station turn right onto the Finchley Road. You may turn immediately right onto Rotherwick Road, one of the original entrances to the suburb or continue to Hoop Lane, where Meadway Gate is approximately one mile from the Finchley Road. The oldest part of the suburb is on Hampstead Way, which leads off the Finchley Road in Temple Fortune.

HIDCOTE MANOR GARDEN (NT) Edwardian and interwar gardens
Hidcote Bartrim, nr Chipping Campden, Gloucestershire GL55 6LR
Telephone: 01386 438333
Website: www.nationaltrust.org.uk/main/w-vh/w-visits/w-findaplace/w-hidcotemanorgarden/

HILLTOP FARM (NT): home of Beatrix Potter from 1905
nr. Sawrey, Ambleside LA22 0LF
Telephone: 015394 36269
Website: www.visitcumbria.com/amb/hilltop.htm

HOMEWOOD country house designed by Edwin Lutyens (1901). The house is privately owned but offers Bed & Breakfast accommodation. Please book or enquire before visiting.
Homewood, Park Lane, Knebworth, Hertfordshire SG3 6PP
Telephone: 01438 812105
Website: www.homewood-bb.co.uk/

ABOVE: *Lucas Square, designed by Geoffry Lucas in Hampstead Garden Suburb (1909)*

LETCHWORTH the town is accessible by railway but is best explored with a car. From a map, one can easily find original parts such as Westholm Green and Eastholm Green and some of the original entries in the Small Cottage Exhibition still stand in Nevells Road. Examples of Parker and Unwin's short terraces may be found around Norton Way.
First Garden City Heritage Museum,
296 Norton Way South, Letchworth Garden City, Hertfordshire SG6 1SU
Tel: 01462 482710
Website: www.letchworthgc.com/placestovisit/history/gardencityheritagemuseum.html

LIBERTY'S the 1927 Tudorbethan building, Great Marlborough Street, London W1B 5AH
Website: www.liberty.co.uk/contact_us/how_to_find_us

MANOR HOUSE, UPTON GREY restored Gertrude Jekyll gardens around an original Tudor farmhouse which was rebuilt as an Edwardian country house. Visitors to the Garden are welcome, by appointment only, on weekdays. There is an admission fee of £5.00 which includes a printed guide and plant list.
The Manor House, Upton Grey, nr Basingstoke, Hampshire, RG25 2RD
Tel : 01256 861035
Website: www.gardenvisit.com/g/manor1.htm
Email: uptongrey@lineone.net

MR STRAW'S HOUSE (NT) an Edwardian house, refurbished in 1923 but unchanged since 1932.Timed visits, booking required
7 Blyth Grove, Worksop, Nottinghamshire S81 0JG
Telephone: 01909 482380
Website: www.nationaltrust.org.uk/main/w-vh/w-visits/w-findaplace/w-mrstrawshouse/

ABOVE: ' *Queen of Time*', *Art Deco ornament (1925) over the main entrance of Selfridges deparetment store*

MUNSTEAD WOOD former home of Gertrude Jekyll, now privately owned with some open days each year. Specific open days are listed in the annual National Gardens Scheme Yellow Book
Website: www.gardenvisit.com/garden/munstead_wood_garden

NEW EARSWICK the 1902 'Garden Village' development is two miles north of York city centre.
Website: www.jrf.org.uk/housingandcare/newearswick/

NYMANS (NT) interwar garden
Handcross, nr Haywards Heath, West Sussex RH17 6EB
Telephone: 01444 405250
Website: www.nationaltrust.org.uk/main/w-vh/w-visits/w-findaplace/w-nymansgarden/

OVERBECK'S (NT) Edwardian house and garden with diverse interwar collections
Sharpitor, Salcombe, Devon TQ8 8LW
Telephone: 01548 842893
Website: www.nationaltrust.org.uk/main/w-vh/w-visits/w-findaplace/w-overbecks.htm

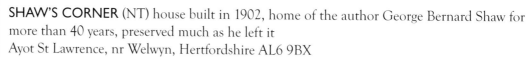

SELFRIDGES the building in Oxford Street (1907-28) displays some remarkable Edwardian and interwar details, including the 'Queen of Time' over the main entrance
Selfridges London, 400 Oxford St, London W1A 1AB
Website: www.selfridges.com/index.cfm?page=1183

SHAW'S CORNER (NT) house built in 1902, home of the author George Bernard Shaw for more than 40 years, preserved much as he left it
Ayot St Lawrence, nr Welwyn, Hertfordshire AL6 9BX
Telephone: 01438 829221 (Infoline)
Website: www.nationaltrust.org.uk/main/w-vh/w-visits/w-findaplace/w-shawscorner

ABOVE: *the terrace, Standen, East Sussex, designed by Philip Webb in 1896*

SISSINGHURST CASTLE GARDENS (NT) interwar gardens set around a Tudor manor house and tower
Sissinghurst, nr Cranbrook, Kent TN17 2AB
Telephone: 01580 710700
Website: www.nationaltrust.org.uk/main/w-vh/w-visits/w-findaplace/w-sissinghurstcastlegarden/

STANDEN (NT) 1896 country house with William Morris interiors
West Hoathly Road, East Grinstead, West Sussex RH19 4NE
Telephone: 01342 323029
Website www.nationaltrust.org.uk/main/w-vh/w-visits/w-findaplace/w-standen/

ABOVE: *the entrance front of Standen*

SUNNYCROFT (NT) largely unaltered gentleman's suburban villa (c.1899)
200 Holyhead Road, Wellington, Telford, Shropshire TF1 2DR
Telephone: 01952 242884
Website: www.nationaltrust.org.uk/main/w-vh/w-visits/w-findaplace/w-sunnycroft/

TOTTERDOWN FIELDS ESTATE the first LCC 'council houses' or 'cottage estate' Head south fromTooting Bec Underground station. Turn left onto Lessingham Road. The estate is concentrated around the grid where Lessingham Road crosses Franciscan Road.

WELWYN GARDEN CITY Hertfordshire. The second garden city is accessible by railway but more easily explored by car. East of the centre, Parkway and the Broadwater Road, many original small and medium-sized houses remain on the Peartree and Panshanger estates.

WHITE HART LANE ESTATE London N17 (now Tower Gardens Conservation area), second LCC 'council houses' or 'cottage estate'. It is the grid of streets between Lordship Lane and Risley Avenue. The Peabody Cottages are adjacent to the end nearest the junction of Lordship Lane and Bruce Grove.

2 WILLOW ROAD (NT) home of the modernist architect Erno Goldfinger
Hampstead, London NW3 1TH
Telephone: 01494 755570 (Infoline)
Website: www.nationaltrust.org.uk/main/w-vh/w-visits/w-findaplace/w-2willowroad/

WYTHENSHAWE Manchester's 'garden suburb' is located north of the airport. Examples of the vernacular style terraces may be found around Wythenshawe market place/bus station. Speculatively built interwar houses may be found around Northenden.

ABOVE: *title page of an Edwardian book on domestic architecture*

BIBLIOGRAPHY

Arber K., *Thirtiestyle*, Middlesex University Press, 2006
Artley A. (ed.), *Putting Back the Style*, Evans Bros, 1982
(Essays by members of the) Arts & Crafts Exhibition Society, Rivington, Percival & Co, 1893
Baren M., *How it all began: stories behind those famous names*, Smith Settle, 1992
Beattie S., *A revolution in London Housing*, Architectural Press, 1980
Blackburne E., *Suburban & rural architecture*, London, 1865
Bosomworth D., *Victorian Catalogue of Household Goods*, Studio Editions, 1992
Brandt Bill, *London in the Thirties*, Gordon Fraser, 1983
Byrne A., *London*, Georgian Press, 1986
Cave C.F., *the Smaller English House*, Robert Hale, 1981
Chambers W., *Treatise on Decorative . . . Architecture*, London, 1791
Cliff S., *English Archive of Design & Decoration*, Thames & Hudson, 1998
Curtis A., *Small Garden Beautiful*, London, 1909
Dillistone G., *Planning & Planting of Little Gardens*, London, 1920
Day L.F., *Ornamental Design*, London, 1897
Deakin D., *Wythenshawe*, Phillimore, 1989
Doré G., *London: a Pilgrimage* (reproduction: Dover Press), 1871
Dyos H.J., *A Victorian Suburb*, Leicester University Press, 1961
Eberlein H.D.& Richardson A., *Smaller English House*, Batsford, 1925
Fletcher B., *The English House*, London, 1910
Foley E., *Book of Decorative Furniture*, London, 1920
Forster E.M., *Howard's End*, London, 1910
Gere C. & Whiteway M., *Nineteenth Century Design*, Weidenfeld & Nicolson, 1993
Gibberd F., *Architecture of England*, London, 1791
Girouard M., *Life in the English Country House*, Yale University Press, 1978
    Sweetness & Light, the Queen Anne movement 1860–1900, Oxford, 1977
Gray A.S., *Edwardian Architecture*, Duckworth, 1985
Gray R., *History of London*, Hutchinson, 1984
Greeves T. Affleck, *Bedford Park – the first garden suburb*, Bedford Park Society, 1999
Hadfield M., *History of British gardening*, John Murray, 1979
Hamerton I. (ed.), *W.A.S. Benson: a biography*, Antique Collectors Club, 2005
Hamilton J., *An introduction Introduction to Wallpaper*, London HMSO, 1983
Hardy W., *A guide to Art Nouveau style*, Grange Books, 1996
Hattersley R., *The Edwardians*, Abacus, 2004
Helm W., *Homes of the Past*, London Bodley Head, 1921
Holme C. (ed.), *Modern Domestic British Architecture & Decoration*, The Studio, 1901
Horsham M., *Twenties & Thirties Style*, Grange Books, 1996
Huggett F. E., *Victorian England as seen by Punch*, Sidgwick & Jackson, 1978

BIBLIOGRAPHY

Hunt J. & Thorpe D., *Gerrards Cross: a history*, Phillimore, 2006
Jackson A., *Semi-detached London*, Allen & Unwin, 1973
Jackson F., *Raymond Unwin*, A Zwemmer Ltd, 1985
Jackson L., *Twentieth Century Pattern Design*, Mitchell Beazley, 2002
Jackson N., 'Speculative Housing in London', Ph.D thesis (University of. Westminster), 1990
Jenner M., *Architectural Heritage of Britain & Ireland*, Michael Joseph, 1993
Johnson A., *How to restore your Victorian House*, David & Charles, 1991
    Understanding the Edwardian and Inter-War House, Crowood Press, 2006
Kerr R.,   *The Gentleman's House*, London, 1865
Langley B., *The Builder's Jewel*, London, 1767
Laver J., *Edwardian Promenade*, Edward Hulton, 1958
Lichten F., *Decorative art of Victoria's era*, London, 1950
Long H., *The Edwardian House*, Manchester University Press, 1993
Loudon J.C., *Cottage Form & Villa Architecture*, 1846
Macartney M.E. (ed.), *Recent English Domestic Architecture I–III*, Architectural Review 1908-10
    Recent English Domestic Architecture V, Architectural Review, 1920 Macintosh C., *Book of the Garden*, Edinburgh, 1853
Manchester Corporation, *City of Manchester Plan*, Jarrold & Sons Ltd, 1945
Mayhew T., *London Labour & the London Poor*, London, 1861-2
Middleton G., *Modern Buildings Vol 2*, Caxton, c.1910
Miller M., *The Complete Guide to Twentieth- century Antiques*, Carlton Books, 2005
Miller M (ed.), *Hampstead Garden Suburb* (Archive Photographs Series), Chalford 1995
Miller M. & Stuart Gray A., *Hampstead Garden Suburb*, Phillimore, 1992
Morris T., *A House for the Suburb*, London, 1870
Muthesius H., *Das Englische Haus/the English House*, Berlin 1904 Translation by Stamp D. Crosby Lockwood Staples, 1979
Muthesius S., *The English Terraced House*, Yale University Press, 1982.
National Trust, *Mr Straw's House*, National Trust, 2004
National Trust, *Standen*, National Trust, 2006
Nicholson P., *Builder's & Workman's Director*, Knight & Lacey, 1825
Nicolson N., *Sissinghurst Castle Gardens*, National Trust, 2006
Olsen D.J., *City as a Work of Art: London, Paris & Vienna*, Yale University Press, 1986
Osband L., *Victorian House Style*, David & Charles, 1991
Pain W., *Builder's Companion*, London, 1762
Priestley J.B., *English Journey*, William Heinemann Ltd, 1934
Quennell C.H.B., *Modern Suburban Houses*, London, 1906
Quiney A., *House & Home*, BBC, 1986
    Period Houses, George Philip, 1989
Reyburn W., *Flushed with Pride: the story of Thomas Crapper*, London/Pavilion, 1989
Richardson C.J., *Picturesque Designs for Mansions*, Atchley, 1870
Richardson T., *English Gardens in the Twentieth Century*, Aurum Press, 2005
Richardson C.J., *Picturesque Designs for Mansions*, Atchley, 1870
Robinson W., *The English Flower Garden*, John Murray, 1883
Sackville-West V. *English Country Houses* William Collins 1945
Sparrow W. S. (ed.), *The British Home of Today*, Hodder & Stoughton, 1904
    The Modern Home, Hodder & Stoughton, 1906
Stamp G. & Goulancourt A., *The English House 1860–1914*, Faber & Faber, 1986
Stevenson G., *The 1930s Home*, Shire Publications, 2006
Stevenson J.J., *House Architecture*, London, 1880
Tilbrook A.J., *Designs of Archibald Knox for Liberty & Co*, Richard Dennis, 1976
Tressall R., *The Ragged Trousered Philanthropists*, Richards /Daily Herald edition, 1927
Turner M., *Little Palaces: The Suburban House in North London 1919–39*, Middlesex Poly., 1987   Unwin   R., *Cottage plans & common sense*, Fabian Society, 1902
Waller P.J., *Town, City & Nation England 1850–1914*, Oxford University Press, 1983
Walvin J., *English Urban Life 1776–1851*, London Hutchinson, 1984
Warren G. & Klein D., *Art Nouveau and Art Deco*, Chancellor Press, 1996
Weaver L., *Small Country Houses of Today*, Country Life, 1910
    The House and its Equipment, Country Life, 1911
Wheeler G., *A Choice of Dwelling*, John Murray, 1871
Yarwood D., *The English House*, Batsford, 1979
Young & Marten, *Victorian House Catalogue*, Sidgwick & Jackson, 1990
Young W., *Town & Country Mansions & Suburban Houses*, London, 1879

INDEX

A

Abbeystead Hall 95
A.E.L. 9
Aalto, Alvar 126, 127
Acetylene 181
Ackock's Green, Birmingham 2
Addison, Dr Christopher 46
Addison Act 47, 115, 123
Admiralty Arch 1
Aesthetic Movement 49
A Foreign Resident 33
air-gas 181
Alderley Edge, Manchester 3
Aldershot 8
Aldridge J. 215
Alexander Morton & Co 52, 211
Alfred Chapman & Co 210, 211
Amalgamated Press 9
Anaglypta 211, 227
Anglepoise 143, 184, 185
aniline dyes 199
Anne of Denmark 18
Architects 10, 11, 12, 22
Architectural Review 31, 91, 119
Architrave 225, 230
Arding & Hobbs 3
Argentina 4, 115
Art Deco 53, 127
Art Nouveau 52, 53, 143, 156, 157, 211, 213
Arts & Crafts 31, 49, 50, 52, 129, 151, 166, 177, 181, 199, 211
Arts & Crafts Exhibition Society 50
Arts & Crafts movement 9, 35, 49, 50, 51, 53, 60
Ascot, water heater 131, 173
Ashbee, C.R. 51
Ashford 5
Atco 141
Aufseeser, Hans 214, 215
Aumonier 60
Austin Reed 115, 129
Autumn tints 203

B

Baillie-Scott 17, 34, 63, 92, 115, 117, 128, 129, 150, 151, 159, 167, 196, 197, 221
Bakelite 127, 179, 189, 203, 231
Banqueting House, Whitehall 18
Bardfield Papers 215
Barking 47
Barlow & Jones 215
Barnet 15
Barnett, Henrietta 40, 41, 83
Barrow 5
Barry Parker 38, 41

basement 23, 25
Bath 18, 19
bathroom 11, 12, 13, 25, 46, 47
Battersea 37, 45
Batty Langley 11
Bawden, Edward 215
Baxendale's 127
bays 43, 117, 121, 139, 145, 146, 147
bay window 25, 25, 25, 25, 31, 31, 43
BBC 191, 193
Beale, James 35
Beaufort Street 135
Becontree 47
Bedford Park 21, 22, 37, 49
bedrooms 25, 34, 37, 43, 45, 46, 47
beigery 215
Belcher, John 19, 33, 197
Bell, Alexander Graham 187
Benson W.A.S. 35, 52, 52, 182, 183
Besant, Walter 2
Bestlite 184, 185
Bidlake W.H. 19, 21, 53, 60, 77, 147, 149, 151, 181
Birkenhead 5
Birmingham 2, 5, 7, 27, 35, 38, 45, 47, 49
Birmingham Daily Mail 2
Blackpool 5, 6
Blomfield R. 103, 197
Blumenfeld R. D. 7
Blyth Grove 67, 70, 71, 140, 141, 201
Bodley G.F. 50
Boer War 45
Boot's chemists 3, 6
Booth, Charles 69
borders 205, 207, 213, 219, 227, 229
Bournemouth 6
Bourneville 38
Bowden, Manchester 3
box hedges 28, 29, 61
Braddell, Darcy 117
Bradford 7
brick 15, 17, 18, 19, 22, 34, 37, 43, 47, 115, 117, 119, 121, 123, 125, 135, 142, 143, 145, 147, 149, 151, 165, 167, 171
Brighton 2, 9, 18
Bristol 2, 45
British Commercial Gas Association 9
Broadcasting House 193
Bromley 8
Brompton Square 59, 187
Bruce Grove 45
Brunswick Square Act 18
Bucklow 124
Builders & Contractors 10, 69
Building News 21, 22

bull's eye glass 221
bungalow 117
bungalows 15
Butterfield, William 143, 210, 211
By-laws 22, 27, 37, 41

C

Cadbury, George 37, 38
Camera Square 58, 115
cames 223
Canada 4
Canons Park estate 13
Cardiff 5
carpet bedding 29
Carr, Jonathan 49
Carter & Co 219
casement 115, 117, 125, 131, 152, 153, 155
Cash, John 3, 177, 201, 221
Cassell's Household Guide 221
cathedral windows 197, 221
Cawardine 185
chalet 117
Chamberlain J.H. 49
Charles Wade Paget 40
Chaucer Road, Cambridge 119
Cheap Cottages' Exhibition 40, 87, 83
Chelmsford 191
Chelsea Park Gardens 58, 59, 62, 65, 73, 115, 135, 147
Chelsea Square 116, 117, 129, 134, 135
Cheshire 37, 119, 124
Chesterton G.K. 91
Chile 115
chimneys 22, 161, 163
Chislehurst 8, 119, 137
Christ's College, Cambridge 4
Church Farmhouse Museum 18
Churchill 6
cigarette cards 9
cisterns 177, 179
Cities in Evolution 5
City of Manchester plan 115, 133
Clapton 29
classically proportioned 18
Clayton & Shuttleworth 6
Clements House 11
Cliff, Clarice 131
Clifton, Bristol 2
Clutha glass 52
coal fires 25
Coal gas 181
cock-loft 71
Cockfosters 15, 119, 121
Coleherne Court 13, 58, 59
Coleton Fishacre 113
Colman's 3
Colour schemes for the Flower Garden 107
conservatory 6, 25
Cooper 131, 202, 203

copper 35, 170, 171, 173, 201, 223
Corbett, Archibald Cameron 11, 71, 84, 85
Cordofan candlesticks 52
cornice 201, 207, 224, 225, 227, 229
Corn Laws 4
Costain 12, 125
Crane, Walter 10, 50
Cotham, Bristol 2
cottage 5, 13, 17, 31, 41, 43, 45
cottage plan 17, 31
Cottage Plans & Cottage Sense 85
cottage style 31
council houses 31, 45, 47
Country Gentleman magazine 87
Country Life 33, 34
Covent Garden 18
Coventry 5
Cragside 33
Crane 10, 50
Crapper. Thomas 177
Creda electric cooker 170, 171
Crewe 5, 41
Crickmer, Courtenay 69
Crittall Ltd 131, 155
Croydon 8
Cubism 53
Curtis A.C. 78, 87
Curton A.W. 139
Curwen Press 215
Cymric 51

D

dado 172, 199, 207, 211, 217, 219, 224, 225, 227, 229
Dagenham 8, 47
Dahlia 29
Daily Express 3
Daily Mail 2, 3, 9, 51
Daily Mail Ideal Home Exhibitions 9, 117, 119, 121
Daily Mirror 3
Daimler 7
Darcy, Braddell 117
Darlington 5
Davis estates 125
Dawber, E. Guy 97
Deane, Humphrey 117
Debenham, Ernest 55
Debenham house 55, 61, 64, 65
Debenhams 52
deposits 15
Derby 5, 45, 47, 123
Derby Corporation 123
Derby Mercury 45
Design & Industries Association (DIA) 52
Design Reform movement 49
De Soissons, Louis 43, 116, 117, 123